China's Rising Research Universities

China's Rising Research Universities

A New Era of Global Ambition

ROBERT A. RHOADS
XIAOYANG WANG
XIAOGUANG SHI
YONGCAI CHANG
Foreword by Ji Baocheng

Johns Hopkins University Press
Baltimore

© 2014 Johns Hopkins University Press
All rights reserved. Published 2014
Printed in the United States of America on acid-free paper

2 4 6 8 9 7 5 3 1

Johns Hopkins University Press
2715 North Charles Street
Baltimore, Maryland 21218-4363
www.press.jhu.edu

Library of Congress Cataloging-in-Publication Data

Rhoads, Robert A.
China's rising research universities : a new era of global ambition / Robert A. Rhoads,
Xiaoyang Wang, Xiaoguang Shi, and Yongcai Chang ; foreword by Ji Baocheng
pages cm
Includes bibliographical references and index.
ISBN 978-1-4214-1453-9 (hardcover : alk. paper) — ISBN 978-1-4214-1454-6
(electronic) — ISBN 1-4214-1453-8 (hardcover : alk. paper) — ISBN 1-4214-1454-6
(electronic) 1. Universities and colleges—Research—China. 2. Education,
Higher—Research—China. I. Title.
LB2326.3.R56 2014
378.51—dc23   2013044776

A catalog record for this book is available from the British Library.

*Special discounts are available for bulk purchases of this book. For more information, please
contact Special Sales at 410-516-6936 or specialsales@press.jhu.edu.*

Johns Hopkins University Press uses environmentally friendly book materials,
including recycled text paper that is composed of at least 30 percent post-consumer
waste, whenever possible.

CONTENTS

Throughout the West, knowledge and understanding of Chinese higher education, and specifically of the Chinese research university, have been somewhat
limited over the years. This is in part a consequence of language and cultural differences but also a reflection of the diverse political and ideological trajectories
of the leading nations of the world. Today, China increasingly finds itself at the
center of a host of complex and far-reaching processes intersecting the cultural,
economic, and political spheres. These intersecting processes are producing an
increasingly interconnected world stage, often described in terms of globalization. Such global processes, of course, implicate the university, which takes on
increasing prominence in the context of a world economy more and more tied
to the production and application of knowledge. This is no less true in such
leading nations as Germany, the United Kingdom, and the United States than
in China. The authors of this volume call the world's attention to this changing
landscape and China's growing role in global higher education.

No other book, to my knowledge, available in the English language captures
the richness and depth of the challenges and opportunities facing our nation's top
universities and their quest to enhance research and further internationalize
their basic practices, including in the area of faculty life. The four universities
highlighted in this book are all critical to the national push to build world-class
universities, each in a unique way. Certainly, Peking, Tsinghua, and Renmin
have played and continue to play leading roles in defining and shaping the
research university ideal in China. Peking is recognized throughout China for
its history of independent thought; Tsinghua is known as the leading Chinese
university in the area of applied science and university-industry innovation; and
Renmin is recognized for its service to the government and the broader society,
most notably exhibiting vast expertise in the areas of finance, management,
international affairs, and law, among others. Minzu University, as the authors
of this work compellingly argue, occupies a special position in China's higher
education landscape, being the key university in service to the nation's ethnic

affairs vision. This role is critical to the further development of a nation as ethnically diverse as China.

The authors of *China's Rising Research Universities* provide a depth of description and explanation through the use of the case study method—perhaps the best way of capturing the complex array of processes operating at an institutional level. Certainly, the opportunity to forge a new, more internationalized vision of the Chinese university is at hand, and the authors offer numerous examples to support such a transformation. In all of the cases noted in the book, the role of internationalization in shaping the nature of the faculty life and work is clearly and powerfully presented. Also, the emphasis placed on the development of research capacity—captured best by the authors' focus on Project 985 funding—reveals the importance the nation's leaders place on developing the productive capacities of leading universities, not only in terms of science and engineering but also with regard to cultural development. We cannot allow the world's best universities to be evaluated only by the revenue-generating model of the research university. A vision of the public enterprise or the public good, emphasizing service to society, must continue to be at the heart of the research university ideal. Such a university mission necessitates a certain level of commitment by national governments to funding universities in service to the people.

Although the case study methodology is helpful in providing a depth of context, it is at the same time somewhat limited in capturing the complexity and diversity of the Chinese research university. China is a nation with a long history, vast lands, and a great population. The society is quite complex and diverse, and these characteristics are reflected by Chinese universities. Though those universities are rooted in the same traditional culture and face some common challenges, nonetheless each is unique. Such differences are difficult to capture in a handful of case studies. Also, some claims are based on the authors' own experience and may not completely agree with the perspectives of others. One of the most important values of a scholarly work is, however, not to convince someone of a particular point of view but to raise critical questions. This book certainly attains such an aim.

China's Rising Research Universities offers an honest and open take on the opportunities of global dynamics and national priorities, and it also explores some critical challenges to the development of the research university. For example, the authors note problems and complexities relating to such issues as academic freedom, institutional autonomy, faculty promotion processes, and faculty peer review. These are legitimate considerations as top Chinese universities move toward a more internationalized model of the modern research university. The authors also raise critical issues about the need for China to further develop research universities with an eye to the nation's unique history and culture. Balancing the forces of internationalization and standardization with legitimate pressures and concerns linked to China's unique background is perhaps the greatest challenge before us. *China's Rising Research Universities* captures this complex challenge like no other book presently on the market.

Ji Baocheng
Professor of Economics
Renmin University of China
President, Renmin
University of China (2000–2011)

We organize this book around rich organizational portraits of our four case studies, with each constituting a separate and unique narrative. These case studies are contained in chapters 1 through 4. A more comprehensive discussion of our findings and their implications follows in the conclusion, including a discussion of the achievements and ongoing challenges of China's top universities.

We begin the book with an introductory chapter that establishes much of the basis for the subsequent chapters. Included in the introduction is our review of four major phases in the development of the Chinese university: (1) the republican period (1911–1949), (2) the socialist period (1950–1977), (3) the Open Door period (1978 to the mid-1990s), and (4) the present period, characterized as one of global ambition (the late 1990s to the present). The latter phase represents our contribution to the evolving narrative that is Chinese university reform. The introductory chapter also highlights several major issues confronting Chinese higher education, including marketization, decentralization, privatization, massification, internationalization, research capacity building, global education pressures, and social inequities. We also highlight the push to build world-class universities while seeking to clarify the basic meaning of *world-class* and noting specific Chinese Ministry of Education initiatives in the form of Projects 211 and 985. We also delineate some of the basic features of the overall Chinese system of higher education as a means to better contextualize our focus on building world-class universities.

Chapter 1, "Tsinghua University and the Spirit of Innovation and Entrepreneurialism," centers on the key role Tsinghua plays in advancing applied research and building extensive ties with business and industry for the purpose of contributing to the nation's economic development. Two key organizational structures at Tsinghua in particular are noted for their contributions to innovation and entrepreneurialism: the university science park, known as TusPark, and the University-Industry Cooperation Committee (UICC). As the nation's leading science and technology university, Tsinghua is held up as an example of the type of university-industry connections needed for promoting the nation's economic interests. Accordingly, the chapter focuses on the university's academic innovation and entrepreneurialism, including its role as a global leader in applied research, which is highlighted by its many forms of international engagement. A key facet of this chapter focuses on how top Chinese research universities such as Tsinghua are increasingly implicated by the nation's growing role in the global, knowledge-based economy. Relatedly, several faculty concerns are raised in light of expanding pressure on Tsinghua professors to contribute in innovative ways to economic development, including challenges associated with generating research revenue, growing pressure to publish in the most elite scholarly venues, difficulties in being promoted, and problems associated with limitations on academic freedom.

Chapter 2, "Peking University and the Pursuit of Academic Excellence the 'Beida Way,'" focuses on the changing context of faculty life at Peking University in light of the university's quest for academic preeminence across a broad range of fields. An important facet to understanding the culture of Beida, as it is known colloquially, is recognizing the importance of its history and the key voice it has assumed relative to Chinese cultural and political life. This includes the significant role Beida faculty and students played in the May Fourth Movement and the subsequent changes in Chinese society enacted during the 1920s, a period often described as the Chinese renaissance. Reflective of Beida's involvement in the nation's transformation is the unique cultural ethos of the university, characterized by its emphasis on inclusiveness, faculty loyalty to the profession, the pursuit of knowledge with skepticism, and a spirit of individualism. Connecting the historic and cultural foundations of the university and its larger role within Chinese society to the growing influence of globalization and the advance of worldwide university competition is integral to this chapter. Additionally, chapter 2 stresses that Peking University is recognized as one of the nation's key cultural institutions in which government leaders and Chinese citizens take great pride. Its leadership role is one of the reasons that it was the first university to adopt academic personnel reform in the early 2000s, which was seen as a necessary step in elevating faculty productivity. Hence, transforming Beida's policies and practices as part of the quest for world-class standing serves as a signpost for the broader Chinese higher education community.

Chapter 3, "Internationalization of Academic Life and the Changing Face of Renmin University," focuses on Renmin's leading role in providing a national voice for international issues as well as its overall efforts to internationalize the campus. Renmin professors, including some of the nation's leading scholars in a variety of key social science disciplines, point to the growing challenges linked to globalization, China's growing role as an economic and political leader, and the importance of scholars increasingly thinking and operating in international terms. Central to our discussion of internationalization at Renmin is former president Ji Baocheng's threefold vision for the university, introduced during his first year in office in 2000: "*da lou, da shi, da qi.*" President Ji's vision essentially aimed to direct the university toward improving facilities, building a great faculty, and embracing a broader vision. The latter two issues are of central concern to our discussion of internationalization at Renmin and are organized around five key themes: (1) the influence of international standards on scholarship, (2) the relevance of experiences abroad, (3) collaboration and partnerships with foreign scholars and organizations, (4) hosting of foreign faculty and students, and (5) the pedagogical and curriculum implications of internationalization. A key discussion in chapter 3 addresses the reality that some Chinese professors see aspects of internationalization as forms of colonialism in which Chinese universities fall under the influence of Western universities and their academic norms. As several professors point out, such influence can at times be counterproductive to serving the needs of Chinese society.

Chapter 4, "China's Ethnic Diversity and the Critical Role of Minzu University," examines the case of the nation's leading minority-serving university. In addition to highlighting organizational challenges confronting Minzu University, the chapter also pays a good deal of attention to China's ethnic minority context, pointing to the diversity of the nation and its related cultural challenges. This leads to a discussion of the important role of the *minzu* college and university system, most notably Minzu University in Beijing. With regard to Minzu, the chapter centers on three "narratives of change" that help to define the present-day organizational context: internationalization, marketization, and ethnocultural development. These narratives are considered in the context of growing pressures on the university to further develop as a comprehensive institution while also serving the nation's ethnic affairs. The chapter also highlights efforts to upgrade the university's research capacity in terms of increased pressure on faculty members to publish more, changes in the promotion process, higher levels of stress reported by faculty members, and emphasis being placed on the quantity of publications rather than their quality.

The conclusion, "Achievements and Challenges in the Quest to Build Leading Universities," summarizes the major findings of the book (and the related empirical project) and considers the future for China's leading universities. Key findings from each case study are highlighted. We identify eight areas of positive change at China's leading universities: infrastructure for research and teaching, research capacity, scholarly productivity, university-industry connections, internationalization, academic quality, faculty promotion processes, and faculty recruitment practices. We then go on to discuss seven areas of concern: institutional autonomy, administrative transparency, diversified funding, faculty empowerment, faculty evaluation and assessment, ethnic affairs and diversity, and questions of colonialism. We conclude the chapter and the book by returning to our central argument focused on global ambition and the overall role of the nation's universities in advancing China's interests worldwide.

We extend our deepest gratitude to all the faculty and staff at Minzu University, Peking University, Renmin University, and Tsinghua University who took the time to meet with us or provide assistance to us in the development of this book. We also thank our students and colleagues for their support and ideas during the years of hard work toward the completion of this project. And we are grateful for the support of our families and friends throughout our careers. Finally, we offer a special thank-you to Greg Britton, Editorial Director, and Sara Cleary, Senior Editorial Assistant, whose editorial work and assistance at Johns Hopkins University Press made this all possible.

China's Rising Research Universities

The Chinese University and the Quest for World-Class Standing

China's Changing Landscape

In August 2010 newspapers around the world reported that China had surpassed Japan as home to the world's second-largest economy. An article in the *New York Times* captured the significance of this development: "The milestone, though anticipated for some time, is the most striking evidence yet that China's ascendance is for real and that the rest of the world will have to reckon with a new economic superpower. . . . Experts say unseating Japan—and in recent years passing Germany, France and Great Britain—underscores China's growing clout and bolsters forecasts that China will pass the United States as the world's biggest economy as early as 2030" (Barboza 2010). Official year-end data confirmed midyear reports, as journalists writing for the *Guardian* in early 2011 confirmed that China had leapfrogged Japan "to become the world's second-largest economy, a title Japan . . . held for more than 40 years" (McCurry and Kollewe 2011). Almost as remarkable, in a 2012 Pew Foundation survey of citizens of fourteen leading nations, China, not the United States, was identified as the world's leading economic power; even Americans gave China the nod over the United States by one percentage point (Rampell 2012).

That China as a nation had come such a long way by the beginning of the second decade of the twenty-first century is startling by most accounts. After all, only a few decades had passed since the nation opened its doors to the outside world under the leadership of Deng Xiaoping. And now almost weekly, or so it seems, a momentous accomplishment is announced. For example, in the fall of 2010 the *Guardian* reported that a Chinese supercomputer had "overtaken the US as home of the world's fastest" (Branigan 2010). This marked only the second time in the history of the supercomputer rankings that a U.S.-based computer had not taken first prize (Japan surprised U.S. computer scientists in 2002 by walking away with the award) (Vance 2010). The Chinese supercomputer was housed in the city of Tianjin, not far from Beijing. The article went on to report that the supercomputer "was developed by the National University of Defense Technology. The system was built from thousands of chips made by US firms—Intel and Nvidia—but domestic researchers developed the networking technology that allows information to be exchanged between servers at extraordinary speeds" (Branigan 2010). This accomplishment was more than a case of Chinese scientists simply adapting Western technology for their purposes, as had been common in the past. The networking technology used to interface among many smaller computers was considered a major technological advance. A related *New York Times* story confirmed the importance of the accomplishment, quoting U.S. professor Wuchun Feng of Virginia Polytechnic Institute and State University (Virginia Tech): "What is scary about this is that the US dominance in high-performance computing is at risk. One could argue that this hits the foundation of our economic future" (Vance 2010).

Similarly, in September 2011 the Chinese government announced the completion of the world's deepest underground laboratory—the Jinping Underground Laboratory in Sichuan province, a collaboration between Tsinghua University and Ertan Hydropower Development Company. The lab was built 2.4 kilometers beneath Jinping Mountain and potentially enabled Chinese physicists to play a leading role in the search for dark matter and the study of neutrinos (Li 2011). Furthermore, in August 2012 the *New York Times* reported that China was moving forward with the development of a "more capable generation of intercontinental ballistic missiles and submarine-launched missiles, increasing its existing ability to deliver nuclear warheads to the United States and to overwhelm missile defense systems" (Bradsher 2012). That China was using advances in science and technology to strengthen its military systems was not too surprising, given, as Shi Yinhong, a professor of international relations from Renmin University, argued, the need to "contain threats from North Korea" and the reality of the continual "high-tech expansion" of the U.S. military (Bradsher 2012).

The reality of a stronger and more assertive Chinese nation-state has become apparent throughout the Asian region. Tensions with neighboring Japan have escalated in recent years over a territorial dispute involving strategically important islands—called *Diaoyu* in China and *Senkaku* in Japan—especially "after

Japan's then prime minister, Yoshihiko Noda, nationalised the three islands Japan did not already own" ("Dangerous Shoals" 2013). Throughout 2012 and into 2013, the tension reached crisis proportion on several occasions, such as when a Chinese patrol plane "buzzed the islands" and Japan "scrambled fighter planes," and then about one month later when "Japanese and Chinese jets sought to tail each other near the islands' air space" ("Dangerous Shoals" 2013). Additionally, disputes in the South China Sea with other Asian nations, such as Vietnam and India, have seen the Chinese government adopt a "hard line" stance, reflective of the nation's growing confidence and assertiveness (Perlez 2012b). Disagreements with neighboring nations, and most specifically with Japan over the Diaoyu-Senkaku islands, have resulted in large-scale protests in major cities such as Beijing, Guangzhou, and Shanghai, leading observers to note the "patriotic fervor" and nationalism arising throughout parts of China (Johnson and Shanker 2012).

Clearly, China's rapid economic and technological rise has contributed to major changes in the international environment as well as the national landscape. In terms of more localized, internal matters, the nation's rapid growth has not been without its problems. Although China made news by surpassing Japan as the world's number-two economy and the United States as home to the world's fastest supercomputer in 2010, a few years earlier it captured headlines for less noteworthy reasons. In 2007 the *Guardian* reported that China had passed the United States as the leading nation in producing carbon dioxide emissions (Vidal and Adams 2007). This occurred years ahead of expectations, another indicator of the rapid growth of China and its overall manufacturing productivity. In fact, seven Chinese cities now rank among the world's ten most polluted cities, and a 2007 World Bank report maintained that annually 460,000 Chinese people die prematurely from breathing polluted air or drinking toxic water (Jackson 2010). Linfen, a city of over four million people in central China's Shanxi province, is considered by some environmental experts to be the most polluted city in the world and has a birth-defect rate "nearly 30 times the worldwide average" (Jackson 2010). Beijing may not be too far behind, as evidenced by several consecutive days in January 2013 when even the Chinese government acknowledged the "hazardous" or "even worse" air quality and ordered government vehicles off the roads and highways in and around the city (Wong 2013). The air quality throughout China's urban centers is a constant reminder of the costs of such rapid economic expansion. A major factor is the heavy reliance on coal, in part driven by the nation's vast coal supplies in its western province of Xinjiang; so extensive are the western deposits that some have described China as the "new Middle East" for coal (Hickman 2011).

Although the national government has taken steps to curb air and water pollution, Beijing's political leaders often face the complex challenge of balancing environmental reform with pressures to sustain economic growth and provide employment for such a large population. The latter concern is a particularly vexing problem for the Chinese government, given significant economic differences between the nation's urban and rural populations, not to mention challenges associated with the nation's great size, regionalism, and ethnic diversity. Indeed, concerns about regionalism and ethnic differences, often linked to economic issues as well, have attracted much attention in recent years, in part due to uprisings by ethnic minority populations in regions such as Tibet and Xinjiang (Branigan 2009; Wong 2010). These are quite delicate matters in China, and maintaining a state of harmony—a central goal under former President Hu Jintao ("Hu Calls" 2011)—often is easier said than done.

Over the years, Chinese leaders have struggled to unify a nation that is geographically vast and far more ethnically and culturally diverse than most outsiders realize. The farther one gets from Beijing, the more challenging it is to advance and preserve national unity. This is not a minor issue, either historically speaking or in the present age. Indeed, as one travels throughout the southern and western regions of China, it is not uncommon to hear sayings dating back thousands of years that hint at the nation's great regionalism and diversity, including one paraphrased as "The emperor has many rules, but Beijing is far away, and the mountains are very high." This expression is commonly recognized among residents of Yunnan province, where large numbers of China's fifty-five official ethnic minority populations reside, including members of the Bai, Dai, and Yi peoples.

National euphoria about opportunities linked to economic growth is somewhat dampened by widespread environmental problems, not to mention the significant challenges associated with maintaining national harmony in the face of economic inequalities. Concerns also arise relating to the nation's positioning within the global political landscape, both in terms of growing opportunities to influence world decisions and with regard to increasing responsibilities to advance peaceful relations worldwide. The reality of such complexities is not to be taken lightly, and China's leaders increasingly turn to the nation's top universities for help in addressing such pressing concerns. This was most obvious at Tsinghua University's 2011 centennial celebration, when Hu Jintao delivered a compelling speech at the Great Hall of the People in Beijing, pointing to the critical role of universities in supporting the nation's economic and social development.

As pride in the nation's accomplishments grows, China's universities increasingly have become a point of focus, both in terms of their responsibilities in contributing to the nation's further development and also as a measure of the nation's progress. This fact has led to major investment by the central government in upgrading the nation's leading universities. China's leaders expect their universities to assume standing among the elite universities of the world—the Harvards, Oxfords, and Stanfords—and at the same time, they hold them accountable for assisting in China's economic and social transformation. Accordingly, the university is called on to educate future generations of Chinese citizens and leaders while advancing forms of knowledge capable of addressing the nation's many economic, technological, environmental, and cultural challenges.

The contemporary Chinese university is defined by its responsibility to the broader society. The government clearly recognizes the role its universities and scholars are likely to play in the future of the nation, and accordingly, since 1995, has adopted major initiatives and channeled massive funds toward the goal of strengthening more than a hundred key universities. The importance of today's universities is especially obvious when one considers the growing role they play in contributing to the expanding knowledge-based economy (Altbach 2009; Collins and Rhoads 2010; Mohrman, Ma, and Baker 2008; Peters and Besley 2006; Slaughter and Rhoades 2004). China's government leaders and policy makers have recognized this as well.

As comparative scholars of higher education, we are greatly interested in the growing importance of China's leading universities. It is hard to imagine universities anywhere else in the world that have faced such a rapidly changing national landscape, given the many changes China has passed through in recent decades. Professors, of course, have been at the center of the changes taking place at Chinese universities, and we are particularly interested in their working lives. They play key roles in the production, management, and application of knowledge, arguably the basic threefold mission of contemporary research universities (Rhoads and Szelényi 2011). Thus, in the following section we further discuss the nature of our interest and the basic strategy we implemented in examining China's leading universities.

Overview of Our Project

The accomplishments and challenges framing the contemporary Chinese context implicate its universities in many complex ways. The broad responsibility of modern universities includes not only their contributions to economic development but also major responsibilities in terms of advancing cultural understanding and promoting national unity. With this in mind, the results reported in this book support our goal of better understanding the contributions of China's universities and their faculty to the nation's expanding role as a global economic, political, and cultural leader.[1] We see a case study approach as the best method for unearthing and describing the institutional complexities of China's leading universities and the work of their faculty.[2] Accordingly, we selected four universities because of their centrality to national concerns and their importance to advancing forms of knowledge capable of serving the nation's pressing needs.

We made a decision to focus our inquiry on universities specifically in Beijing, given that the city is akin to what Paris is to France—a center for university life and home to many of the nation's top universities.[3] Limiting our case studies to one city also served the purpose of making our collaborative efforts more workable. Thus, the primary sites for our analysis are Tsinghua University, Peking University (also known as Beijing University), Renmin University, and Minzu University. All four universities are located in Haidian District, the famous university district of Beijing; indeed, all four are situated along the same main thoroughfare, known as *Zhongguancun*. These universities also were selected because they are included in two major Ministry of Education (MoE) initiatives that began in the mid- to late 1990s, known as Project 211 and Project 985 (we describe these projects in greater detail later in this chapter). These major national initiatives are critical to the changes we discuss throughout this work, being the key sources of funding for elevating Chinese universities in terms of their disciplinary foundations, internationalization, and research capacity.

We present key findings in the form of rich and intensive case studies conducted at the respective universities. Throughout our collaborative project we stressed forms of empirical inquiry consistent with the interpretive social science tradition.[4] Additionally, we drew insight from previous social science research focused on academic culture, which we define as the norms, values, beliefs, and practices associated with university life. Here, the work of Burton Clark and William Tierney proved particularly insightful.[5] Our understanding of academic culture parallels to some extent previous work on organizational culture, wherein institutions are seen to exhibit unique cultural qualities and forms.[6] Hence, although the four universities included in our study are somewhat similar in that they are all included as part of Projects 211 and 985, each institution is seen as having distinct cultural characteristics. Capturing the uniqueness of these four universities was part of our overarching goal.

We relied a great deal on data collection strategies commonly associated with case study inquiry but informed by the ethnographic tradition.[7] Specifically, we used the following data collection tools: semistructured interviews,[8] informal interviews (including casual discussions with key informants), observation/participant observation, and document collection and analysis. The broad array of data collection tools is consistent with Norman Denzin's discussion of the use of triangulation as a strategy for strengthening qualitative social science research (Denzin 1989). The results of our case studies form the bulk of chapters 1 through 4.

In addition to conducting four case studies, our overall project also relied on informal interviews and observational data collected at ten additional universities. Most of these universities were visited as part of the lead author's year as a Fulbright scholar to China (2010–2011), during which he taught at Minzu University and presented more than two dozen lectures at universities throughout China. As part of this effort, informal discussions were held, often in a group or focused-dialogue format, centering on changes in Chinese higher education and similarities and differences between Chinese and U.S. universities. Such discussions were held at the following universities: Beijing Normal University, Beijing University of Chemical Technology, Dalian University of Technology, Guangdong University of Foreign Studies, Jinan University (in Guangzhou), Sichuan Normal University, Southwest University, Wuhan University, Yunnan University, and Zhejiang University. Visits to these universities added another layer of richness to our overall understanding of changes at Chinese universities and combined in dynamic ways with the insider knowledge of the three coauthors, all of whom have years of experience living and working at Chinese universities.

The primary thrust of our study focused on changes in faculty life at China's top universities. The empirical inquiry revolved around the following basic research question: Given major policy initiatives by the Chinese MoE, most notably the implementation of Projects 211 and 985, how are the working lives of professors[9] changing at the nation's leading universities? The focus on professors' working lives reflects our view that faculty are the critical link in raising the quality and improving the overall operations of the academic enterprise. We recognize that key administrative personnel and students also are involved in efforts to strengthen universities, but we find it most helpful to consult with professors. Thus, we contend that developing a deeper sense of how faculty experience and perceive changes in university life is critical to understanding the transformation of the contemporary Chinese university.

A Brief Sojourn to the Past: The Historical Development of the Chinese University

To better understand the complexities of the contemporary Chinese university, particularly the established and emerging research universities, we find it helpful to explore important developments over the years. This is in keeping with our conviction that present-day opportunities and challenges confronting today's universities must be interpreted in light of the unique history and culture of higher education in China. Furthermore, although Chinese educational policy makers and institutional leaders may look beyond the nation's shores to chart a course for the future of their universities, the adoption of new structures, policies, and practices is likely to take on unique forms when transplanted to China's cultural and political landscape.

We see four primary reform periods in the development of the Chinese university, largely corresponding with political and social changes taking place in the broader society: (1) the republican period (1911–1949), (2) the socialist period

(1950–1977), (3) the Open Door period (1978 to the mid-1990s), and (4) the present period, characterized as one of global ambition (the late 1990s to the present). Here, we draw extensively from two key works: *The Alienated Academy: Culture and Politics in Republican China, 1919–1937,* by sinologist Wen-Hsin Yeh, and *China's Universities, 1895–1995: A Century of Cultural Conflict,* by educational comparativist Ruth Hayhoe.[10]

The Republican Period

The first major reform period in the development of the Chinese university largely parallels the rise of the Chinese republic at the dawn of the twentieth century. In the late 1800s and early 1900s, during the final years of the Qing Dynasty, the idea of the university was firmly planted in Chinese soil. Although a handful of universities already existed, including missionary-focused institutions such as Shanghai's St. Johns University (founded in 1879), it was not until the founding of the likes of Peking (1898), Fudan (1905), and Tsinghua (1911) that a more nation-focused notion of the university took root. Here, for example, Yeh pointed out that Fudan University in Shanghai stressed "national learning," translated as "the articulation, in Chinese, of ideas that addressed Chinese concerns and facilitated social and political changes in China" (Yeh 2000, 105).

The Chinese university of the early twentieth century had a distinctive identity linked in part to a coming together of East and West, with teaching methods and conceptions of knowledge influenced both by Chinese traditionalism, mostly in the form of Confucianism, and Western modernist thought, associated with scientific rationality and empiricism. Additionally, curricula and educational practices influenced both by capitalism and Christianity were quite prominent in the functioning of the missionary universities (Hayhoe 1996). This was a period in Chinese history marked by increased openness, perhaps even a degree of vulnerability, to the West. In this regard, analysis of the influence of American and European university ideals in China is difficult to disentangle from elements of the cultural and economic colonialism also occurring at that time. However, as the nationalist movement grew in power and vitality, Western cultural influence increasingly was called into question. This is clearly evident in the anti-imperialist movements of the early 1920s, launched to a great extent by the May Fourth Movement of 1919, resulting in attacks against missionary universities such as St. Johns, which "was increasingly the target of accusations of cultural imperialism" (Yeh 2000, 84).

Although it can be said of the late nineteenth and early twentieth centuries that the university per se was relatively new to China, higher learning certainly was not; China had already established a system of imperial examinations and structured learning opportunities known as *shuyuan*, which included libraries and opportunities for intellectual discussion led by widely recognized scholars (Hayhoe 1996, 10–12). However, during the 1800s and leading up to the increased influence of Western universities around the turn of the century, this form of higher learning had limited impact on the nation's economic growth and development. As Rui Yang pointed out, "Chinese higher education continued to train Confucian scholars with little knowledge of the outside world. Although Western models had already demonstrated their strength, China's communication with the West was thus intentionally hindered" (R. Yang 2004, 315). Yang went on to note that such training focused on acquiring "encyclopaedic knowledge based on Confucian values, which in practice served only the aristocracy" (2004, 315). Many colleges and universities were founded after the elimination of the imperial examination, a system used to award administrative posts within the government. This was a transitional period in China's history, marked most emphatically by the end of the Qing Dynasty in 1911 and the rise of the modern Chinese nation-state under the leadership of the Chinese Nationalist Party or Kuomintang (KMT). Sun Yat-sen (Sun Zhongshan) played a prominent role in the overthrow of the Qing Dynasty and became the early leader of the new Chinese republic. Hailing from Guangdong (he was Cantonese), Zhongshan University in Guangzhou stands as a tribute to his achievements as a republican leader and a reminder of his place in Chinese history.

The transition from empire to republic, combined with the coming together of East and West, produced a period of great experimentation in the form and structure of the Chinese university. Such vast reform may also be understood as a consequence of the lack of a strong central government during the years 1911 to 1927 (Hayhoe 1996; Yang 2004). But Western influence, in the face of growing nationalism, increasingly was interpreted as imperialist. Hence, by the late 1920s and early 1930s, and captured most prominently by the Nationalist Party's Northern Expedition, the Chinese cultural and political landscape made it more and more difficult for Western models of university life to thrive (Yeh 2000).

The Socialist Period

The second reform period in the development of the Chinese university followed the rise of the Mao-led communist movement and a restructuring of the university in the early 1950s in a manner consistent with the Soviet model. Ka Ho Mok addressed this period in the evolution of the Chinese university: "Soviet influence was reflected not only in the organization and administration of higher education but also on the way that textbooks, teaching methods and classrooms were designed" (Mok 2005a, 63). The reorganization of Chinese higher education under Soviet influence involved nationalizing "all higher education institutions, including all public, private, and missionary universities and colleges" (Mok 2005a, 63). The development of the university thus followed a trajectory consistent with Soviet-based socialist ideals, combined, of course, with the unique characteristics of Chinese culture and social customs.

A core component of the Soviet-influenced system was academic specialization. As Hayhoe explained, "The emphasis in higher education under Soviet influence was very much on the formation of a highly disciplined elite corps of specialists in all of the areas needed by the new socialist state" (1996, 81). Additionally, the Soviet model of science stressed a bureaucratic "reordering of knowledge from above," in part to better serve centrally coordinated industrial development plans (76). What resulted was the development of highly specialized universities that were centrally controlled and administered. Hayhoe further noted, "The primary concern was to restructure the whole higher education system in ways that would ensure its direct service to the economic and social goals of the First Five-Year Plan. Thus, the main consideration in the patterns of knowledge was a functional one in terms of personnel training. It led to an eclectic set of institutional types, each with its own distinctive curricular rationale" (76).

Donghui Zhang argued that the Soviet influence over Chinese higher education actually weakened from about 1958 to 1976 (2012). In fact, she sees the communist period as being composed of two stages, with the first roughly covering 1950 to 1958, where Soviet influence was "big brotherly" in nature, and the second 1958 to 1976, when China turned inward "and closed its doors to the world" (2012, 402). This is most apparent by the shift in national policy leading to the Cultural Revolution in 1966, wherein the nation's universities were mostly closed to regular students and academics, the exception being the use of the campuses for training peasants, workers, and soldiers for participation in the Red Guard. Many universities opened in the mid-1970s, but participation was limited only to those students capable of meeting the political scrutiny of socialist ideology—meaning those who were poor or working-class. It was not until 1978, when a formal entrance examination was reintroduced, that the political litmus test largely was dropped and access to the university expanded to all classes within Chinese society.

The Open Door Period

The third period in the development of the Chinese university followed the death of Mao and the reopening of universities in the aftermath of the Cultural Revolution. This period in Chinese higher education largely reflected government-enacted reform policies (often described as the "Open Door" policies) under the leadership of Deng Xiaoping, from roughly 1978 to the mid-1990s (Cheng 1986; Hayhoe 1989, 1995, 1996). In addition to the reopening and restoration of the university, this period also is marked by greater openness to the world community, evidenced in part by larger and larger numbers of students and professors traveling abroad as well as by China becoming a host for foreign students and scholars. During this period of higher education reform, a system once steeped in Soviet specialized knowledge systems turned back again to ideals grounded in Europe and the United States, with the latter nation by this time widely recognized as the world leader in terms of the quality and capacity of its research universities.

Kai Ming Cheng argued that a key facet of university reform during this period was the granting of increased autonomy to universities, evidenced at two levels: (1) at the macro level in terms of the overall system being less centrally controlled by the central government, and (2) at the institutional level in terms of greater decision-making ability being given to university leaders (1986). In summarizing key reform documents of 1985, Cheng noted that in addition to major cities being granted the authority to run their own universities (an example of greater macro-level autonomy), the institutions themselves were given the right to train and enroll self-supporting students, to develop their own syllabi and course materials, to accept research commissions, to cooperate in research and technological development projects, and to appoint and remove vice presidents and other cadre at various administrative levels (Cheng 1986, 256–257). These were important changes in terms of enabling universities to chart aspects of their own institutional trajectories. The Open Door policies and the nation's momentous economic strides provided a foundation for further strengthening the universities, especially in light of their growing importance to an emerging knowledge-based economy.

The Global Ambition Period

The present period of university reform in China may be characterized by the nation's growing global ambition, defined to a great extent by the impact of globalization and China's increasingly prominent place in the world. The global ambition period is marked by the nation's economic strength and the related national effort to build or further develop world-class universities.[11] Accordingly, there is strong governmental and institutional support to build top research universities capable of both contributing to economic development and attaining world standing comparable to that of the best Western universities.

The global ambition period highlights the growing challenges China faces as it increasingly integrates into a host of world systems, including those of an economic variety. Writing about this period in Chinese higher education reform, Ka Ho Mok argued,

> China's accession to the World Trade Organization has unquestionably subjected the mainland to keener regional and global competitions and challenges. Real-

izing the newly emerging knowledge economy requires competent and highly qualified and professional people, the Chinese government believes the changing domestic, regional and global social and economic environments have rendered its higher education systems inappropriate and less competitive in the global marketplace (2005a, 62).

A key facet to addressing the competitive challenges noted by Mok is the merging of many specialized universities, developed under the influence of the Soviets, to create comprehensive universities better suited to serve the needs of a global society. As an example, one of the nation's top universities, Zhejiang University, represents the 1998 merger of four separate universities: Hangzhou University, Zhejiang Agricultural University, Zhejiang Medical University, and Zhejiang University. The effort to build comprehensive world-class universities brings us to the contemporary state of the Chinese university and a number of pressing issues that shape the present-day experiences of the nation's professors —matters that are of deep concern to us as scholars of academic culture and university life.

Several major changes arise within the context of the global ambition period; such changes offer both challenges and opportunities to the nation's universities. These challenges and opportunities relate to issues of marketization, decentralization, privatization, massification, and internationalization. Additionally, universities face unique pressures related to the national quest to expand research capacity, the necessity to prepare students for an increasingly global employment environment, and the expectation to address the nation's goal of fostering harmony in the face of both major economic differences between urban and rural citizens and significant ethnic tensions between minority populations and the Han majority. These and other issues are central to our discussion in the following section as we expand in greater detail on the challenges and opportunities associated with the present period of global ambition.

Challenges and Opportunities: An Academic Revolution of Sorts

The present, more globally oriented period of Chinese higher education is marked by increased financial support for its top universities, beginning during the mid-1990s. Through highly funded national initiatives, China's MoE has set its sights on elevating the operations and status of its top universities. Project 211 was launched in 1995 to advance the educational capacity and international competitiveness of roughly a hundred of the nation's top universities; funding focuses on strengthening management systems, research capacity, and key disciplines, including those contributing directly to the advance of science, technology, and culture. Project 985, initiated in 1998, focuses primarily on a smaller subset (thirty-nine) of the nation's top universities and seeks to elevate these institutions to world-class status, particularly in terms of research, teaching, and international engagement. These policies combine with nation-wide massification initiatives to create an academic revolution of sorts in China, the pace and scale of which calls to mind the dramatic transformation of U.S. higher education following World War II and extending through the 1960s, documented by Christopher Jencks and David Riesman in their classic work *The Academic Revolution* (1969). For scholars of higher education, the contemporary Chinese university offers an exciting laboratory for studying the impact of reform initiatives on key institutional actors such as faculty.

China since the early 1980s has shown a growing openness to the West and to the ways of Western universities. With the passing of Mao Zedong in 1976 and the subsequent rise to power of Deng Xiaoping, China's place in the world began to change. Although Deng never held the formal leadership positions of president or general secretary of the Chinese Communist Party (CCP), he nonetheless was the indisputable leader of the nation in the post-Mao era. It was under Deng's early guidance, in the form of the nation's Open Door policies, that China began to lay the foundation for increased marketization, although a more complete embrace of market principles arguably did not take place until the early 1990s. The shift to marketization affected the nation's universities as well as other key institutions and social systems. Thus, marketization is a key initial step in a long road leading to a series of important developments in higher education. In what follows, we highlight many of the significant changes that continue to define and shape the present-day higher education context in China.

Marketization

National policies implemented in the early 1980s promoted greater individual and family responsibility in terms of funding social programs, including higher education. This resulted in the implementation of tuition and fees at universities throughout the country. Tuition and fees became particularly important at institutions excluded from national funding initiatives implemented in the mid- to late 1990s. Such colleges and universities increasingly had to rely on market strategies for their survival; this included viewing students as key actors within a consumer market, given heightened competition among universities to generate tuition revenue.

The 1980s and 1990s saw a shift in China toward increased marketization, as well as deregulation and privatization; this corresponded with global anti-Keynesian trends, stressing that marketization and "the private sector approach is comparatively superior to traditional approaches adopted in the public sector" (Mok 2000, 111). Despite numerous shortcomings associated with such arguments, including the obvious challenge of addressing non–revenue generating public-good concerns, the reality is that governments throughout the world found it increasingly difficult financially to meet the higher education needs of burgeoning national populations. Mok argued that the shift during the Open Door period was quite dramatic in China, pointing out that the national government underwent an ideological change. This resulted in a new social policy paradigm: "New values stressed personal interests, material incentives, differential rewards, economic efficiency, market distribution, and competition. In short, efficiency replaced the traditional goal of equality, and the government relaxed its control over the public domain and abandoned its role as provider of comprehensive services" (Mok 1997c, 262). Hence, higher education was no longer defined simply as a public good to be provided by the state. Instead, the system was targeted for marketization with the help of varying levels of governmental support, depending on the competiveness and rank of the universities (with the top universities receiving higher levels of national support).

Most recently, China's expanding role as a global economic player further linked its universities to marketization. This trend is global in nature, and numerous scholars have discussed and debated the significance and benefits of it (Altbach 2001, 2003; Marginson 1995, 2006; Marginson and Considine 2000; Peters and Besley 2006; Slaughter and Leslie 1997; Slaughter and Rhoades 2004; Rhoads and Liu 2009; Rhoads and Torres 2006). Marketization, in part, is tied to the increased commodification of higher education. We see commodification as involving the treatment of university outputs—such as students and graduates, curricula and course offerings, and research findings and related ideas or inventions—as products to be marketed to various consumerist entities. This broad process of linking university commodities to revenue-generating sources, most notably business and industry, and defining students and families as potential consumers is seen as key to generating diverse sources of market-driven revenues. In part, this reflects the growing prominence of market forces operating throughout Chinese society and goes hand-in-hand with the decentralization of higher education (Mok 1999, 2000, 2002).

Decentralization

Decentralization of higher education also must be understood first and foremost as part of the larger sociopolitical changes that took place throughout Chinese society in the post-Mao era. Under Mao, the nation's colleges and universities functioned within an apparatus of centralized governmental control. However, this educational governance system began to loosen up in the post–Cultural Revolution years and especially during the era under Deng's leadership, as revealed in key government documents such as "Decision of the Central Committee of the Chinese Communist Party on the Reform of the Educational System." There was a growing sense that the need for change and innovation within the educational system required greater levels of institutional autonomy. Along these lines, Mok wrote, the government acknowledged that "over-centralization and stringent rules would kill the initiatives and enthusiasm of local educational institutions" (2002, 261).

The decentralization movement was reflected in two related trends: (1) reduction in funding from the national government (except for the top hundred or so universities included in Projects 211 and 985) and (2) increased decision-making ability on the part of institutions and educationalists. Here, Mok characterized the decentralization of Chinese higher education in terms of the following ideas:

> devolving decision making from the central government to individual higher education institutions. Realizing the importance of professional knowledge and technical know-how to the success of China's modernization and admitting the state's insufficient financial resources to create adequate educational opportunities for the citizens, the state has allowed more autonomy and flexibility to local governments and educationalists in directing the course of educational development (2002, 261).

Thus, although greater institutional autonomy relative to the national government may be understood as a byproduct of the decentralization movement, such reform was advanced with the coinciding expectation that provincial governments would increase their financial investment.

Along with the shift to higher levels of institutional autonomy, there also came a social charge to better serve the nation's needs, including the growing numbers of Chinese citizens desiring access to higher education. This pressure to expand enrollments produced the financial necessity to develop alternative revenue sources and further commercialize aspects of higher education services, including by increasing the number of non-degree or certificate students. The consequence for many colleges and universities is that decentralization shifted the educational cost burden to local, provincial, and private sources (Mok 2000, 2001). The present-day funding structure is particularly challenging for those institutions ineligible for Project 211 and 985 funding. The quest to be part of these highly funded projects, mostly during the early years of the twenty-first century, fueled widespread institutional pursuit of status and ranking within the Chinese higher education system; the hope of many university presidents at that time was to join the elite class of institutions included in the national government's sponsorship.

Privatization

Coinciding with marketization and decentralization is the adoption of more flexible policies for the development of a private sector. The institutions that resulted are people-run, nongovernmental postsecondary institutions often termed *minban* schools and described by some scholars as constituting the privatization of Chinese higher education (Cheng 1999; Mok 1997a, 1997b, 1997c, 2000, 2005b). These types of institutions have added new options for college-aged adults, especially those with low scores on the national university entrance exam known as the *Gaokao* (high school students must do extremely well on this intensely competitive, one-time exam in order to gain admission to the better national and provincial universities). *Minban* schools tend to differ from the more academically oriented colleges and universities in that they mostly are "practically oriented . . . with the nature of their courses lying mainly in vocational and technical, as well as in business and commercial spheres" (Mok 1997b, 560).

The privatization of higher education in China, while part of the changing national sociopolitical landscape, may also be understood as part of a global phenomenon influencing educational systems around the world. Fazal Rizvi described the basic belief structure of such a trend: "There is an almost universal belief that the state should no longer be asked to fund the growth of the higher education sector but that there should be greater reliance on private sources to meet even the existing commitments" (Rizvi, 2006, 66). Some see this global push as part of the advance of neoliberal ideology, although the Chinese educational policy context does not perfectly match the neoliberal model, given the ongoing heavy involvement of the central government in coordinating such important functions as the university admission process, including its role in managing the *Gaokao*. But what is clear, even in China, is that private sources of revenue, including reliance on tuition and fees, are increasingly needed to offset the growing costs of an expanding higher education sector.

Massification

Another key feature of the changing higher education landscape in China is the pressure to expand, as part of the movement toward a mass conception of higher education access (Hayhoe 1995). Massification in many ways reflects widespread social pressure to make higher education accessible to larger and larger numbers of people, who increasingly must compete for positions within the labor market. Also, from the perspective of government and industry, there is the need for greater numbers of educated workers capable of operating in ever-diversifying and increasingly global businesses and industries. Then there is also a growing sense of status and opportunity associated with possessing a college degree.[12] All these forces combine to make access to higher education socially significant.

Martin Trow divided the world's higher education systems into elite, mass, and universal, arguing that elite systems enroll under 15 percent of the traditional college-aged group, mass systems enroll 16 to 50 percent, and universal access is achieved when over 50 percent are enrolled (Trow 2006).[13] Each type emphasizes different educational goals and objectives: elite systems emphasize "shaping the mind and character of a ruling class . . . for elite roles"; mass systems focus on "transmission of skills and preparation for a broader range of technical and economic elite roles"; and universal higher education is characterized by the "adaptation of the 'whole population' to rapid social and technological change" (Trow 2006, 243). Of these three categories of national academic systems, clearly China falls into category two—that of mass higher education.

As evidence of China's massification, Beijing MoE data revealed that in 1990 less than 5 percent of Chinese young adults of college-going age (eighteen to twenty-two years old) were enrolled in higher education institutions.[14] Ten years later, in 2000, that figure surpassed 10 percent. In 2002, only two years later, enrollment of this age group reached Trow's threshold for mass higher education at 15 percent, and then only three years later, in 2005, it surpassed 20 percent (Brandenburg and Zhu 2007). Most recently, World Bank data from 2006 to 2009 show a steady year-by-year increase, culminating in 2009 with a 25-percent participation rate.[15] Although this amounts to an incredibly rapid level of expansion for a twenty-year period, China still lags behind some of the most developed nations, where higher education participation rates approach 50 percent among leading nations (D. Yang 2004).

Increased student enrollments have not necessarily seen corresponding levels of expansion in terms of faculty, staff, and facilities. Consequently, faculty tend to report relatively high teaching and advising loads, which further complicates national efforts to expand research capacity; indeed, it is quite common for Chinese professors to advise countless master's students and spend endless hours supervising thesis work, which remains a mainstay of graduate education in China. Students, too, experience the pitfalls of rapid expansion. Student services, including residential facilities, have been hard pressed to meet the growing needs of burgeoning student populations. For example, it is not unusual for Chinese students living in the dormitories to have as many as six or seven roommates, squeezed together in crowded rooms with two to four sets of multitiered beds. Additionally, many universities that once housed faculty and staff on campus as part of the socialist ideal of the *danwei* (a community of workers) have converted such facilities to student housing.

Internationalization

The Open Door policies of the 1980s marked the beginning of the internationalization of the Chinese university, as cultural exchange among students and scholars became a vital component of the universities. Today China is the world's leader in sending students abroad. *China Daily-USA*, for example, reported that China had 1.27 million students abroad at the end of 2010, with Western nations such as Australia, Canada, France, Germany, the United Kingdom, and the

United States (the top destination for Chinese students going abroad) among the lead countries in hosting such students (J. Chen 2011). Additionally, many Chinese universities have added international programs to their curricula, such as Chinese language study for foreign students, as part of a nationwide effort to become a world leader in exporting higher education (by hosting foreign students, a university is essentially exporting higher education as part of the knowledge industry). Related to this trend, universities offer a growing number of courses in English, as part of the strategy for attracting more international students and scholars.

Another aspect of internationalization, in part driven by massification goals, is that the government has adopted a more open stance toward partnerships between universities and foreign postsecondary education providers. This policy shift has resulted in the opening of numerous branch campuses on the part of foreign universities, such as the United Kingdom's Nottingham University campus at Ningbo in Zhejiang Province, which former premier Wen Jiabao visited in April 2011 (Sharma 2011). Also, many universities have developed collaborative degree programs in which students spend a portion of their program of study at a Chinese university and another portion at a foreign university. Given the overwhelming number of young people interested in pursuing the baccalaureate, the Chinese government sees foreign partnerships as part of the solution to widespread demand.

Research Capacity Building

A central aspect of recent university reform that lends additional support to the academic-revolution argument is the increased focus on strengthening scholarly productivity and overall research capacity. The goal of advancing academic science and expanding university research has, of course, international implications, given the transnational nature of modern-day scientific inquiry (Altbach 2009). This transnational quality adds to the overall expense of expanding research capacity.

Numerous scholars have examined efforts by Chinese universities to expand and elevate institutional structures, including educational and research processes (F. Huang 2005; Mok 2001, 2002). Monies from Projects 211 and 985 have been critical to achieving such objectives. But government funding alone cannot meet the demands of building top academic science programs, and consequently, Chinese universities such as Tsinghua University and Zhejiang University have sought to raise research revenue through university-industry ties, especially in the applied sciences and engineering. For example, both universities have heavily invested—with the help of national, provincial, and municipal funding—in the development of industrial research and science parks designed to bridge the gap between university research and the needs of business and industry. These science parks, in part, are to serve as incubators for the development of new products, businesses, or even entire industries. With the development of Tsinghua University Science Park, simply known as TusPark, and Zhejiang University National Science Park, these two universities have adopted the entrepreneurial characteristics of top U.S. research universities, where university-industry structures like these are quite common and academics in the applied sciences are often viewed as both scientists and inventors.[16]

One key to building world-class universities, as has been pointed out by Kathryn Mohrman, Wanhua Ma, and David Baker, most specifically in their elaboration of the Emerging Global Model, is diversified funding. Such funding is of course critical to supporting academic science and expanding research capacity. Accordingly, today's Chinese universities seek to access a range of revenue sources to support the academic science enterprise, including the following: taking advantage of government research funding opportunities at all levels (i.e., national, provincial, and municipal); greater interaction with and applications to foreign and international funding agencies, such as the Ford Foundation, the World Bank, and UNESCO; greater emphasis on connecting research to the needs and interests of business and industry (as in the examples of Tsinghua and Zhejiang); institutional development strategies to expand philanthropic activity; and the implementation of faculty promotion and reward policies and practices emphasizing funded research and grant writing.

Global Educational Pressures

In terms of curricular development, Chinese universities have had to concern themselves with global relevance and competitiveness, necessitating revisions of academic programs and curricula. A major shift here has been the effort to better prepare students for an increasingly global employment environment, leading to the expansion of English as both an area of study and, in many classrooms, a language of instruction (Rhoads and Liang 2006; Ross 1993). Driven in part by marketization, Chinese universities have reexamined degree programs and credentialing. The national government has played a key role here as well, given that the Chinese economy still functions on the basis of strong centralized mechanisms, including government control over numerous fields and industries. In fact, a yearly concern of the central government is the percentage of college graduates who successfully find employment. Efforts to prevent high unemployment among college graduates, which could lead to social unrest, are a central component of the national government's initiatives to promote a harmonious society.

Social Inequities

Although ethnic minorities in China account for less than 10 percent of the overall population, given the overall size of the society this still amounts to a minority population about one third the size of the entire U.S. population. Chinese universities, like universities in other parts of the world, have a special responsibility to advance national interests, including concerns linked to maintaining social stability, promoting equal opportunity, and advancing cross-cultural understanding. In particular, the nation's universities have been called upon to address widespread social inequities among China's rural and urban populations and between the Han majority and the fifty-five officially recognized ethnic minority groups. The development of multiple campuses devoted to ethnic minorities as part of the *minzu*[17] university system, including Minzu University of China (MUC) in Beijing, is seen as critical to elevating educational opportunities for ethnic minorities as well as strengthening the cross-cultural communication abilities of both the Han majority and ethnic minorities. Although the original goal of the *minzu* university idea was to provide training for communist cadre and government officials, who would then work and serve in minority regions, more recently *minzu* universities have focused on a variety of intellectual fields for the purpose of strengthening ethnic culture and heritage. There is some debate about the precise role of *minzu* universities, and some of the issues associated with them can be quite sensitive within the context of Chinese politics. We address facets of this debate in our chapter about MUC, arguably the key *minzu* university in China.

Additional Considerations

In addition to the aforementioned major points, which include both challenges and opportunities confronting Chinese universities in the present-day context, other issues also are important to consider. The fact that issues or problems might arise in the context of rapid student expansion and dramatic institutional and curricular change, not to mention the significant push to expand research capacity, is hardly surprising. For example, there have been reports in recent years of high levels of plagiarism discovered in papers published by Chinese faculty (Friedman 2010). In fact, several of the nation's leading scholars have been found to have violated scholarly norms and crossed the lines of plagiarism (T. Chen 2011). As evidence, one study reported that 31 percent of papers included in a leading scientific journal between 2008 and 2010 were found to include unoriginal material without proper citation (T. Chen 2011). Some speculate that great pressure on Chinese scholars to produce at higher and higher levels may be contributing to shortcuts taken by some professors; indeed, plagiarism may result from high levels of stress caused in part by an overly quantitative approach to faculty evaluation and promotion practices. We highlight issues relating to this in a couple of our case study chapters.

There also are concerns about whether the central government's funding of its top universities benefits all of society or perhaps only subsectors—such as the urban middle and upper classes, whose children are most likely to score high enough on the college entrance exam to attend the Fudans, Tsinghuas, and Zhejiangs of China. Some of these concerns were pointedly noted in a speech by Zhu Rongji, the nation's premier from 1998 to 2003, at the centennial celebration of Tsinghua University in April 2011. Zhu's comments criticized a key higher education planning document—"The Outline of the National Plan for Medium- and Long-Term Educational Reform and Development (2010–2020)"—describing it as not much more than "empty talk" (Yeung 2011). The reform document targets the college participation rate of high school graduates at 40 percent, to be achieved by 2020; if reached, this would amount to an increase of 15 percentage points in a matter of less than a decade. Zhu, who formerly served as the founding dean of Tsinghua's School of Economics and Management, raised questions about the goal to elevate a group of universities, including Tsinghua, to world-class university status, in light of such widespread economic disparities between rural and urban populations. Implicit in his criticism were questions about the degree to which people living in China's underdeveloped countryside are likely to benefit from increased spending on the nation's top universities. According to Linda Yeung, writing for *University World News*, "Zhu's remarks also sparked off renewed debate about the need for academic freedom and institutional autonomy, and possible leadership ambivalence in providing greater freedoms" (Yeung 2011).

High levels of academic freedom and institutional autonomy are common characteristics of world-class universities. There appears to be growing recognition among some university leaders that such issues must be addressed in the coming years. One university president told us that expanding academic freedom was a crucial step still to be taken by leading universities. Among those faculty members willing to speak out about the issue, there was general consensus that much room for improvement exists.

Many of the issues highlighted in this section, and indeed throughout this chapter, reappear in the context of our discussion of the four case studies to be presented in chapters 1 through 4. For now, though, we find it helpful to shed some light on what is actually meant by *world-class* university status, given the prominence of such rhetoric relative to Chinese higher education reform.

The Push for World-Class University Standing

At the heart of efforts to reform China's top universities is the importance that the national government places on developing world-class research universities. Of course, China is not alone in such a quest. Other nations, including some of its neighbors in the form of the Russian Federation and the Republic of Korea, are also intent on such a goal (Froumin 2011; Rhee 2011). This worldwide push to build research universities, documented to some extent by Altbach and

Jamil Salmi (2011), is seen to be critical to strengthening national economies. But this global trend raises a variety of issues, including most notably a basic question: What does a world-class university look like? Writing for the World Bank, Salmi began his book *The Challenge of Establishing World-Class Universities* (2009) with a similar essential question: What does it mean to be a world-class university? He argued that the term *world-class* has come to signify "the capacity to compete in the global tertiary education marketplace through the acquisition, adaptation, and creation of advanced knowledge" (4). Of course, as Salmi noted, status as world-class is not a matter of self-proclamation but instead generally "is conferred by the outside world on the basis of international recognition" (2009, 4). For years, as Salmi explained, such status was offered mostly on the basis of institutional prestige, with traditional university power-houses such as Harvard, Yale, Oxford, and Cambridge basking in the sunlight of academic elitism. However, in recent years global ranking schemes based on various quantifiable measures have emerged as key sources for granting world-class status. Two of the more noteworthy global rankings that have gained some level of credibility are the Academic Ranking of World Universities (ARWU) of Shanghai's Jiao Tong University and the Times Higher Education (THE) rankings. Along these lines, Niancai Liu, a collaborator with Salmi and Director of the Jiao Tong University Center for World-Class Universities, has played a key role in advancing the measurement of various institutional outcomes to assess world-class standing.[18] Liu, along with Qing Hui Wang and Qi Wang, also has documented the efforts of his own university—Shanghai Jiao Tong—to attain world-class standing as a research university (Wang, Wang, and Liu 2011).

There is a general belief among national leaders that presently China lacks the kinds of universities typically defined as world-class. There are of course exceptions to such a position, with some scholars and policy makers seeing the nation's top universities, including the likes of Fudan, Peking, Tsinghua, and Zhejiang as already world-class or on the cusp of achieving such status. Some of the global rankings support the latter argument; Peking University (or Beijing University) was ranked forty-fifth in the 2013–2014 THE rankings, followed by Tsinghua at the fiftieth position. No other Chinese university appeared in the top two hundred, although Fudan and the University of Science and Technology of China were listed as part of the group between 201 and 225. Several others were included among the overall list of four hundred. Perhaps it is noteworthy here that Salmi suggested that there may only be thirty to fifty legitimately world-class universities in the entire world. However, we see such thinking as rather narrow—perhaps even elitist—in terms of delineating what constitutes world-class; most certainly, we believe that China's top universities should be included in any discussion of what it means to be a world-class university, if for no other reason than to add some diversity to the discussion of what constitutes world standing among postsecondary education institutions.

The 2013 Jiao Tong ARWU rankings painted a less favorable portrait of Chinese universities than the Times Higher Education rankings, listing Fudan, Peking, Shanghai Jiao Tong, Tsinghua, and Zhejiang among a group ranked 151–200. Nanjing, Sun Yat-sen, and the University of Science and Technology of China appeared in a group ranked between 201 and 300. In all, a total of twenty-eight Chinese universities were ranked among the top five hundred. If Hong Kong is included, that total increases to thirty-three. To offer some perspective on the road ahead, assuming that Chinese leaders will continue their quest to be part of the discussion of university pre-eminence and that these rankings will continue to hold some significance (this may in fact be somewhat of a stretch), presently the United States has 17 of the top 20 and a total of 149 among the top 500 universities, by far the most among nations (here we are referencing the 2013 Jiao Tong ARWU rankings).

Although the rankings have been highly criticized, they do in fact largely depend on quantifiable outputs. The ARWU includes measures of alumni and staff winning Fields Medals and Nobel Prizes, measures of highly cited researchers, number of articles published in *Nature* and *Science*, number of articles indexed in the Science Citation Index Expanded (SCI Expanded) and the Social Sciences Citation Index (SSCI), and per-capita performance (controlling for size of the university). The Times Higher Education rankings include thirteen measures covering the following five areas: (1) teaching (the learning environment), (2) research (volume, income, and innovation), (3) citations (research influence), (4) industry income (innovation), and (5) international mix (staff and students). We point out here that the categories of research and citations account for 30 percent and 32.5 percent of the overall result respectively, thus highly favoring universities with massive research enterprises such as major medical centers. This latter point was stressed at a 2011 Paris conference focused on rankings and accountability organized by UNESCO, the OECD's Programme on Institutional Management of Higher Education (IMHE), and the World Bank. A keynote speaker at the conference pointedly lamented, "There are about 15,000 higher education institutions in the world, and people are obsessing about 100—less than 1 percent of the world's institutions" (Marshall, 2011). It was also pointed out that the global rankings mostly measure research quality and capacity, not the quality of the educational experience for students. Most likely, only research universities may reasonably be compared across national boundaries. Simon Marginson and Marijk van der Wende made a similar point when they noted, "Global comparisons are possible only in relation to one model of institution: that of the comprehensive research-intensive university. This model of HEI [Higher Education Institution] is the only one sufficiently widespread throughout the world to lend itself to the formation of a single competition" (2007, 308).

Salmi tended to support the use of outcome measures such as those used by the ARWU and Times Higher Education, arguing that "world-class universities are recognized in part for their serious outputs. They produce well-qualified graduates who are in high demand on the labor market; they conduct leading-edge research published in top scientific journals; and in the case of science-and-technology-oriented institutions, they contribute to technical innovations through patents and licenses" (Salmi 2009, 6). In actuality though, data from the United States suggest that the production of technical innovations, through such measures as patents and licenses, is in no way limited only to science and technical universities but in fact reflects a serious institutional commitment to research, often measured by research expenditures (Rhoads 2011).

A key aspect of the quest for world-class status is recognition that higher education markets are increasingly globalized, thus adding to a sense of growing international competition for students, faculty, administrators, and research funding. This point is highlighted by Ben Wildavsky in *The Great Brain Race: How Global Universities are Reshaping the World* (2010). He pointed out that students increasingly have a global brand mentality and often pursue their scholarly interests regardless of national boundaries. Obviously, such trends are more likely to apply to students with greater financial means, but these same dynamics also have increasing weight among faculty and administrators. Such conditions offer significant motivation for national governments to seek to advance universities capable of developing a global brand. In fact, as the knowledge- and information-based, high-tech economy becomes increasingly influential, the role of universities is likely to expand. Hence, building universities capable of competing in a global marketplace seems like a reasonable concern and a wise investment.

In their discussion of the Emerging Global Model, Mohrman, Ma, and Baker highlighted a number of features that apparently compose this emerging university ideal, including global mission, worldwide recruitment, and global collaboration with other universities (2008). They also discussed the importance of "research intensity," which, of course, in an age of big science is increasingly a global venture. Their work, as well as that of Salmi and Wildavsky, clearly highlights the importance of broad forms of global engagement, from recruitment of students and faculty to the ways in which research is emphasized and conducted. The importance of engaging in high-level research certainly seems central to any reasonable notion of world-class university standing, especially in light of the growing importance of knowledge- and information-based industries.

A key facet of China's overall effort to develop and/or strengthen world-class

TABLE 1
Original Project 985 Universities (9)

Fudan University
Harbin Institute of Technology
Nanjing University
Peking University
Shanghai Jiao Tong University
Tsinghua University
University of Science and Technology of China
Xi'an Jiao Tong University
Zhejiang University

universities is elevating the quality and quantity of academic research conducted by faculty members. Some scholars and institutional leaders believe that China largely lacks such high-level research, perhaps with some exceptions at a handful of the most highly regarded universities ("China Lacks" 2010). This perspective appears to be widely shared among institutional leaders and policy makers engaged in refashioning China's top universities.

The emphasis placed on elevating research, including expanding research capacity, is apparent in key government documents relating to Projects 211 and 985. For example, the 1999 MoE document "Action Scheme for Invigorating Education Towards the 21st Century," regarded as the starting point for Project 985 and one of the most important documents guiding Chinese higher education, points to the importance of strengthening research at key universities as well as implementing high-level research and creative talent. At the time, nine universities were invited to participate in Project 985 (see table 1). Later, thirty additional universities were added to the project (see table 2). The importance of supporting and expanding research is also evident in subsequent documents from the MoE, including "The 2003–2007 Action Plan for Invigorating Education." The latter document's significance in guiding university research development in China was highlighted in a March 2004 speech by then–minister of education Zhou Ji, who noted, "This new Action Plan will continue to implement the 985 Project, the 211 Project, and the High-Level Innovative Talents Project" (Zhou 2004). Zhou went on to add that new plans would also be launched to strengthen postgraduate education, further stimulate scientific and technological innovation, and enhance social science research. He further maintained that, "It is expected that via these programs and projects, the new Action Plan will offer an overall coordination for the development of various disciplines, talent training, science and technology innovation, the establishment of teaching and researching cohorts, and international cooperation and exchanges. As a result, remarkable improvements could be witnessed in the key universities and key disciplines."

TABLE 2
Additional Project 985 Universities (30)

Beihang University
Beijing Institute of Technology
Beijing Normal University
Central South University
Central University for Nationalities
China Agricultural University
Chongqing University
Dalian University of Technology
East China Normal University
Huazhong University of Science and Technology
Hunan University
Jilin University
Lanzhou University
Nankai University
National University of Defense Technology
Northeastern University
Northwest A & F University
Northwestern Polytechnical University
Ocean University of China
Renmin University of China
Shandong University
Sichuan University
South China University of Technology
Southeast University
Sun Yat-sen University
Tianjin University
Tongji University
University of Electronic Science and Technology of China
Wuhan University
Xiamen University

Another key MoE document, "The Outline of the National Plan for Medium- and Long-Term Educational Reform and Development (2010–2020)" (hereafter, simply "The Outline"), which took more than five years to complete, is regarded by government officials as the most important document for guiding China's higher education during the second decade of the twenty-first century. Here, MoE officials are likely to disagree with Zhu Rongji's criticism at the centennial celebration of Tsinghua University in April 2011. "The Outline" also stresses the elevation of university research:

> by encouraging universities to contribute to innovation in knowledge, technology, national defense, and regional innovation systems. Research in natural science, technological science, philosophy, and social sciences shall be carried out in a big way. While serving national objectives, higher education institutions shall also give their researchers a free hand to explore the unknown, and intensify basic

research. Research in applied sciences shall be strengthened with the main thrust to be focused on major practical issues.

Overall, "The Outline" points to the ongoing importance China's leaders place on developing universities and their research capacity and in this light serves to reinforce and extend the goals and objectives of Projects 211 and 985. Such initiatives, seen in their broadest perspective, may be understood as having two linked aims: (1) strengthening the ability of university science and research to address national interests, including enhancing economic development, and (2) raising the world-wide standing of universities in a manner consistent with the nation's growing ambitions. But government-funded initiatives like those highlighted here address only about a hundred of the nation's universities. Accordingly, we see the need to provide some basic background information about the size and scope of higher education in China in its totality, so as to better ground the case studies to be presented in chapters 1 through 4.

Chinese Higher Education by the Numbers

The Chinese higher education system has evolved to be one of the world's largest, with some 2,305 colleges and universities defined as "regular institutions" by the MoE. These institutions operate at three governance levels: the national, provincial, and municipal.[19] The national universities, of course, are the most prestigious and are far more likely to be known outside of China. Additionally, there are 796 institutions focused only on some type of graduate education and 384 adult higher education institutions, which mostly engage in vocational training. Finally, there are 812 *minban* schools, which may be divided into two categories: domestic and international. Domestic *minbans* are managed by Chinese nationals, and international *minbans* are managed by foreigners, although the latter must be partnered with a Chinese university. Combining the different types of institutions yields a total of nearly 4,300 higher education institutions, a figure comparable in size and diversity to the United States when both four-year and two-year institutions are included.

Recent figures from the MoE reveal that student enrollment in higher education is now over twenty-three million, counting only undergraduates and graduate students enrolled in regular colleges and universities and the specialized graduate institutions. Additionally, there are close to thirteen million more students enrolled in adult education, including web-based programs, advanced degree or certificate programs for people already employed, non-state and private certificate programs, and in-service training programs. Finally, recent counts point to nearly 118,000 international students, who are typically treated as a separate category among university enrollment numbers.

Of the 2,305 regular colleges and universities, only 547 are classified as comprehensive; these colleges and universities are reflective of the shift from the Soviet model of the highly specialized university toward the European/U.S. models of universities with broad (comprehensive) academic programs and curricula. However, the legacy of Soviet influence endures to this day, as revealed by the significant number of highly specialized colleges and universities, including those focusing on the following primary fields: science and technology (821), finance and economics (242), teacher training (189), medicine and pharmacy (163), agriculture (81), art (79), political science and law (69), language and literature (48), physical culture (30), ethnic nationality (18), and forestry (18).

Reflective of the nation's concern and commitment to addressing ethnic minority issues, including social unrest mostly in its western and southwestern regions, the eighteen special ethnic nationality colleges and universities primarily report to the State Ethnic Affairs Commission (as was noted previously, these are commonly described as *minzu* colleges and universities). Fifteen of these institutions are regular universities offering a range of academic programs but specializing in education and research related to ethnic minorities. Ethnic universities of this type are regionally dispersed so as to best address China's diverse ethnic populations. Comparatively speaking, these universities share some characteristics in terms of their cultural and ethnic missions to U.S. Historically Black Colleges and Universities (HBCUs) as well as some Hispanic Serving Institutions (HSIs).

The vast size and diversity of Chinese higher education makes it difficult to draw firm conclusions about the system as a whole. Indeed, we are of the conviction that analysis of Chinese higher education benefits from a fine-tuned, focused, empirical investigation. In other words, there is little benefit to conducting comparative analysis of national universities with provincial or municipal ones or comparing *minbans* to publicly funded colleges and universities. A better approach is to examine in some detail the differential sectors of the overall system. Along these lines, and given our interest in national initiatives to expand and enhance research capacity and increase internationalization, our concern necessarily leads us to focus on those universities designated by the central government to receive extra funding as part of Projects 211 and 985. Such a goal resulted in four intensive case studies conducted at the nation's leading comprehensive universities.

The Chinese University as a City of Infinite Variety

Writing about the move toward mass higher education in East Asia in 1995, Hayhoe raised a provocative question about possibilities for China: "Is there the possibility of an Asian multiversity emerging in the Chinese context?" (Hayhoe 1995, 312). Of course, her reference to the multiversity built upon Clark Kerr's classic work *The Uses of the University* (1963), which described the U.S. research university of the early 1960s. The multiversity, for Kerr, defined the basic operations of the university in terms of three important functions: research, teaching, and service. The functions of the multiversity were to be tied to the growing knowledge industry, and in fact, from Kerr's point of view, the university should serve as the leading social institution in producing and applying knowledge for the purpose of serving national development, including, most importantly, economic development. His vision sought to challenge traditional thinking, which often viewed the university simply as an institution engaged in educating future generations of civic, cultural, and economic leaders. For Kerr, the university should be "a city of infinite variety," characterized by Hayhoe as "a complex, diverse entity with greatly fractionalized power; the multiversity is massive in size, has many levels, serves diverse populations" (1995, 307).

In drawing on Kerr's vision, Hayhoe raised the possibility that China, some sixteen years ago, was moving toward the development of its own isomorphic version of a comprehensive multiversity. Although we need not reach any definitive conclusion with regard to her question, it is nonetheless helpful to ponder the degree to which a Chinese version of the multiversity is sprouting up from Chinese soil, although certainly evidencing forms of influence from the West in general and the United States in particular. We consider the manner and form of points of divergence, given the unique qualities of Chinese society and culture. This is an important facet to our intellectual endeavor in this book—to raise questions about the contemporary structure of the Chinese research university, mindful of models it presumably may be seeking to mirror in some rather confounding and multiplicitous ways but also paying great attention to cultural influences deriving from Chinese society. The mixture of Chinese culture and influences from the West is likely to yield organizational forms reflective of the sort of "infinite variety" that makes universities such intriguing cultural spaces.

Writing in 1995, Hayhoe certainly could not have predicted very easily that only some seven years later Chinese higher education participation rates would reach the magical threshold that Trow described as mass higher education—the 15-percent mark. And now, a decade and a half later, higher education participation rates in China seem to be progressing toward 30 percent, with the nation perhaps heading toward universal levels of postsecondary participation (50 percent, based on Trow's thinking). These more recent enrollment developments are captured to some extent in Hayhoe's 2011 collaborative effort with Jun Li, Jing Lin, and Qiang Zha, *Portraits of 21st Century Chinese Universities: In the Move to Mass Higher Education*. This book highlights changes linked to massification for twelve Chinese universities. But participation rates alone do not capture the essence of the multiversity, nor do they tell the entire story of the revolutionary changes taking place in China. Consequently, there is a great need to deepen the discussion of the contemporary Chinese university. Expansion of the student population certainly is a beginning point, but much more is going on, and a good deal of it affects the working lives of professors.

The research enterprise is a key facet of the modern university, or multiversity if one prefers, and such endeavors come with many complexities, including vast differences among scholars based on their disciplinary orientations, institutional variations, and, of course, individual dispositions and preferences. Because of these complexities, we subscribe to the value of the case study approach to illuminate aspects of "a city of infinite variety," especially as such variety applies to the working lives of professors.

Throughout our writing, we stress the idea of the Chinese university as a center of diverse activities that is not simply engaged in educating the next generation of Chinese leaders but also serves in a wide range of capacities, including most importantly its role in the production, management, and application of knowledge. This is a critical function of the modern university in an age dominated by global forces. And although many university actors play key roles in the production, management, and application of knowledge, Rhoads and Katalin Szelényi (2011) saw faculty as particularly pivotal to these complex processes. We concur and thus choose to turn our attention to the work of Chinese professors, which we explore in the light of thick description generated through case study inquiry.

CHAPTER ONE

Tsinghua University and the Spirit of Innovation and Entrepreneurialism

Tsinghua University, commonly described as the "MIT of China," is consistently ranked as one of the two best universities in the nation, along with neighboring Peking University. Most see it as the nation's top university in terms of science, technology, engineering, and mathematics (STEM). The university is especially renowned for its applied science and engineering programs and their extensive connections to business and industry. Since the 1980s there has been a well-known saying at Tsinghua: "No matter which door you open at Tsinghua, you will find a company inside." But while the university is highly recognized for graduating some of China's leading scientists and engineers, it also is known for cultivating many high-level government officials, including President Xi Jinping, former president Hu Jintao, former premier Zhu Rongji, and the chairman of the National People's Congress Wu Bangguo. Given its many accomplishments beyond simply STEM-related fields, Tsinghua is recognized as a truly comprehensive university earning worldwide recognition in such global ranking schemes as the Times Higher Education World University Rankings and the QS World University Rankings, where in the 2013–2014 versions Tsinghua occupied the fiftieth and forty-eighth positions, respectively.

Tsinghua is widely recognized as the most entrepreneurial university in China. The physical embodiment of the university's entrepreneurial spirit is captured by Tsinghua University Science Park, simply known as TusPark, located in a high-tech zone of Haidian District near the southeast corner of the campus. Covering an area of some twenty-five hectares, TusPark comprises twenty buildings, including twin high-rise structures, and primarily serves as a center for technology transfer, company incubation, and talent cultivation. In keeping with the university's focus on innovation and entrepreneurialism, the park has built extensive business relationships with leading international corporations, including Google and Microsoft, while offering incubator support to many less well-known start-up companies. Together, major corporations and start-ups make use of TusPark's business and research support, taking up residence within the 690,000-square-meter facility. TusPark, with its focus on the application of scientific innovation, is a critical component of the university's economic development mission. It also is a sight to behold; its lavishness was captured to some extent by Jeffrey Young, writing for the *Chronicle of Higher Education*: "The science park for China's leading technological university feels like a fantasyland of entrepreneurship: gilded lounges, grand banquet rooms, a museum and movie theater on site—all packed into a set of matching skyscrapers around a central plaza that resembles New York City's Rockefeller Center" (2010).

The reality of the entrepreneurial spirit of Tsinghua is also evident in a 2011 report issued by the Intellectual Property Owners Association, which listed the top three hundred organizations (mostly corporations) in terms of patents granted by the U.S. Patent and Trademark Office. Although corporations dominated the list, Tsinghua University was included among fourteen universities. It was the only non-U.S. university to make the list, with 104 patents awarded. The only universities with more patents were the University of California system (349), MIT (174), Stanford University (155), the University of Wisconsin (136), Cal Tech (134), and the University of Texas (122) ("Tsinghua Joins" 2011). This is no small accomplishment for Tsinghua.

Of particular interest to us is the transformation of the university over the past fifteen years or so—what we define as the global ambition period of China's higher education development. It is a period that includes the advent of Project 211, in 1995, and then a few years later the addition of Project 985. Tsinghua's great progress was put on stage at its centennial celebration in April 2011, when China's leading government officials praised the university for its service to the nation and university publications hailed its many accomplishments, including the fact that it has been the academic home to two Nobel laureates, Yang Zhenning and Li Zhendao, the great mathematician Hua Luogeng, and the prominent Ming historian Wu Han.

Of course, the development of the university into a widely recognized research university has been the result of many factors, including strong government support, broad-based market activities, and deep engagement with international

academic circles. And although the university actively explores numerous opportunities to strengthen its linkages with business and industry, it also is highly
engaged with national and provincial government agencies and places great
emphasis on serving the needs of Chinese society. However, it is the spirit of
innovation and entrepreneurialism that has come to define the core of Tsinghua's culture. Accordingly, we begin our discussion of Tsinghua and its innovative spirit with a review of its historical roots, which in part form the basis
for its present-day development and emergence as a leader in Chinese higher
education. As is the case with all the case studies presented in this book, our discussion is based on analyses of key institutional documents, a thorough review
of relevant literature, and formal and informal interviews conducted with key
faculty members and administrators.

Tsinghua's Unique History

Tsinghua University is located in the northwest part of Beijing, to the east of
and across the street from another prominent university—Peking University.
The center and older section of the campus is located at a site that 150 years ago
served as the royal courtyard during the Qing Dynasty and the Ming Dynasty
before that (some refer to this area of the campus as the Tsinghua Garden).
Indeed, some people subscribing to *Fengshui*, the Chinese art and practice of
creating harmonious environments, believe this is the reason that the university
has spawned so many great thinkers and national leaders. When present-day
tourists visit the famous Lotus Pond and *Huang Dao* (abandoned island), they
can still see relics dating back to the early years of the Qing Dynasty.

In 1911, the funds used to build what then was called the Tsinghua School
(it also appears as Tsinghua College in some texts) were monies returned to
China as a consequence of its overpayment to the United States and the Boxer
Indemnity Fund, a form of financial restitution demanded of China following
the end of the Boxer Rebellion.[1] Owing to influence from the United States on
early operations of Tsinghua College, its primary audience was Chinese students
preparing to study in the United States under the Boxer Indemnity Scholarship Program. Not too surprisingly, the development of the school with the
indemnity remission funds was interpreted in divergent ways among Chinese
and U.S. observers. From a Chinese point of view the school was more likely
to be defined as a "cynical American scheme to subject China to commercial
exploitation" than "an act of benevolence" or "good will," as some Americans
were apt to describe it (Hunt 1972, 540–541). As is often the case, the actual facts
were far more complicated.

Tsinghua College was founded as a middle and high school to prepare students to study abroad, with the major destination being America's universities;
in fact, many of its faculty members were recruited from the United States. By

the late 1920s many of Tsinghua's graduates had returned to China and helped to transform the school into a four-year university. The transformation of Tsinghua in 1928 to university status was a sign of the nation's progress toward higher education independence. However, the historic connections of the university to its U.S. counterparts remained visible on campus: many of the early buildings were designed by an American architect and modeled after Thomas Jefferson's university—the University of Virginia. During the early years of the university, many famous U.S. scholars were invited to the campus, and the departments and schools were established on the basis of the American university model, including implementation of the idea of general education as a core component of undergraduate education.[2]

In 1937, as the Japanese army invaded and occupied the eastern region of China, the university moved to the city of Kunming in the southwestern province of Yunnan, where it merged temporarily with two other major universities —Peking University and Nankai University, the latter originally located in Tianjin, to the east of Beijing. Together, these three universities formed Southwest United University (in some literature *United* is translated as *Associated*).[3]

For roughly eight years, and during the war, United University proved to be a great success. The university was marked by its superb faculty deriving from the three eminent universities and a relatively liberal academic environment, in part the outcome of its distance from the temporary capital of Chongqing. Faculty and students alike were inspired to excel, and a sense of unity emerged as a motivating force and a necessity for the anticipated reconstruction of their invaded motherland. Although the material conditions were spartan, the morale and learning environment were characterized by vitality and hopefulness. Such a quality became widely known as the United University spirit, which later contributed to the core culture of the three universities. Nobel Prize–winning physicists Li Zhendao and Yang Zhenning (also known as Chen-Ning Franklin Yang) graduated from United University. In 1955, alumni of United University accounted for close to 25 percent of the total members of the Chinese Academy of Sciences (118 of 473) (Z. Huang 1986; F. Zhou 1990).

After the establishment of the People's Republic of China in 1949, Tsinghua University and other universities alike turned to the Soviet Union's model of higher education, emphasizing lengthy periods of time for knowledge acquisition (five or six years for undergraduate study was generally the norm) and more narrowly defined areas of specialization. These were seen as key strategies in imparting applied knowledge to meet the demands of industrialization under a communist planned economy. After 1952, when the Ministry of Education introduced the National College and Department Adjustment program, Tsinghua was transformed into a polytechnic university, with most of the natural science, humanities, and social science departments leaving to join other universities.

The transformation to the Soviet model, of course, greatly influenced the structure, function, and culture of the university. As a consequence of this dramatic ideological and utilitarian shift, Tsinghua became a paramount university in terms of cultivating engineers with both "red" and "specialized" knowledge characteristics. These qualities were seen as crucial to the construction of national industries under the communist model of planned economic development. After the end of the Cultural Revolution, a period on campus marked by widespread political struggle among divergent student factions (Hinton 1972), national and provincial governments filled their staffs with Tsinghua alumni, many of whom had been model engineers within medium and large state-owned companies. A statistic from the early 1990s revealed that more than three hundred high-ranking national or provincial officials had graduated from Tsinghua University. The rise of loyalist engineers to technocratic positions within the government helped to create a new class within communist China and was described by the American sociologist Joel Andreas as the "rise of red engineers" (2009).

During the early 1980s, Tsinghua re-established itself as a comprehensive university, resuming academic studies in the areas of the natural sciences, humanities, and social sciences. Within a national context increasingly characterized as reformist and "open," the latter point with reference to foreign nations, especially those of the Western world, the university gradually adjusted ideas and methodologies linked to a planned economic system and moved in the direction of market-oriented economic models. This led to a broadening of its exchanges and collaborations with Western countries and their respective universities. In many ways, the culmination of this shift was marked by the 1994 founding of TusPark, whose development was vigorously encouraged by both the Ministry of Education and the Beijing Municipal Government. Further solidifying its ties to business and industry, in 1995 the university established the University-Industry Cooperation Committee (UICC), which served as a second key connection between the university's applied science operations and the needs of society. Additionally, in 1996 the university collaborated with the southern city of Shenzhen to build the Research Institute of Tsinghua University in Shenzhen (RITS), which adopted a market-driven model and eventually included four major research centers: the Center for Optomechatronics and Advanced Manufacturing, the Center for Electronics and Information Technology, the Center for Advanced Materials and Biotechnology, and the Center for New Energy and Environmental Technology. RITS was developed in conjunction with the national plan to further develop the Shenzhen special economic zone of Guangdong Province and in so doing take advantage of the economic strength of the neighboring city of Hong Kong. Tsinghua's presence in southern Guangdong served the university well, especially in terms of the growing connections to Hong Kong corporations and the city's business elites. Several billionaires donated hundreds of millions of RMB through the Tsinghua Education Foundation to build magnificent buildings at the Tsinghua campus, including a new library, student center, economics and management school, public administration school, law school, and architecture school, among others.

At the same time that Tsinghua was making entrepreneurial inroads throughout China, the national government expanded its already strong support for the university. With the implementation of Project 985 in 1998, the university, along with Peking University, received preferential support from the central government in the form of extra funding each year in the neighborhood of 600 million RMB annually (1.8 billion RMB over three years). This funding was in addition to Tsinghua's normal governmental allocation and in part was aimed at advancing the institution as a world-class research university. Increased governmental funding, combined with numerous entrepreneurial initiatives, substantially altered the condition and morale of the university. In a matter of only a few years, faculty salaries doubled. The infrastructure, including scientific laboratories and related equipment, was expanded and dramatically upgraded. Library holdings and research-oriented databases grew substantially, and greater attention was paid to the beautification of the campus buildings and grounds. The university also successfully recruited greater numbers of foreign scholars for short- and long-term participation in research and academic life. In short, the university increasingly took on some of the basic features and characteristics of a world-class research university, including most notably its global engagement.

Today, some see the university as having already achieved world-class standing and point to such indices as the Times Higher Education and QS World University Rankings. But others are not convinced and see the need to strengthen the university's academic programs and overall research capacity. Such skeptics are more likely to note the relatively low ranking of the university in the Shanghai Jiaotong Academic Ranking of World Universities, where recently it was listed within the 151–200 range. They also are likely to raise concerns about academic freedom, seen by many as an absolute quality of world-class universities.

Tsinghua now enrolls a little over 15,000 undergraduates and close to 16,000 graduate students, including some 8,400 doctoral students. The university student population also includes approximately 2,300 international students, combining both the undergraduate and graduate levels. The university comprises sixteen schools and fifty-six departments in a full array of fields, including aerospace technology, architecture, economics and management, education, engineering (chemical, civil, electrical, mechanical, and materials science), finance, humanities, journalism and communication, law, life sciences, medicine, natural sciences, public policy and management, and social sciences. Additionally, the university employs over 3,100 faculty members and more than 1,200 postdoctoral researchers.

Tsinghua has become a point of attraction for both visiting foreign scholars and visitors seeking to take in the sites of China's most famous science and technology university. For many of China's governmental leaders, the university, with its multitude of compelling scholarly accomplishments, has become a source of national pride. The university's special relationship with top Chinese officials also is reflected in the extensive support it receives from the government, and to some extent, in the extra degree of institutional autonomy it enjoys (Pan 2007). Such relations are important to explore as part of understanding Tsinghua's place in the national higher education landscape.

Governmental/Administrative Relations and Research Complications

With the establishment of the new China under the Mao-led communist revolution, Tsinghua was favored both by the national government and the Beijing Municipal Government; consequently, the university has enjoyed substantial funding relative to the vast majority of Chinese national-level universities. Because of its strong relationship with both the local and national governments, conservative and utilitarian characteristics predominate in the organization's culture. Although such characteristics may not hinder the university's ability to produce excellent engineers, there is some sentiment that they may limit the development of original knowledge and world-class science. This question has been widely debated over the years, both in academic circles and public venues. But even one of the nation's greatest scientists (considered the father of China's rocket science program), the late professor Qian Xuesun, who returned to China from the United States in 1955, once asked, "Why do China's universities fail to produce more master-level talents?"

Questions about the nation's production of top scholars and scientists are often directed at Tsinghua, given its leading position among Chinese science and engineering universities. A professor of law with whom we spoke offered a response: "Because administrative sectors intervene too much in academic affairs, organizing excessive forms of evaluation and assessment activities. This results in too much quantification of performance criteria, and in turn, people's hearts and minds become too blundering." The professor went on to add, "The government controls too much, so this limits the universities and their ability to produce outstanding talent, just like children may fail to learn to walk skillfully if the parents control too much all the time."

Other faculty members pointed to problems with basic research mechanisms, including most notably research funding. For example, professors noted that although national, provincial, and municipal levels of government implement and support diverse research centers and talent development programs and institution- and discipline-based funding sources also exist, too many of these opportunities are oriented toward the official status and titles of applicants, as opposed to being idea-driven grant competitions. Some faculty noted that simply because a project is funded at a higher level (such as at the national level), or in terms of a larger amount of money, does not necessarily indicate that the research outcomes are any better.

Other serious research issues were noted by Shi Yigong and Rao Yi in their 2010 article published with *Science* (Shi and Rao 2010). They argued that widespread problems—some of which are structural and others cultural in nature—are limiting China's potential to advance scientific innovation. At the heart of the problem is a research funding system that is heavily bureaucratic and open to favoritism. They pointed out that the top-down approach employed in China "stifles innovation and makes clear to everyone that the connections with bureaucrats and a few powerful scientists are paramount, dictating the entire process of guideline preparation. To obtain major grants in China, it is an open secret that doing good research is not as important as schmoozing with powerful bureaucrats and their favorite experts" (Shi and Rao 2010, 1128). They went on to argue that this aspect of the scientific culture "even permeates the minds of those who are new returnees from abroad; they quickly adapt to the local environment and perpetuate the unhealthy culture" (1128). Thus, instead of spending their time on serious scholarly endeavors, such as participating in seminars, working in laboratories, or mentoring graduate students, Chinese researchers must spend a good portion of their time developing relationships and making connections.

A faculty member with whom we spoke suggested that in order to apply for major research funding one must spend about 30 percent of one's time preparing the proposal and about 70 percent "behind the curtain" (*muhou* in Chinese), making inquiries as to who may be on a particular review committee and then taking action to place oneself in good standing with the committee members. This professor suggested that many Tsinghua faculty members are reluctant to behave this way, and so they may not appear to be as successful in terms of their research accomplishments. Faculty also noted that similar problems exist with editors of key journals. Overall, these cultural norms limit the advance of science in China and partially address the question raised by the late Qian Xuesun.

Part of the problem, according to faculty members, is that too much of the research enterprise is controlled by administrators and governmental officials, who are sometimes one and the same, given that Chinese universities are run to a great extent by the government. Some research problems are locally rooted within the university itself, such as when academic administrators have too much control over research funds or operate in overly bureaucratic ways. A faculty member argued that oftentimes administrators are too conservative in interpreting government regulations, which may unnecessarily limit opportunities for professors. Although many Tsinghua faculty members might hope to operate with great integrity, the fact that much of the administrative process is out of their hands leads to frustration and the feeling that they have no choice but to participate in behind-the-curtain processes.

Numerous faculty members called to mind examples of their frustration with confusing administrative processes and overly bureaucratic decision making, some offering heart-wrenching stories of anguish. For example, a sociology professor described a scenario involving a PhD candidate's publication requirements, noting that the student had published two journal articles, as required, but that one of them was in a journal not included on the university's official list. The journal was considered A-level, which is the highest rank possible, but because it was not on the university's list, it could not be counted. As this professor explained, "When the candidate's dissertation was submitted for approval the committee in charge decided that the student was not qualified to submit the dissertation." After extensive follow-up with numerous administrators, the professor concluded that although the university had the opportunity to be more flexible with regard to rules generated by the MoE, it refused to do so. In an exasperated tone, the professor noted, "So, why do they emphasize a student's publications? The main purpose is to raise the quantity of publications of the whole university. This way of evaluation is more like the Great Leap Forward. It is not done on the basis of a scientific attitude."

Philip Altbach and Gerard Postiglione, in their paper "Hong Kong's Academic Advantage" (2012) noted some problems inherent in the scholarly systems at Chinese universities, including at universities such as Tsinghua. One concern they pointed to is the need to limit administrative control of universities; Altbach and Postiglione tended to support the "de-administration of universities," as it is framed in China's 2020 blueprint for higher education development, known as the "Outline for Education Reform and Development (2010–2020)." From such a perspective, the government primarily serves in a broad steering capacity and is less involved in the regular, day-to-day operations of the universities. But Altbach and Postiglione expressed pessimism about whether such a shift was likely to actually take place, pointing to the case of South China University of Science and Technology in Shenzhen, where efforts to limit administrative control were not entirely successful.

In addition to complexities associated with research funding, faculty members also raised issues of academic freedom and concerns about the degree to which Chinese scholars are able to pursue a full range of scholarly interests. These issues seemed especially salient to professors working in the humanities and social sciences, where not everyone has a keen sense of what can and cannot be researched. For example, one faculty member discussed conducting extensive field work in the countryside, focusing on the oral histories of farmers, only to discover that no publisher in China would touch his book manuscript. The professor in question is now considering looking for a foreign publisher, but this may be just as problematic, although in different ways (such as problems relating to language differences). This example points to the conclusion that some issues may be too sensitive to study. In fact, there is a saying in China: "Research without prohibition, but publish with discipline" (*yanjiu wu jinqu, chuban you jilu*), which essentially means that one can theoretically study just about anything, but when it comes to publishing the process is much more regulated and supervised. Issues of academic freedom are imperative to address if top universities such as Tsinghua truly hope to solidify their standing among the world's best universities.

Despite some of the research obstacles presented in this section, there is much for Tsinghua faculty members to be excited about in the short term and the long term, including most notably the extensive funding associated with Projects 211 and 985. The first-term (1999–2001) and second-term (2002–2004) funding of Project 985 substantially improved the infrastructure of the university's schools and departments. Although Project 211 funding is smaller, its funds also have helped to strengthen the university by supporting a host of academic activities. As a consequence of these projects, the university's spending on teaching and research grew significantly from the mid-1990s to the present. Indeed, these projects were widely applauded by the Tsinghua faculty. For example, a mathematics professor likened the funding support to "receiving charcoal during a cold and snowy winter."

Funds from Projects 211 and 985 have been especially helpful as research seed money for the projects of junior faculty. Obtaining such funds typically does not require the behind-the-curtain efforts often necessary in pursuing major grants, such as the larger, more prestigious national awards. Along these lines, a professor of law noted how much easier it is to access 211 or 985 funds. A faculty member in electrical engineering explained that the first term of 985 funding was a bit like scattering seeds, "but the second term funding helped us to build experimental platforms." And a faculty member in education likened the initial 1.8 billion RMB allocated to Peking and Tsinghua each, as part of Project 985, to pie falling from the sky—*tianshang diao xianbing*.

A professor of mathematics saw the increased funding as critical to eroding the last vestiges of the narrowly focused Soviet model that had once defined universities such as Tsinghua. This professor contrasted Tsinghua's transformation with that of another famous university: "Harvard's transformation from a religious college to a modern university took over eighty years, but maybe Tsinghua will need less time to finish the job. . . . We've spent about thirty years so far, but our transformation may need a little bit more time. . . . The key is that we have a clear idea about where we should go." According to this professor, the path for the university involves moving from "indoctrinating teaching" to forms of education in which critical thinking and creativity are promoted.

Although this section raises some evidence of problematic administrative and governmental involvement in the university research enterprise, particularly with regard to research funding decisions, the reality is that without extensive government involvement in Tsinghua, it is highly unlikely that the university could have attained its present-day success. Correspondingly, without strong ties between the government and Tsinghua administrative officials, it is unlikely that the university would have the degree of autonomy that it has. In fact, in a case study of autonomy at Tsinghua and the role of officialdom, Pan Su-Yan made just such an argument: "The political affiliations between Tsinghua's senior administrators, government officials, and national leaders were an important factor in helping Tsinghua successfully attain some level of university autonomy, even though these affiliations inevitably invited the state's political influence on the university" (Pan 2007, 122). Pan went on to argue that interweaving politics and academic governance is a double-edged sword: It can place the university under greater supervision, but when personnel affiliated with the university hold government offices, it can help to protect the university from certain governmental constraints (2007, 122).

A Tsinghua faculty member noted that part of the challenge with such close ties to the government is that the university is often in the position of having to address a short-term, government-driven agenda. Further, the senior administrators are appointed by the government mainly on the basis of political credentials, rather than on the basis of academic or administrative expertise. Certainly, university-government relations are complicated in China, and there clearly are multiple perspectives about the role governmental officials ought to play in operating the university.

Despite some disagreement about the precise role of government in university operations and in shaping academic science, there is no denying that rising expectations from governmental leaders about the importance of university research has contributed to new expectations for faculty members, including those at Tsinghua. These new expectations present a challenging new environment for academics working at top Chinese research universities.

Rising Expectations and Pressure for Faculty

With higher levels of research funding and greater scholarly expectations, Tsinghua's faculty members face a professional environment much different from that of fifteen or twenty years before. With so much emphasis on basic and applied research across a wide spectrum of disciplines, some faculty raised concerns about whether the quality of education may be adversely impacted. Faced with greater expectations to pursue funded research and engage in empirical inquiry, some fear that they will be left with little to no time for teaching and working with students. Accordingly, faculty expressed concerns that students, as well as the educational mission of the university, may suffer. Faculty members subscribing to such fears saw Tsinghua's 3.6 billion RMB in annual research spending (as of 2011) as a warning signal alerting the academic community to potential problems—such as lesser focus on the educational mission of the university.

Increased research funding is only part of the issue. There is also the matter of the rising pressure on Tsinghua faculty to publish more and more, and in the top journals in their respective fields. Clearly, the threshold for faculty promotions is getting higher and higher. But rising requirements are not the only problem; fierce competition among the faculty for limited promotions also adds fuel to the fire. For example, a university may require a minimum of five publications in A-level (top-level) journals for a given promotion period, but many faculty members may in fact publish well beyond the minimum. Because limited slots exist across the university, faculty at Tsinghua and elsewhere in China must compete against one another for such promotions. So, for example, if Tsinghua is granted forty new full professor titles (*zheng jiaoshou*) to be awarded to qualified associate professors (*fu jiaoshou*) for a given year, the number of qualified associate professors may be two hundred, resulting in a potential success rate of only one in five. This is a hypothetical example but is one repeated time and time again at top universities such as those profiled in this book. Universities are essentially mandated to maintain a certain number of full and associate professor positions, and increasing this number involves gaining the approval of the appropriate government officials.

Another added element relative to newly hired Tsinghua faculty is a six-year trial period, at the end of which the *jiangshi* or lecturer (this position is roughly equivalent to the rank of assistant professor at many Western universities) must either earn promotion to associate professor or leave the university. If successful, the new associate professor earns higher levels of professional security. This new policy is a bit reminiscent of how tenure works in the United States, given that an assistant professor typically gets six or seven years to either earn tenure at her or his respective university or leave the faculty.

With faculty spending greater percentages of their time on research and publishing, some Tsinghua faculty believe that the learning atmosphere is increasingly compromised. A sociology professor commented, "There used to be time for students and faculty to sit and talk about books, discuss and describe their key themes and content. Ask questions about the books. But now this is quite rare. It's a kind of setback. As teachers, we find ourselves somewhat helpless to prevent this setback." Similarly, a professor of law believed that faculty increasingly relied on PowerPoint (PPT) presentations because their lectures could be "reproduced" again and again, without too much time and energy spent on course preparation. But this professor believed that overreliance on PPT as an instructional method was partially to blame for decreased motivation on the part of students. As he explained, "Now students don't even bother to read the textbooks. They just want to read the teacher's PPT. After the teacher's lecture, students will ask whether they can get a copy of the PPT or not. Or they will ask which part of the PPT will be on the test."

One might argue that students, like their professors, are also faced with rising pressures linked to greater and greater competition within the society. Faculty face competition as part of the promotion process, whereas students experience it in their preparations for the job market. Part of the issue is China's one-child policy and the responsibility children eventually assume for their parents. This increases pressure to find a good job upon graduation. And if concerns about finding a job become the driving force in the academic lives of students, then motivating them to pursue learning for learning's sake may be a difficult task.

What one hears in the voices of Tsinghua professors, both in terms of their own academic experiences and those of their students, is the powerful role of competition in Chinese society, particularly within the context of the modern university. Here, we are reminded of Susan Shirk's 1982 book *Competitive Comrades*, in which she highlighted a paradoxical quality to the academic struggles of Chinese high school students. She found that students did not simply conform to the Maoist vision stressing egalitarianism and collectivism; they also engaged in intensely competitive and individualistic endeavors as a means of achieving academically and furthering their career possibilities. The latter, as she explained, was the consequence of the social realities of China, wherein one faces the pressures of living within a massive population offering limited resources and opportunities. We saw elements of this type of competiveness at Tsinghua and at the other universities highlighted in this book. There is little doubt that some of the competition is reflective of the longstanding realities of life in such a populous nation, as Shirk found in the case of high school students some thirty years ago. But other facets of the competition are more recent in origin and are likely tied to the increasing influence of market forces on Chinese institutions, including at the nation's leading universities. Such market pressures certainly influence organizational life and decision making at Tsinghua and are increasingly affecting the daily lives of faculty members. But faculty members also have numerous opportunities to benefit from the university's growing marketization. For those professors engaged in applied science research, the entrepreneurial ventures of the eye-catching TusPark are a good place to invest their time and energy.

Advancing Entrepreneurialism at Tsinghua: The TusPark Story

Since the early 1990s, and following national efforts to open the society to market forces and international engagement, Tsinghua has actively embraced marketization. Such an embrace was manifested in developing Tsinghua University Science Park, or TusPark, building extensive collaborations with business and industry, advancing its own economic enterprises, and cooperating with other economic initiatives to build R&D centers, such as the previously noted Research Institute of Tsinghua University in Shenzhen (RITS). The goal is not only to produce enormous economic benefits but also to generate broader social benefits.

The road toward marketization, though, was not always a smooth one. For example, money given to the university to build a new library, eventually to be named after the donor—Shao Yifu, a famous Hong Kong media mogul—was met with much resistance by a group of university elders in the early 1990s. In light of the fact that Shao only donated roughly half the building costs, with the remaining funds coming from the government, the elders opposed naming the library after one individual. A commonly heard complaint went something like this: "A capitalist gave a piece of his stinking money and so why do we need to erect a monument for him? How could this be a fitting thing to do as communists?" Because of such opposition, the ceremony for naming the new library had to be suspended. Shao, as is to be expected, was quite unhappy. Given that he is very influential in Hong Kong, his unhappiness and attitude toward Tsinghua may have influenced other Hong Kong business leaders. In the subsequent years Hong Kong was a wasteland in terms of financial giving to the university. But this incident was only a minor setback for the entrepreneurial ventures of the university.

After the central government implemented its market economy policy around 1992, attitudes toward donations began to change. Under this new climate, characterized by diverse revenue-seeking endeavors, Tsinghua reversed its decision and decided to hold a dedication ceremony for the new library in September 1994, naming it YiFu Hall. This seemed to mend the relationship between Tsinghua and Shao, and it opened the door for attracting more and more donations from Hong Kong and abroad. Today, if one strolls through the eastern area of the campus, it will be impossible to miss the dozen or so magnificent new buildings built using the donations of wealthy business leaders.

The most visible manifestation of Tsinghua's efforts to advance its entrepreneurial interests is TusPark, established in 1994 as one of the earliest university science parks in China. In 2003, TusPark was rated as the only A-level university science park in China, and it was only recently that several other university science parks were upgraded to this level. TusPark has continuously contributed to scientific innovation and entrepreneurialism at a regional and national level, and after some eighteen years it has established an unparalleled reputation as a university science park. Indeed, it is no stretch of the imagination to say that TusPark has become a famous brand throughout China and around the world. TusPark now has branches in more than thirty major cities in China, including Guangzhou, Kunshan, Nanjing, Shanghai, Tianjin, and Xi'an.

The heart of TusPark is located in Zhongguancun, a business area within Haidian District that is home to many high-tech industries. The overall enterprise involves more than four hundred domestic and international companies, including the likes of Juniper, Sohu, Google, Sun Microsystems, and Microsoft. Additionally, the research park supports Tsinghua's own high-tech companies in the form of Tongfang (which produces digital household appliances), Unisplendour (which specializes in information technology and communications), and Chengzhi (which focuses on pharmaceutical, health, and technology products). Other less well-known start-up companies also occupy space at TusPark, working with Tsinghua faculty and staff to turn cutting-edge applied research into innovative products. The idea of bringing established companies such as Google and Microsoft into the same university science facility as start-ups reflects Chinese business thinking at work: Building relationships and connections with others is critical to advancing company goals—it is what the Chinese call *guanxi* (which may be translated as *connections* or *relationships*). Even the open spaces and social activities at TusPark are designed to expand such relationships; hence, new start-up companies have the opportunity to interact with executives, mid-level management, researchers, and technicians from established companies, presenting potentially win-win opportunities. As a consequence, this unique entrepreneurial atmosphere has attracted venture capitalists interested in investing in the development of new technologies, such as communication systems. Additionally, some of Tsinghua's research institutes also occupy office space, rubbing elbows with business-minded entrepreneurs. TusPark has attracted great interest among other domestic and foreign universities.

Although the TusPark model has drawn much praise, it nonetheless has faced criticism relating to the strong financial backing of the Chinese government. For example, an article in the *Chronicle of Higher Education* pointed out, "Some foreign corporations have criticized the park's model as offering an unfair level of government support" (Young 2010). The article went on to note that one British corporation had filed a complaint with the European Union against one of TusPark's spinoff companies, "arguing, among other things, that the company was competing unfairly because its research costs were so heavily subsidized by the Chinese government" (Young 2010). Inarguably, the massive TusPark enterprise brings Chinese and Western entrepreneurial practices together in previously unimagined ways.

The idea of constructing TusPark arose back in 1993. An ad-hoc committee was formulated, and Rong Yonglin, a well-regarded professor of chemistry and a graduate of Tsinghua's chemical engineering department, was appointed as the leader of the group. The group's early plans drew the attention and support of both the local and national governments. In July 1993, the Beijing Municipal Government approved a location and the basic plans for a Tsinghua science park. At a 1994 meeting of key university and department senior leaders, important planning and operational goals were developed: (1) TusPark should learn from other successful science and high-tech centers, such as California's Silicon Valley, North Carolina's Research Triangle Park, the Tsukuba Science City of Japan, and the Hsinchu Science and Technology Park of Taiwan; (2) the park should garner government funding as part of Beijing's High-Technology Industry Development Experimental Zone in Haidian District (the Beijing district where most of Beijing's universities, such as Tsinghua, Peking, and Renmin are located); and (3) the development and operation of TusPark should be organized like a modern business enterprise. The Tsinghua Science Park Development Center was established, and Mei Meng, a highly respected professor of business and management and a graduate of Tsinghua's automation department, was nominated as the general manager. The goals described above came to define the essential operational enterprise of the park.

From the start, TusPark was intensely focused on its mission of innovation and technology transfer, paying great attention to talent development, information dissemination, and company incubation. During an interview, Rong Yonglin noted that the vast majority of university science parks fail, in part because it is too tempting to turn the ventures into real estate projects. As he explained, "The real estate business is much quicker. You just construct buildings and sell them to whoever wants to pay. The initial capital investment is paid back in a short period of time. But when it comes to science parks, universities normally do not have enough capital to finish such a grand construction project completely on their own. They are easily tempted by the choice of turning a science park into a real estate venture that is more profitable." But as he went on to argue, such a strategy would not yield a technology transfer center focused on talent development, innovation, and company incubation. This form of economic development requires a major financial investment and a steadfast commitment on the part of university leaders. Rong maintained, "TusPark benefitted from both," adding, "Building a science park is a systematic, long-term project. You have to have a huge amount of initial capital to start the construction. And then it takes a very long time to choose and attract appropriate high-tech companies, to invest and develop start-up companies, and eventually to yield returns." The money and commitment seem to have paid off, and Rong fondly recalled what one foreign visitor recently said to him, "If you want to see science parks, you can't miss Tsinghua Science Park in Beijing."

As noted, a major function of TusPark is incubating new companies. This point was reinforced by Luo Jianbei, senior vice president of TusPark, during an interview: "To evaluate whether a university science park fulfills its purpose, one important criteria is whether it can develop enterprises that truly contribute to the nation's economy. This means that we have the function of incubation, technology transfer, and entrepreneur development." The incubation of new companies goes hand in hand with technology transfer and the development of entrepreneurial talent, and it involves working closely with applied scientists and business personnel. Often, university staff are needed to bridge the two groups. Such staff must understand both academic science and business processes. TusPark places great emphasis on providing this kind of support to new and innovative ventures arising from Tsinghua's applied research.

Understanding the Unique Tsinghua Spirit and Culture

TusPark was created and developed in a manner consistent with the spirit and culture of Tsinghua. TusPark did not give rise to such a culture, but it was the realization of it. This is another factor contributing to its success and making it difficult to replicate. "Action speaks louder than words," or *xinsheng yuyan* in Chinese, is a motto widely embraced. This characteristic facet of Tsinghua's culture is largely evident in the way applied research and science form the thrust of the university's engagement with the broader society.

As a science-driven, research-intensive university, Tsinghua defines TusPark's broad goals in terms of creating knowledge, initiating innovation, and contributing to society. The university's effort to continually promote the application of new knowledge toward advancing society is implemented largely through the University-Industry Cooperation Committee (UICC), founded in 1995. The committee is composed of leading faculty, researchers, and administrators and is directed by professor and vice president Kang Kejun. The UICC serves as a platform for accelerating the university's technology transfer and is an important mechanism for strengthening collaboration with industry. The multifaceted mission of the UICC may be understood in this manner: (1) to strengthen cooperation, especially with regard to the exchange of talent and information, between university and industry; (2) to study the trends of technology development so as to accelerate research toward development, especially in areas of greatest value to the national economy; (3) to assist enterprises in solving technical and managerial problems arising during development, thereby strengthening overall competitiveness; and (4) to serve as a bridge between domestic and overseas enterprises, facilitating the flow of talent and information in both directions. Furthermore, the UICC promotes exchange and cooperation among Tsinghua's academic departments and research centers with various industries, both home and abroad.

So far, the UICC has recruited to its membership nearly 150 domestic partners; these are business leaders who represent companies covering the majority of the nation's key industries, including electrical power, petroleum, metallurgy, chemical engineering, mechanical engineering, and information technology. Furthermore, many of the UICC business members come from leading national enterprises in their respective industries, and they work to develop partnerships that serve both Tsinghua and their companies. A good example here is the collaboration between Tsinghua scientists and Ertan Hydropower Development Company, which established the China JinPing Deep Underground Laboratory (CJPL) used for the China Dark Matter EXperiment (CDEX) program. The underground lab is the deepest in the world and offers Tsinghua physicists the opportunity "to join efforts across the globe to detect dark matter, observe neutrinos, and watch for exotic particle physics phenomenon" (Normile 2009, 1246).

In terms of more applied research, the UICC has helped Tsinghua to establish a next-generation Internet technology and application joint laboratory with China Telecom to study core technologies and business applications. Another example is the university's long-term cooperation with the Shenhua Group, a state-owned energy and mining company (primarily coal mining), to conduct renewable energy exploration, including studies of hydropower. Additionally, the UICC cooperates with governmental organizations and high-tech industrial zones in a range of provinces, such as the Shenzhen economic development zone, offering supportive partnerships on the basis of industrial and business needs. According to university data, since its establishment in 1995 the UICC has helped to form more than thirty joint research institutes and has signed more than 1,600 contracts relating to research cooperation with domestic and international partners; proceeds from the latter contractual relationships have resulted in an estimated income of some 850 million RMB for the university.

The UICC has also developed partnerships with forty multinational companies, mostly by establishing joint research institutes, setting up research foundations, or developing specific university-industry cooperative programs. This level of international collaboration has resulted in numerous research and educational benefits. For example, Procter and Gamble and the Tsinghua Arts and Science Research Center jointly developed an innovative design competition, and Siemens provided funding for Tsinghua students to attend the annual meeting of Nobel laureates. Another outgrowth of UICC efforts has been the regular recruitment of corporate executives from multinational enterprises (MNEs) as guest speakers or consultants, including such notables as IBM president and

CEO Ginni Rometty, Microsoft founder and chairman Bill Gates, and Dell chairman Michael Dell. This has strengthened the ties of the university to important global enterprises such as Toshiba, Toyota, Siemens, Intel, Hitachi, Hewlett-Packard, Kone, General Motors, and Sony, among others.

Finally, key findings deriving from joint research activities initiated through UICC leadership have had significant applied value. Two examples here are the Tsinghua-Boeing Joint Research Center, established in October 2010, and the Toshiba-Tsinghua Energy and Environment Research Center, established in June 2011. This facet of the UICC has helped to promote the university's international influence and contributes to cultivating the global vision of faculty and students. Perhaps most pertinent to the educational mission of the university, the UICC has contributed in significant ways to the development of student talent in the area of applied research and innovation.

The work of the UICC and the operations implemented and advanced by TusPark have helped to strengthen ties between Tsinghua's educational and research missions and the broader society. Tsinghua's early industry relations were mostly short-term and problem-based (often addressing technical problems) and most likely involved an individual professor rather than being linked to a faculty team or university research center. These early connections were characterized by Tsinghua faculty as "short-term and loose." But today, the relationships are better characterized as strategic and long-term, with both the university and specific companies reaping benefits. Often, the involvement of Tsinghua is "more hearty and substantial," involving interdisciplinary teams of scientists and advanced students. The interactions are more extensive, and deeper relationships are formed. For example, today it is common for technical staff from various industrial or business enterprises to come to university laboratories and work with Tsinghua professors. Professors and advanced students may work on site at companies as well, potentially conducting experiments and analyses alongside technical staff.

But such heavy engagement in industry has not been without its complications. Some faculty discussed Tsinghua's entrepreneurial success in terms of a 2001 decision by China's State Council (the nation's chief governmental body) to introduce a buffer between the university and its industry-oriented enterprises, based on some negative experiences in the late 1990s. Prior to the 2001 decision, university-based enterprises produced money and jobs for the broader society, but these ventures also carried economic and legal risks. A number of faculty members opposed this form of entrepreneurial activity on the grounds that such enterprises "damaged the purity of the academic atmosphere." Consequently, a decision was made to separate the university from such revenue-seeking enterprises. In December 2003 Tsinghua Holdings Company Limited was formally established, marking the beginning of a new journey for the university. Henceforth, the academic side of the campus would no longer take legal or economic responsibility for major entrepreneurial ventures. This also meant that Tsinghua's companies, including Tongfang, Unisplendour, and Chengzhi, were reformed, dropping *Tsinghua* from their corporate name and formally separating their financial operations from the university's.

The official severance of the academic mission of the university from the more entrepreneurial, revenue-generating activities satisfied some of the Tsinghua faculty, although others simply saw it as legal maneuvering; the latter group continued to express concern about the academic image of the university being threatened by so much economic entrepreneurialism. The fact that some groups within the university may not fully subscribe to the organization's dominant norms, of course, is not an unusual development. Most universities are composed of differing subcultures holding diverse attitudes, values, and beliefs. We see the same thing at U.S. universities, for example, where some faculty fully subscribe to the revenue-generating ventures of the modern research university, whereas others see such initiatives as compromising the pursuit of knowledge for its own sake.

Entrepreneurialism and Talent Cultivation

Both the UICC and TusPark aim to strengthen educational and career opportunities for Tsinghua students. An important facet of the UICC is talent cultivation (or talent development), commonly expressed in Chinese as *rencai peiyang*. In terms of talent cultivation, the UICC has helped to establish important internship opportunities at leading Chinese companies for more than three hundred PhD students. Further, the UICC has held forty-three job fairs exclusively for nineteen UICC members (companies) during a recent five-year period, and forty UICC members have employed some 480 Tsinghua graduates. Recent years have seen increasing numbers of top graduates opt to work at key state-owned enterprises in less-developed western areas of the nation. In all, Tsinghua's students, especially its graduate students, have reaped huge benefits from the relationships spawned by the UICC.

Although TusPark is a critical platform for university-industry innovation, it also serves an important role in Tsinghua's educational mission: cultivating student entrepreneurs and providing entrepreneurial education. After more than ten years of exploring a range of educational practices, TusPark established its own entrepreneurial education system. The science park cooperates with various Tsinghua departments, centers, or organizations to provide entrepreneurial education consisting of three basic components: (1) formalized instruction in entrepreneurial education, including courses, hands-on experience, and tutorials; (2) the development of platforms for students gaining entrepreneurial experience; and (3) venture incubation. The entrepreneurial educational mission of the university is captured by Mei Meng, president of TusPark (formerly the general manager of Tsinghua Science Park Development Center) in the course of an interview: "Innovation is everywhere and is a kind of mindset. We hope to provide more opportunities for students to get involved in innovation and the entrepreneurial environment, so that they can advance future opportunities in innovation."

Formalized instruction in entrepreneurial education includes first and foremost the implementation of courses focused on theories of entrepreneurialism; such courses also are likely to include materials and lessons outlining the basic elements of business ventures, typically incorporating the opportunity for students to develop their own professional business plans. Additionally, formalized education and entrepreneurship training includes educational activities offered by the university's youth league and the School of Economics and Management.

TusPark also provides students with access to entrepreneurial experience, giving them the platform to formulate ideas and put them into practice. For example, every year the university has a business plan competition, for which TusPark offers funding, venues for making business presentations, contact with experts, and a rich and diverse alumni network. Students gain precious experience by participating in or attending the competition. Additionally, TusPark has established an entrepreneurial base (similar to a center) for university students to explore actual business endeavors. The base relies on resources from TusPark's incubator services and encourages student entrepreneurs to interact with existing enterprises, including start-up and established companies. Presently, there are three entrepreneurial bases: the Tsinghua MBA Training Base, the Social Practice Base for Graduate Students, and the Science Park Internship Base. Through such programs students get actively involved in TusPark operations and acquire direct experience in the development of innovative and cutting-edge enterprises. A key facet of these programs is the opportunity student entrepreneurs have to build connections with potential business partners, including venture capitalists.

The third facet of entrepreneurial education at Tsinghua is focused on venture incubation. This arm of the educational program focuses on assisting students in developing potential start-up companies based on their own innovative ideas and applied research. Data from 2003 revealed, for example, that one-third of the forty start-up companies calling TusPark home were created by students. In support of these student-led endeavors, TusPark provides a full set of services to assist students, including office space, seed grants, connections to a vast alumni network, entrepreneurial tutorials, and so forth. Business ventures initiated by students are different from other formalized start-ups in that those of the students are far more fragile in nature. Student ventures tend to reflect their strong mastery of technology but often lack the necessary funding, business acumen, and market vision to more fully develop as revenue-generating enterprises. This leads to a high rate of failure among student-initiated endeavors. But failure is only defined in a short-term sense; the big picture centers on helping students to better understand the complexities of bringing applied research and business innovation together in the development of successful enterprises. Hence, the long-term goal is producing Tsinghua graduates with entrepreneurial knowledge and skill sets.

Promoting Innovation through Internationalization

Another aspect of the Tsinghua innovative spirit involves a heavy focus on internationalization. As an integral part of higher education, internationalization is playing an increasingly important role in the development of the modern Chinese university. Internationalization has become a core component of the mission of prestigious universities such as Tsinghua and is seen as critical to the cultivation of student talent and to advancing innovative research. The idea of internationalization embraced at Chinese universities tends to emphasize learning from experience abroad, expanding horizons beyond the interests of the more localized context, and interacting on the basis of cross-cultural and multicultural knowledge and understanding. To achieve these aims, top universities such as Tsinghua focus on developing multi-level and wide-ranging educational and research partnerships with world-class universities in varying parts of the world.

After the founding of the People's Republic of China, the internationalization process of Tsinghua was closely interrelated with the reform and opening up of the nation. This occurred after the realization that the early communist strategies of focusing on a highly centralized, planned economy and a semi-closed country did not meet the nation's most pressing needs. Consequently, Deng Xiaoping initiated a process of reforming and opening up Chinese society in the late 1970s. For example, in 1978 Deng Xiaoping made the important decision to expand the scale of the nation's student and scholar exchange program. Based on this specific policy shift, China sent fifty students to study abroad in the United States, including nine students from Tsinghua. However, the international cooperation of Tsinghua and other top universities was mostly unidirectional during this early phase of the Open Door period, and the number of students actually studying abroad was rather small. At the time, Chinese universities were ill-prepared to openly embrace fuller forms of internationalization, as many campus leaders and policy makers worried that China was vulnerable to the colonial influence of Western nations, including the influence of university students and scholars. Some worried that the culture, as well as the national identity of its citizens, might lose elements of distinctive Chinese tradition if exposed too rapidly or extensively to Western academic norms.

Confidence in the ability of the Chinese people and the nation's institutions, including its universities, to withstand Western influence gradually grew, and in 1992 Deng Xiaoping gave his famous Southern Tour Speech. As part of his visit to several southern cities, including most notably Guangzhou and Shenzhen, Deng emphasized the importance and necessity of deepening the opening-up process. He put forth a variety of programs and policies, and many new breakthroughs in internationalization were soon to follow. During this period of the early 1990s, Tsinghua University was more fully internationalized.

These changes must be understood in the context of the broader opening up of the nation, as part of the massive reform of Chinese society. Increasingly, Chinese policy makers, institutional leaders, and faculty members believed that the universities could greatly benefit from working with prestigious foreign universities. At Tsinghua, developing exchange programs and partnerships with foreign scholars and institutions was seen as a way of furthering innovation in education and research. Such innovation was believed to be critical to the university's international recognition for education and research. This critical repositioning of the university was consistent with the general zeitgeist, which recognized that China's development was in fact inseparable from that of the outside world. China went from a state of closed-door stagnation to a state of open-door innovation in only about fifteen years. Today's campus visitors often are surprised by the degree to which Chinese academic communities have embraced aspects of different parts of the world.

For Tsinghua, the 1990s marked the beginning of a major push to attain educational and scientific prominence at a global level. Throughout the 1990s it pursued such goals in a variety of arenas, but most notably academic research. In 2003, the university explicitly defined its development strategy and its goal of achieving world-class university standing by 2020; it also identified the goal of achieving "leading" world-class university status by 2050. These goals involved a heavy dose of internationalization, in keeping with the idea that academic science of the highest quality typically is international in scope. Hence, advancing Tsinghua as a world-class university required further developing international cooperation with top research universities around the world.

In the mid-1990s, former Tsinghua president Wang Dazhong (president from 1994 to 2003) put forward a new vision of the university aimed at establishing a comprehensive, research-oriented, open university. The idea of an open university had two layers of meaning. The first meaning reflected openness to the society, which was meant to capture the obligation of the university to serve the economic construction and social development of the nation. This was seen as the natural outgrowth and extension of Deng's Open Door reforms. The second level of meaning was intended to promote international exchange and cooperation. President Wang, during an interview, captured this facet of the open university idea: "International exchange and cooperation should serve the mission of the university; it should serve to improve the cultivation of talent, research, and faculty qualities. We may learn from the Western developed countries at the beginning of the international exchange and cooperation, but then we should digest what we have learned and find our own way. Through international exchange and cooperation, we should enhance our reputation in the world."

Tsinghua has built relationships with more than two hundred universities from more than forty countries and regions (here *regions* references such locales as Hong Kong and Macau, part of China but having a special classification). Additionally, Tsinghua has become a key locale for hosting international conferences; during one recent academic year the university hosted over seventy international conferences including nearly nine thousand participants, with more than three thousand coming from foreign countries.

One aspect of internalization has been the university's increased participation in regional, university-level associations, such as the Association of Pacific Rim Universities (APRU), which was formed in 1997, and the Association of East Asian Research Universities (AEARU), founded in 1996. The APRU seeks to build on the combined strength of major research universities in the region with the primary objective to contribute to the economic, scientific, and cultural advancement of the Pacific Rim nations. The AEARU functions as a forum for the presidents of leading research-oriented universities in East Asia, seeking to implement exchange programs among the respective universities. The broad expectation is that cooperation on the basis of common academic and cultural issues will not only benefit the universities and their academic communities but will also strengthen social, cultural, and economic development in the region.

Another key form of international collaboration has been the development of joint research institutions. A case in point is the Brookings-Tsinghua Center for Public Policy (BTC), founded in 2006 as a partnership between the university and the Brookings Institution in Washington, DC. Based at the School of Public Policy and Management, the BTC produces important and innovative policy research in support of China's development and for the purpose of advancing China-U.S. relations. A second example is the Tsinghua–Johns Hopkins Joint Center for Biomedical Engineering Research, established at the university in 2008 and housed within the School of Medicine. This collaboration focuses on cutting-edge research in neuroscience and neuroengineering, tissue engineering, medical imaging, and biology in medicine. The center offers state-of-the-art research facilities, promotes the exchange of scholars and students between the two universities, and organizes joint conferences and educational activities. These joint research centers, along with numerous others, including a collaborative effort between Tsinghua and Columbia University scientists in the area of advanced genome technology, highlight the innovation and strength of Tsinghua's advanced science programs as well as its prominent reputation globally. The fact that it is able to form transnational partnerships with such highly regarded elite research universities is suggestive of Tsinghua's growing status within the global higher education arena.

The Internationalization of Faculty Life

Any discussion of internationalization at Tsinghua must place great emphasis on academic life, particularly in terms of the knowledge production and potential innovation of professors as scholars and scientists. Faculty members, of course, directly influence the construction and development of disciplines as well as the cultivation of student talent. Also, given the emphasis on Tsinghua as an engine for entrepreneurial science and innovation, it is most helpful here to focus on how internationalization helped to advance the scholarly contributions of the faculty.

Internationalization of the professorate is a method for improving the competitiveness of any university. This is clearly evident when one examines the diverse makeup of the faculty at leading universities around the world. Tsinghua has long placed great importance on the recruitment of well-known scholars from around the world. Some estimates suggest that the university has hosted more than ten thousand foreign experts and teachers over the past ten years; many of these scholars played significant roles in advancing the educational and scholarly mission of the university and deserve some credit for the present-day standing of the university's departments as well as the overall development of the university.

In the contemporary context, Tsinghua has continued to stress the value of foreign talent and has participated in numerous programs to recruit professors from abroad. One national program is the Project of University Academic Innovation and Intellectual Introduction, also known as Project III, jointly implemented by the MoE and the State Administration of Foreign Experts Affairs in 2006. This program seeks to recruit a thousand leading scholars from the world's top hundred research universities and institutes and offers funding to build a hundred innovative research bases or centers focused on research cooperation and scholarly exchange. Tsinghua is home to three such bases: one focused on intelligence and networking systems (the Base of Intelligence and Networking Systems), a second focused on cutting-edge issues and their mathematical applications (the Base of Several Frontier Issues and Their Applications in Mathematical Sciences), and a third studying water and environmental pollution controls (the Base of Water Environment Pollution Control). In the past few years, these centers have achieved substantial results in the areas of scientific research, talent development, and disciplinary advances and in terms of attracting leading overseas scientists. For example, since the implementation of the three centers, foreign experts have supervised nearly a hundred graduate students and jointly trained fifty doctoral students.

Other programs also have been critical to recruiting foreign talent, including the Tsinghua Global Scholars Fellowship initiative and the Chair Professorship Fund. The former includes funding to support the recruitment and maintenance of foreign scholars doing cutting-edge research in key disciplines (the "key disciplines" are determined annually by the university issuing guidelines and a report to the MoE and the State Administration of Foreign Experts Affairs). Similarly, the Chair Professorship Fund supports the recruitment of renowned international professors to serve as chair professors (these are mostly visiting appointments, with the foreign professors required to spend roughly three months per year at Tsinghua). Chair professors typically agree to a three-year appointment and are expected to participate in a research group. In addition to the chair professor being funded by the university, the research group also is supported to the tune of one million RMB annually. As a consequence of these and other programs, Tsinghua has recruited nearly four hundred distinguished, visiting, and advisory professors in recent years. According to university data, Tsinghua hosts an average of a thousand long-term and short-term foreign experts from about fifty countries every year. These experts are mainly from developed nations such as those of the European Union as well as nations such as the United States and Canada. Approximately 50 percent come from the natural sciences and engineering, 43 percent from the social sciences and humanities, and 7 percent from law and medicine.

Many of the long-term foreign faculty recruited by Tsinghua are Chinese expatriates, and some opt to take more permanent positions at the university, such as the previously noted Nobel laureate Yang Zhenning, who joined the faculty of Tsinghua's Institute for Advanced Study upon his retirement from the State University of New York, Stony Brook in 1999. More recent is the addition of Andrew Chi-Chih Yao, a Chinese-born American computer scientist and computational theorist and recipient of the prestigious Turing Award in 2000 (Hvistendahl 2009). He too joined the Institute for Advanced Study and also became the director of the Institute for Theoretical Computer Science.

Some minor controversy has surrounded the recruitment of famous foreign professors, with some Chinese scholars arguing that the expats should be "excluded from any projects that touch on China's national interests" (LaFraniere 2010). A case in point is Tsinghua's recruitment of molecular biologist Shi Yigong from Princeton University, whose arrival and perceived favored treatment supposedly "caused an outcry among principal investigators in China" (Qiu 2009). Indeed, there are vast salary differences between some Chinese expats and nationals working at the same university.

Despite the Shi Yigong example, Tsinghua's reception of foreign experts generally is characterized as highly enthusiastic and welcoming. In fact, throughout the institution's history, faculty and staff have prided themselves on paying great attention to connecting foreign experts to the campus academic community; Tsinghua professors and students alike are known to embrace the opportunity to learn from foreign scholars, seeking to advance both their understanding of foreign universities and their particular disciplinary knowledge. As evidence, Purdue University engineering professor Gavriel Salvendy, in 2001, was brought to Tsinghua as the founding dean of the newly established industrial engineering department, quite a forceful decision even by today's standards. This spirit of openness to international scholars is another key element of the university's culture and contributes to the innovative nature of the students and faculty. In turn, foreign experts have had a significant influence on the university, helping to promote students' understanding of multiculturalism and improving the level of internationalization of the curriculum. Relatedly, many have developed new courses, especially at the graduate level. They have also introduced new teaching methods and styles of classroom management. Many have collaborated with Tsinghua faculty and students in organizing jointly sponsored conferences, developing and conducting research projects, presenting conference papers, and producing and publishing research papers and reports. For many short- and long-term visiting professors, collaboration often continues even after they leave Tsinghua and return to their home universities.

Although foreign experts have made innumerable contributions to the university's internationalization, and by most accounts enjoy their time at Tsinghua, some have faced difficulties in carrying out their teaching or research assignments. For example, some foreign experts have been unhappy with the teaching load or felt that their professional knowledge and talent was not fully utilized in the process of course construction. Some found China's higher education system to be too institutionalized and overly bureaucratic. The fact that many things are accomplished by drawing on interpersonal relationships tended to hamper their experience. Challenges have extended to the personal realm as well; many foreign experts have noted difficulties with interpersonal communications, pointing to linguistic and cultural differences. This has at times limited their ability to develop deep and meaningful friendships with Chinese scholars. It seems as though the university might benefit from a more comprehensive analysis of the overall experience of foreign experts, both in terms of their experiences as well as those of Tsinghua faculty and students interacting with them.

Students and Internationalization

Internationalization of the university also is embodied by the enrollment of foreign students. In December 1950, fourteen students from Eastern Europe enrolled at Tsinghua, marking the first time the universities of the new China had accepted foreign students. Today, Tsinghua offers thirty-eight baccalaureate programs, ninety-nine master's programs, and seventy-eight doctoral degree programs for international students. Eleven of the master's programs and one of the doctoral programs are delivered in English. Most of the doctoral programs in engineering encourage the enrollment of students who are skilled in English but lack Chinese language proficiency. Moreover, Tsinghua offers non-degree programs such as advanced study (including student exchange and joint research) and Chinese language study. More than two hundred non-degree courses are taught in English at both undergraduate and graduate levels.

In 2012, more than 3,500 international students from 108 countries studied at the university, with 75 percent pursuing formal degrees and the remaining students engaged in advanced studies, joint research, or Chinese language study.[4] Countries sending the largest number of students are as follows (in rank order): the Republic of Korea, the United States, Japan, France, Germany, Canada, Malaysia, Singapore, the United Kingdom, Australia, Indonesia, Thailand, Italy, Vietnam, and Russia. Foreign student involvement is higher at Tsinghua than at all or nearly all Chinese universities, with many foreign students receiving financial support in the form of funding from three potential sources: the China Scholarship Council (CSC), the Beijing Government Scholarship (BGS), and the Tsinghua University Scholarship (TUS). For the academic year 2012–13, 31 percent of degree-pursuing international students were awarded scholarships.

There are of course many differences between Chinese culture and the cultures from which many of the international students come. These differences present enormous challenges to international students lacking familiarity with Chinese customs and the lifestyle of the nation's college students. It is not uncommon for such challenges to lead to a variety of frustrations or in some cases serious psychological maladies, such as depression. This is particularly a concern for those international students having little to no Chinese language ability; lacking Chinese language skills can make even the most simple of daily tasks difficult to negotiate.

In addition to enrolling large numbers of foreign students, Tsinghua has paid great attention to encouraging its own students to study abroad. There are several important support programs for fostering increased study abroad, including programs supported by the Chinese Scholarship Council. There are also collaborative study programs with foreign universities, such as the MIT-Tsinghua International MBA Program, a collaboration between the Tsinghua School of Economics and Management and MIT's Sloan School of Management. Launched in 1997, the program has produced more than 6,700 Tsinghua MBA graduates, many of whom have gone on to play important roles in business in China and around the world. Many other similar partnerships enable a wide array of Tsinghua students to gain valuable experience abroad; this furthers both their disciplinary knowledge and their employability in the globally linked Chinese economy.

Concluding Remarks

Our intent in this chapter is to capture key aspects of the organizational culture of Tsinghua University, with a particular focus on its strong commitment to innovation and entrepreneurialism. We note how the university has placed great emphasis on connecting the production and management of knowledge to applications that might benefit society, especially in terms of economic development. The concern for economic development is particularly evident in the university's commitment to the following key objectives: (1) advancing industrial and corporate partners; (2) furthering technology transfer; (3) incubating innovative ideas through an emphasis on applied science; (4) developing and supporting start-up companies; and (5) cultivating talent, both in terms of students and faculty. Two key organizational structures for achieving these objectives are TusPark and the University-Industry Cooperation Committee (UICC), although a variety of small and more focused mechanisms operate as well. Clearly, the university is highly tied to business and industry and has been for some time.

Although Tsinghua is best known for its applied science and engineering programs, most of its other academic programs are highly regarded. However, when it comes to the social sciences and humanities, the university often takes a backseat to its neighbor, Peking University, or to nearby Renmin University. Tsinghua's science and engineering programs cast a huge shadow, one from which it is hard for other academic operations to escape.

Another key point to make is that extensive governmental support has been critical to the university's success over the past two decades or so. It is especially worth noting the contributions of Project 985 and to a lesser extent Project 211. The funds from these projects have helped university scholars and scientists to sidestep some of the problematic aspects of grant seeking and have strengthened the university's effort to build greater research capacity. Additionally, the national and municipal governments have supported the university's marketization by also offering expensive real estate and financial support. Tsinghua is influenced by interwoven governmental and market-oriented forces. This is not academic capitalism in the strictest sense but instead represents a combination of public and private initiatives, reflecting to some extent a coming together of socialist and capitalist economic forces. Government officials believe that providing the university with such massive support will create a new model of university innovation and entrepreneurialism, which other Chinese universities will follow. Thus, our analysis of Tsinghua stresses its engagement with the society in the form of marketization (reflecting its entrepreneurial spirit) but also the strong involvement and support of the government.

Internationalization is another key facet of the culture of Tsinghua and is directly tied to the university's focus on advancing innovation. Since its founding as the Tsinghua School, as a result of the Boxer Indemnity Fund remission monies, Tsinghua has been an internationally oriented educational enterprise. Even after it escaped the direct influence of the United States, the university maintained strong international ties. The international aspects of the university highlighted in this chapter point to the ways in which the university engages with the international academic community, especially in terms of advancing cutting-edge science. Such efforts enhance the university's strong emphasis on innovation and entrepreneurial thinking and add to the overall efforts to further develop as a world-class research university.

The period from the early 1990s to the present has been one of vast change for Chinese higher education. As we note in the introduction, it is a period marked by global ambition, and this certainly has been the case for Tsinghua. These times have been particularly interesting for Tsinghua faculty members, both in terms of challenges and opportunities. For example, they have faced great challenges in dealing with larger and larger numbers of students, all while being confronted with a changing research environment. A major facet of the change in research operations has been the reality of higher expectations in terms of scholarly productivity. The result for many has been increased stress and to some extent frustration relating to a lack of control over the academic mission of their university. Some faculty see the education of undergraduate and graduate students as potentially compromised in the new research-focused environment. These same faculty members also tend to raise questions about whether the heavy emphasis on innovation for the sake of entrepreneurialism and revenue generation may corrode aspects of the academic culture, such as the pursuit of ideas for the sake of advancing knowledge. Many of these faculty members would prefer to see the university become a little more balanced, focusing less on serving business and industry and more on educating students and generating knowledge without regard for revenue potential.

Still other faculty members voiced optimism about the new opportunities emerging in the increasingly competitive research and funding environment, including opportunities related to the expanding ties to business and industry. These faculty members are more likely to benefit from such growing opportunities and in some sense are seen as the victors in an academic environment increasingly shaped by applied science innovation and marketization.

Most faculty—whether highly invested in innovation and marketization or not—tend to agree that administrators and government officials continue to be the key decision makers and that such a situation may at times limit the ability of universities like Tsinghua to achieve true world-class standing. This is particularly true with regard to research funding processes and academic freedom. Strong government involvement has, however, contributed to some extent to the higher levels of autonomy enjoyed by the university and its faculty. Such complexities mark the quest of leading Chinese universities for world-class standing.

CHAPTER TWO

Peking University and the Pursuit of Academic Excellence the "Beida Way"

China's dramatic economic growth over the past three decades has spurred numerous writers to assert the nation's return to glory. Using rhetoric that borders on the apocalyptic in some cases, especially with regard to the Western world, books such as Martin Jacques's *When China Rules the World: The End of the Western World and the Birth of a New Global Order* (2009), David Smith's *The Dragon and the Elephant: China, India and the New World Order* (2007), and Robyn Meredith's *The Elephant and the Dragon: The Rise of India and China and What It Means for All of Us* (2007) have further spurred a growing interest in everything Chinese. Beyond the imagery of China as a fire-breathing dragon intent on consuming the world is the reality that the nation has returned in some sense to assume a key role in the world's economic and political stage, as captured by John Bond, former chairman of HSBC: "The timing does not matter, but we in the West do need to prepare ourselves, particularly our young people, for a powerful and exciting re-emergence of China on the world scene. The first of the ancient, historic powers to return to glory" (Smith 2007, 94). Similarly, Ruth Hayhoe, writing in 2005, noted, "Many people would agree that one of the striking phenomena of the late twentieth century has been China's stunning economic resurgence, after more than a century in which its people suffered from invasions, wars, and internal political strife. Most governments and large corporations now see it as essential to articulate a China strategy in order to deal effectively with this new manufacturing powerhouse" (575–576).

China's economic success certainly has captured the world's attention, and obviously the country's significance in the geopolitical arena is on the rise. But China has international objectives other than simply asserting itself economically and politically. China's leaders and the nation as a whole also place great emphasis on the cultural forms that make China a unique force in the world. Accordingly, many desire that the nation's top universities, as exemplars of Chinese culture past and present, achieve worldwide recognition. Hence, efforts by the Ministry of Education (MoE) to strengthen universities are not simply intended to enhance their role in promoting economic development but also reflect the government's commitment to its best universities attaining world-class standing. This involves reaching higher levels of institutional attainment, including by advancing research capacity and the general production of knowledge. Nowhere is this thirst for academic achievement and global recognition more apparent than at the nation's leading university—Peking University.

In 1998, Peking University, also known as Beijing University and, colloquially, Beida, celebrated its centennial. The fact that the nation's president at the time, Jiang Zemin, delivered a keynote speech in honor of the university is testimony to its social significance. Additionally, the Post and Telecommunications Ministry issued commemorative stamps for the occasion, and the country's astronomers named an asteroid after the school (Tempest 1998). During one public event, a top Chinese Communist Party (CCP) official proclaimed, "I have just received great news. Our mountain climbing team has just conquered a peak in Nepal. Now there's the spirit of Beijing University for you!" (Tempest 1998). Timothy Weston, in the introduction to his book covering the history of the university from 1898 to 1929, acknowledged the importance of the centennial celebration: "Celebrations to mark such occasions are common enough, but this one, attended by some fifty thousand people, was a veritable extravaganza that made it abundantly clear that Beijing University occupies a particularly distinguished place in Chinese modern history" (2004, 1). He went on to add, "In myriad ways the commemoration stressed that Beida's greatness resides in an ineffable spirit born of its heroic history and that the university is recognized by Chinese the world over as having been at the forefront of China's quest for dignity and glory in the modern world" (Weston 2004, 1–2).

As applied research and innovation mark the culture of Tsinghua, Beida also exhibits a unique cultural ethos, primarily grounded in the university's quest for academic excellence, which serves as a political and cultural signpost for the broader society. The university's influence is evident in many historical accounts of student and faculty accomplishments, most notable of which is the role faculty and students played in leading what became known as the May Fourth

Movement (because it was linked to demonstrations on May 4, 1919). Known also as the New Culture Movement, this period of several years was marked by political and cultural fervor that challenged foreign imperialism, elevated populism, and refashioned Chinese nationalism. Beida students also played leadership roles in the Tiananmen Square protests of 1989, when thousands of students throughout the nation sought to spur the central government toward more rapid democratization.

The leadership contributions of Beida go far beyond activism; indeed, the university's image and identity are most centrally tied to the significant scholarly achievements of its many great professors over the years. Beida's faculty and academic programs represent the heart and soul of the university and are what the nation's leaders most often herald in proclamations of its greatness. When President Jiang Zemin celebrated the university's first hundred years with his May 4, 1998, keynote address at the Great Hall of the People, he announced a new MoE project to strengthen the university even more, Project 985.

The focus of this chapter is Beida's institutional emphasis on the pursuit of academic excellence. We examine the ways in which national initiatives such as Project 985 have contributed to furthering the university's research mission as well as its standing in the world of higher education. Related to this, we examine how changes related to strengthening the university's research quality and capacity affect faculty members and their working lives. In order to more fully understand the contemporary context of faculty life at Beida, we explore the university's rich and storied history.

The Historical Legacy of Beida

The northwest corner of Beijing is home to China's two most famous and influential institutions of higher learning, Peking and Tsinghua Universities. They are separated only by the busy Zhongguancun thoroughfare, which divides Haidian District from north to south. Few dispute the fact that the two are ranked first and second in terms of China's greatest universities, although determining which is first is not so easily resolved. Even in the global ranking schemes, the two have switched places from year to year on a few occasions. However, when it comes to measures of their cultural and political contributions to the nation, there is little dispute that Beida's star shines a little brighter.

Peking University was founded as the Imperial Peking University and was China's first modern university. As such, it was at the center of the country's major intellectual movements of the twentieth century, including the introduction of Western forms of learning, a revived interest in Buddhism, and a reinterpretation of Confucian and other branches of Chinese traditional learning (Lin 2005, 1). The founding of the university was discussed by Ruth Hayhoe in her book *China's Universities 1895–1995: A Century of Cultural Conflict*: "The

Imperial University . . . was almost the only institution introduced under the influence of progressive intellectuals involved in the brief Hundred-Day Reform Movement of 1898 to survive the conservative backlash to this movement. It was patterned after the University of Tokyo, which in turn had been influenced by both French and German academic patterns" (1996, 18). The university's progressive roots proved resilient, although certainly there were times when these institutional qualities were deemed dangerous, such as during the Cultural Revolution, when the university, like others throughout China, closed its doors to normal operations.

The Imperial University of Peking is considered the first government-established institution of higher education founded on a Western model. As of 1919, the Imperial University "was [still] one of only three government-established universities and the only one located in the capital and completely financed by the central government. It was considered the leading institution of higher learning in the country" (Chow 1960, 48).

Western-style colleges and universities arose in China upon the ruins of traditional Confucian academies, which offered advanced learning but bore little semblance to the university ideal (Yeh 2000, 1). In some sense, the founding of the first universities reflected "a delayed but critical response to the Dynasty's political failures after the Opium War and to the profound sense of intellectual failure stemming from that defeat" (Yeh 2000, 1). With the nation's doors forced open by their defeat, Chinese intellectuals experienced a variety of reforms launched under widespread Western influence, including the founding of new universities such as the Imperial University of Peking. The establishment of Peking is generally viewed as a landmark in the history and trajectory of Chinese higher education, even though it took almost two decades for it to take shape as a modern university. This came later, when Beida President Cai Yuanpei launched the reform of the university in the late 1910s.

Following the revolution of 1911, the Imperial University was renamed the National Beijing University (*Guoli Beijing Daxue*). Several years later, Beida, as it was known by then, played a lead role in the May Fourth Movement, when its students protested their government's weak response to the concession of Shandong Province to Japan as part of the Treaty of Versailles. The May Fourth demonstrations "resulted in a series of strikes and associated events amounting to a social ferment and an intellectual revolution" (Chow 1960, 1). In time, the term *May Fourth* came to take on a deeper meaning, suggesting to some extent the intellectual and political vitality of the nation.

The May Fourth Movement was one of the most controversial episodes in Chinese history. For some Chinese, the movement marked a form of national renaissance or liberation. For others, it was a complete catastrophe. In many ways, the movement epitomized the cultural conflict between the radical, liberal revolutionists and the traditional nationalists. The former proclaimed that the movement was a "Chinese Renaissance" analogous with reformation or enlightenment, at least in its cultural significance. The nationalists criticized the movement for damaging traditional cultural forms and corrupting the youth by teaching them to act contrary to traditional moral principles (Chow 1960, 338–344).

Regardless of the interpretation, the May Fourth Movement signified a new chapter in Chinese history. In a broad sense, the movement marked an intellectual revolution that shook the cultural foundations that had given form and substance to Chinese thinking for thousands of years. For example, with the contribution of Peking University scholars, ideals associated with democracy and science came to have greater influence in Chinese culture and politics. Elements of these new forms of thought in turn shaped views about social and economic transformation, particularly in terms of addressing the nation's widespread poverty and underdevelopment. The nature of the influence of May Fourth thinking was captured to a great extent by Chow Tse-tsung (also Zhou Cezong) when he wrote that the movement "was actually a combined intellectual and sociopolitical movement to achieve national independence, the emancipation of the individual, and a just society by the modernization of China. Essentially, it was an intellectual revolution in the broad sense, intellectual because it was based on the assumption that intellectual changes were a prerequisite for such a task of modernization . . . and because it was led by intellectuals" (Chow 1960, 358–359).

The May Fourth Movement was closely tied to the open-minded and progressive thinking of Beida professors and students. This is captured by the launch of two progressive journals involving the Beida academic community, *New Youth* and *Renaissance*. These intellectual venues, and the broader movement that spawned them, are generally associated with the growth of cultural iconoclasm and the rise of socialist thought in China, which were spearheaded to a great extent by Beida's progressive faculty, including the likes of philosopher and essayist Hu Shi, a leader in the country's New Culture Movement during the late 1910s. Thus, the relationship between Beida and the May Fourth Movement, and the related restructuring of Chinese political and cultural thought, came to define the core of what the university stood for, offering a foundation to the academic lives of faculty and students alike. In a sense, both the movement and the university came to be synonymous with the nation's political and cultural progress.

Another unique facet to Beida's history is the early reform it underwent in moving from governmental control to a true academic community. The university was not the first founded in China, but arguably it became the nation's first modern university. A key figure in this transformation was the university's former president Cai Yuanpei. In the late 1910s and early 1920s, Cai, "a traditionally educated scholar with an innovative bent" (Israel 1998, 119) introduced key elements of the German university ideal. Nearly as soon as he took office, in 1916, Cai started the project to transform Beida into a legitimate public university—arguably the first in China. From Cai's perspective, a university ought to be defined by relations characteristic of an academic community rather than serving as an official agency or extension of the government. He considered the university to be "a universal meeting ground where different ideas and values of Orient and Occident, antiquity and modernity, could be studied objectively, debated freely, and selected discriminately" (Israel 1998, 119). To enact this idealized vision, Cai recruited to the university a host of intellectual luminaries, all with divergent personalities and perspectives on the world. Some were radical scholars, such as the two cofounders of the Chinese Communist Party (CCP), Chen Duxiu (also Chen Tu-hsiu) and Li Dazhao. Chen was a revolutionary socialist, educator, philosopher, and author, and Li served as professor and dean of Beida's library. Other professors brought in by Cai were less radical but just as influential, including skeptical historian Gu Jiegang and Qing Dynasty loyalist Gu Hongming. In all, Cai's reforms set the stage for the high-level intellectual work that came to symbolize Beida for years to come, all the way to the early days of Mao's revolution and up to the Cultural Revolution in the middle 1960s (Israel 1998, 119–120).

Between the late 1930s and the late 1940s, during the time of the war with Japan, Peking University and two other universities—Tsinghua and Nankai—formed Southwest Associated University (also known as Xinan Lianda or simply Lianda). In early 1937, spurred by the Japanese occupation of the northern provinces, students and faculty members of the three universities were forced to relocate to Changsha, the capital city of Hunan province. At that time, the associated university was called Changsha Temporary University, although Changsha was not considered an ideal location for the campus. It was not long before groups of students and faculty continued their trek west to find a more desirable locale for the temporary university. In May 1939 they reached the city of Kunming and formed Southwest Associated University, which served as an academic home to students and faculty through the remaining war years. Although the university operated under poor conditions, it became known for the remarkable quality of scholarship produced by faculty across disciplines; the university also educated a generation of students who would go to provide important forms of intellectual leadership throughout the Chinese academy (Hayhoe 2005, 57). It was during the time of Lianda, arguably, that the intellectual ideals and values that came to define Peking University and the Beida way were first planted. As John Israel noted in his book *Lianda: A Chinese University in War and Revolution*, "War brought tens of thousands of students closer to the people. Back-country travel to reach refugee campuses brought young scholars into contact with laborers, peasants, and tribal minorities" (1998, 387). The juxtaposition of everyday, down-to-earth struggle with vibrant intellectual exploration formed the unique context for academic life at Lianda, leading Israel to describe it as "both the high point of achievement and the harbinger of the precipitous decline of China's liberal academic tradition" (1998, 381).

After the founding of the People's Republic of China, the central government took over and nationalized all higher education institutions in the early 1950s; these institutions were restructured under the influence of the Soviet Union (Min 2004). In May 1952, the MoE issued a plan for national higher education adjustments requiring institutions to focus on "the needs of national construction" by strategizing about their own particular strengths and conducting "their work in order of importance and urgency" (Yang 2000, 321). There also was a good deal of concern expressed about the imbalance of geographic distribution and the needs of the rural areas (Yang 2000). As part of this national reform, Chinese universities increasingly copied the structures and operations of the Soviet model rather than looking to Western universities, such as those in Germany, the United Kingdom, and the United States. The Soviet model was applied with little regard for the characteristic qualities of Chinese society and culture. In the 1960s, Chinese higher education policies were influenced by political ideologies such as those arising during the Great Leap Forward. This served to alienate many intellectuals, including faculty teaching at Peking University. With the breaking of relations with the Soviet Union later in the 1960s, the government resumed earlier attempts to achieve some sense of balance between Confucian traditions and Western forms of teaching and learning. This trend developed fairly smoothly until the onset of the Cultural Revolution in 1966.

During the Cultural Revolution, almost every facet of the nation's higher education system, including Chinese academic traditions, Western academic influences, and changes adopted under Soviet influence, was destroyed (Min 2004). For instance, the national examination for college entrance was abolished from 1966 through 1977, and many professors and intellectuals were perceived as counter-revolutionaries and tormented by menial work assignments or more serious forms of punishment. Additionally, the Ministry of Education ceased to function during the late 1960s and early 1970s.

Following the implementation of Deng Xiaoping's Open Door policies, primarily during the 1980s, the university evidenced increasing levels of international engagement, both in terms of sending students and scholars abroad and hosting foreign visitors. The biggest transformations, however, were to come in the 1990s with the implementation of new governmental programs, Projects 211 and 985, the latter being of most importance to the development of China's elite universities.

Project 985 was first announced by former CCP general secretary and then-president Jiang Zemin at Beida's centennial celebration at the Great Hall of the People. The early objectives of Project 985 funding focused on strengthening nine top universities—including, of course, Peking—with the goal of establishing them as world-class universities. Additionally, Peking, along with Tsinghua, was targeted for the highest level of 985 funding, in the form of 1.8 billion RMB every three years. Beida's most-favored status was not only a reflection of its historical relevance in Chinese society; its selection also reflected the scholarly accomplishments of its faculty across the pure and applied sciences, arts and humanities, and social sciences. In terms of the pure and applied sciences, disciplines such as medicine, computer science, chemistry, mathematics, and physics have garnered much attention at the university. With regard to the humanities and social sciences, fields such as Chinese language, philosophy, history, business, economics, politics, law, and sociology have stood out over the years. Another indicator of Beida's preferential treatment is its number of academicians in the Chinese Academia of Sciences (CAS) and the Chinese Academia of Engineering (CAE); the university ranks first in total academicians in these two prestigious organizations.

The implementation of Project 985 at Beida mostly involved further developing the university's international competitiveness and enhancing its academic operations, including strengthening the university's overall research enterprise. To accomplish these objectives, Beida's leaders paid great attention to faculty recruitment. In the early 2000s, Beida enhanced its efforts to attract superb scholars both nationally and internationally. By 2010, most of the faculty members working at the university had visited or worked at foreign universities. Additionally, in one recent ten-year span the university appointed over six hundred new professors, with one-third coming from universities outside of China. Recent years have witnessed even greater emphasis on internationalizing the university, in part as a consequence of recognizing the growing significance of a global, knowledge-based economy. For example, over the past few years the university has appointed hundreds of foreign experts and scholars to visiting or guest faculty positions, including visiting research fellows. Faculty and students at the university consistently speak of the important contributions foreign scholars make to the overall mission of the university, particularly in terms of their teaching and research. They clearly play a critical role in promoting the objectives of Project 985 and contribute in significant ways to further developing the university as a global force.

The Contemporary Institutional Context

Beida's campus is located on a beautiful and spacious plot of land (over 270 hectares) not far from the Yuanmingyuan Garden and the famous Summer Palace. The university includes some 36,000 full-time students, including roughly

14,000 undergraduates, nearly as many master's students, and some 8,000 doctoral students. The university also serves more than 10,000 adult part-time students and more than 52,000 online students. Additionally, there are more than 3,700 international students, with the vast majority pursuing formal degree programs. Beida has just over 2,100 full professors, almost the same number of associate professors, and a much smaller number of lecturers and assistant professors. The university's large percentage of full and associate professors in part reflects its high status within the nation's higher education system.

The university has fifty-three major schools and departments and offers some 105 undergraduate programs, 291 graduate programs, and 241 doctoral programs. In addition to the formalized curriculum, the university is also marked by a vibrant student body, with over two hundred student organizations and annual programs such as the International Cultures Festival, a campus-wide celebration of the university's foreign student population.

The university's website, in the form of the "President's Message," highlights several facets about the university, noting that it is "regarded as a symbol of modern Chinese education" and that its "democratic administration" has placed "great emphasis on academic freedom and scientific research." It goes on to state, "The student body, faculty, and alumni . . . have made significant research achievements and generated an incredible number of works of scholarship in both the arts and the sciences," adding that the university has "produced a great number of scholars in various areas of concentration and specialty." The latter point is partially supported by university data regarding faculty membership in exclusive scholarly associations. Namely, the university boasts having fifty-three members in the Chinese Academy of Sciences (CAS), seven members in the Chinese Academy of Engineering (CAE), and fourteen in the Third World Academy of Sciences (TWAS). The "President's Message" closes by noting that the university "has high hopes of becoming a world-class university in the 21st century."

The Beida campus is a must-see destination for tourists visiting Beijing. Its historic contributions to Chinese society and its present-day ambience, including the shady, tree-lined campus streets and walkways, make it an important physical and cultural space in the Chinese landscape. The importance of the campus was acknowledged by *TIME Asia* in a 1999 article, which listed Peking University as one of the fifty places that define modern China ("China's Amazing" 1999); Beida was included along with such important locales as Hong Kong, Shanghai, Xi'An, the Pearl River Delta, and the Great Wall.

Beida's Cultural Ethos and Identity

The university is marked by a great sense of pride in its past accomplishments as well as a hopeful vision of what lies ahead. There is great stress placed on pursuing meaningful academic community, which former university president Cai Yuanpei saw as critical to an authentic university. Some see the core of Beida as residing with its strong faculty, a point also articulated in the famous inaugural speech of former Tsinghua president Mei Yiqi back in 1931: "The reason why a university has the qualification to be regarded as a place of higher learning is not because it might own some impressive buildings and first-class facilities, but absolutely because of the many excellent scholars and professors who are working there."[1] Along these lines, many Beida faculty with whom we spoke attributed the university's superior academic environment to the great accomplishments of past professors. Some of the university's current academics relish stories of past accomplishments by noted professors and point to the importance such stories or "tales" play in giving meaning to the modern-day Beida experience. One senior faculty member talked about the importance of the university's long history and described how the stories give meaning to the present and help to sustain the unique culture of the university.

Throughout the twentieth century, the legend and popularity of Peking University spread throughout China. Even folks living in the remote and rural regions of the country are likely to look to the university with a bit of awe, perhaps noting a major accomplishment by saying, "Oh, that is Beida's style." Or they might say, "Beida is just Beida." "That's the Beida way"—*"Beida jingshen"* is the expression typically used in China to capture this facet of Beida. Such kinds of comments are not uncommon and reflect a sense of national pride in the university. Along these lines, some even look to the university as having mystical powers, pondering the likely location of such powers and typically pointing to the Unknown Lake (*Wei Ming Hu*) or Liberal Arts Pagoda (*Bo Yia Ta*), two favorites for visitors. It is a Beida tradition to spend important and reflective moments in solitude at such locales, and it is not uncommon to hear stories of inspiration centered on the lake or the pagoda. A faculty member with whom we spoke shared his experience. He spoke of getting his PhD at Beida and then being faced with many difficult choices. It was his doctoral supervisor who finally convinced him to take a post at Beida. As he explained, "The key point is that my doctoral supervisor convinced me to believe that Beida has something unique in terms of the ethos of Beida. What is it? At first I did not understand, even though I had worked here as a post-doc for two years. However, a decade has now passed and I have come to an insight about this university and what makes it so special—Beida's cultural ethos is embedded in the beauty of the Unknown Lake and the Liberal Arts Pagoda."

Beyond mysticism, there are more palpable elements that have come to capture the core ethos of the university and its faculty, including inclusiveness, loyalty to the profession, pursuit of knowledge with skepticism, and a spirit of individualism. In what follows, we highlight these facets of Beida's culture.

Inclusiveness

Inclusiveness refers to a general tendency of the academic community to encourage diverse voices and perspectives. Beida has a tradition of openness to divergent points of view. This was partially captured by the following comments from a senior professor: "Beida is always adhering to an ideal of governance that incorporates inclusiveness. This is generally perceived as one of the traditions of the university, a quality that we've inherited from the evolution of the university. This inclusiveness, in some sense, is similar to academic freedom, but in the Chinese context. We appreciate this tradition of divergent voices."

The university stresses an idealized vision of academic community whose mission involves cultivating student talent and producing and disseminating knowledge. But it is widely recognized that to accomplish such goals the university must be open to differences, most notably differing opinions and perspectives. As one faculty member noted, "Beida's idea of inclusiveness is a foundation for realizing the goal and mission of the university." And a senior faculty member and a dean similarly commented, "I have never regulated faculty members too much, which might kill innovative passion and creativity. Take myself as an example, I am a professor . . . and have experienced academic freedom since the very beginning when I came to the institution" (Wang and Liu 2002).

Loyalty to the Profession

Faculty also take great pride in their working lives as professors and generally expressed a very positive attitude and commitment to the academic profession in interviews. Some had been offered lucrative opportunities in the business world but preferred the lifestyle and environment of the university. A faculty member in economics spoke of having had several options at one point in his career—"Either working as a senior official in governmental agencies or working as a senior manager at a major company, where the salary was much higher than that of university professor." He chose an academic career, though, mainly because he enjoyed the lifestyle of being an academic. Another professor spoke of his sense of obligation to his particular school, likening it to "a ship sailing the ocean with no lifeboats." As this professor went on to explain, "I see no other option but to hold on and make it safe for the voyage. The reason is simple—I have been working here for more than a quarter century and I like many of my colleagues. I am very loyal to the school. I would never do anything to hurt the school. We need to treat it like it is our own property to safeguard."[2]

Another professor spoke of the joy he experienced in interacting and mentoring students: "To tell you the truth, I keep my current post first and foremost because I like the work—it fills me with enthusiasm and energy. Every day, when I enter into the classroom and interact with the students . . . they are so young and energetic. They make you feel younger and more energetic, more than you really are. I relish this kind of feeling. So I would never leave my current position." From this faculty member's perspective, working at Beida is a far better option than working as a civil servant or in some other field. He noted how much he loved doing research and being a Beida professor. As he concluded, "To be a teacher at Beida is my lucky choice."

Pursuit of Knowledge with Skepticism

Another quality that faculty at Beida value is skepticism when it comes to the production and transmission of knowledge. This, in part, reflects Beida's leadership role as the nation's first true university and is believed to be crucial to fostering critical thinking and creativity among students. Such skepticism involves encouraging students to question values, modes of living, social norms and customs, and moral ideals, both past and present. This facet of Beida at times situates the university in opposition to elements of traditional Chinese thinking.

Symbolically speaking, the Liberal Arts Pagoda, located on the banks of the Unknown Lake, signifies the university's commitment to the pursuit of truth, regardless of where the truth might point. The pagoda is seen as a kind of torch or beacon emphasizing the value of truth. This point of view is captured by a common expression at Beida: "Everyone is equal before the truth." This is often interpreted as meaning that authority should not be worshipped above the truth. Of course, such a perspective runs counter in some ways to traditional Chinese thought.

Chinese culture has long stressed the importance of authority, including paying great respect to the knowledge and understanding of elders and government leaders. Generally, those occupying lower-level positions in society, such as students, dare not oppose or question those above them. For instance, during Mao's leadership, many Chinese became ardent followers of his thinking without ever seriously challenging his ideas of social structure or Marxism in general. However, as an example of Beida's ethos favoring a healthy dose of skepticism, Professor Liang Shu-ming raised serious questions about the degree to which Marxist class theory actually accounted for the complexities of Chinese social structure. Liang, considered one of the last neo-Confucianists, was famous for both his work in classical philosophy and his critique of Marxism. He argued that Chinese rural society could not be easily analyzed along class lines, despite the obvious economic disparities. Liang posited that within the same rural family lineage one commonly found economic divisions of the poor and the wealthy. The dominant Marxist interpretation suggests violent revolutionary confrontation within the same family lineage, necessitating the poorer relatives overthrowing those of a higher economic standing. For Liang, this was unacceptable in the Chinese context.

To raise critical questions during Mao's regime was quite extraordinary. Professor Liang's challenge to dominant Marxist thought is an example of the kind of courage epitomized by the Beida ethos. Another example of such intellectual courage was exhibited by Ma Yanchu, a former president of Beida, who in the 1950s challenged the thinking of many senior government leaders, including Mao, in terms of whether or not the society benefitted from having such a large population. Although Mao favored high population growth, Professor Ma, an economist, disagreed and in 1957 published his famous article "On a New Strategy of Population" in the *People's Daily*. Professor Ma instead proposed that any increase in the population must coincide with similar growth in the national economy. Professor Ma's thesis earned him distinction as the so-called "Thomas R. Malthus of China" and resulted in him being accused of counter-revolutionary thinking. He subsequently faced a choice: Deny his thesis and continue as Beida's president or step down from his post. He chose to resign and stated, "It does not matter whether or not I am supposed to quit my office as president of the university, but I must follow the truth. I do not think it a political issue, but only a purely academic one. In this sense, I am not anti-revolutionist, but a positive promoter of truth. . . . I proposed my thesis about population for the county's future development and interests of the people, so I am not afraid of anything in order to hold to the truth" (Xiao 1998, 95–96).

The stories of Liang Shu-ming and Ma Yanchu resonate in the hearts and minds of Beida students and faculty and contribute to the seriousness with which the academic community supports the skeptical pursuit of knowledge. This aspect of the university's culture has contributed to movements not only to advance the university as a progressive space within Chinese society but also to strengthen a civic democracy stressing elements of freedom and social justice beyond the campus walls. To challenge authority requires equal doses of courage and wisdom. This is particularly true in Chinese society, where despite the influence of institutions such as Beida, traditional forms of Chinese thought, including Confucianism, tend to stress obedience among younger generations, including university students. Beida has a history of its faculty and students raising critical questions, most obviously in the May Fourth Movement and the Tiananmen Square student demonstrations. Such bravery, though, is not without consequences, a case in point being Beida student leader Wang Dan, who served prison time for his leadership role in the Tiananmen Square democracy protests (Erlanger 1998).

Spirit of Individualism

There is a saying that if a student is not willing to be different, then she or he should not opt to attend Beida. The university, as one faculty member noted, is viewed as a "paradise for talent and creativity but a purgatory for mediocrity." This spirit of individualism is a source of pride among academics at the university and is evidenced to some extent in the academic lives of Liang Shu-ming and Ma Yanchu. A senior Beida professor known for his knowledge of Chinese culture commented that the spirit of intellectual individualism was deeply embedded in the culture of Beida and is reflective of what is known as the "Beida way." As he pointed out, this quality has been fostered by the generations of skeptical scholars who have populated the campus. Israel, writing in *Lianda*, offered support for such comments, noting that even in the early years of the university's development, "Tolerance of learned eccentricity was part of Beida's tradition of academic freedom" (Israel 1998, 120).

Influenced by this ethos of individualism, or what Israel called "the Beida spirit of laissez-faire individualism" (1998, 120), Beida faculty tend to speak passionately and fondly of their university and its academic culture. The fact that past professors, and university presidents as well, have paid a heavy price for their independent thinking is seen as a great value to be cherished, and it is a source of pride for many of the professors with whom we spoke. From their perspective, few institutions if any can come close to matching Beida in terms of its emphasis on individualist thinking and concomitant willingness to challenge dominant practices. In a very real sense, this facet of the university's ethos, along with the additional qualities discussed in this section, set it apart from other universities in the quest for academic standing. But again, there have been times when individualist thinking has resulted in serious consequences.

Beida and the Culture War

Like many top research universities worldwide, Beida has targeted the goal of being a world-class university. Its inclusion in Project 985—indeed, its preferential status in the project, along with Tsinghua—further fueled the quest to enhance the university's standing. And like most Chinese universities, Beida has followed a prescribed plan for achieving institutional objectives, typically updated every several years in the form of a strategy or development document. For example, in 1994 Beida's administration developed an initial plan to strengthen the university with "The Outline of Development and Reform." This was then revised in 2002 in the form of "Action Plan for Shaping Beida as a World-Class University from 1995–2015," which was then revised again in 2008 as "The Strategic Guidelines for Beida's Development." More recently, the university administration produced a new plan, "The Strategic Plan for Shaping a World-Class University from 2012–2020." The revised rendition obviously placed great emphasis on the university's elevating its standing. For example, one of the documents noted that the proper path for Beida to attain world-class university standing was to further reform the organization and governance of the university. Several reforms were noted: (1) to reshape a new, more dynamic Beida by building more comprehensive disciplines, developing more rational institutional structures, and adding greater competitiveness, efficiency, and effectiveness; (2) to focus more on preparing talent in terms of a proper mix of creativity and practical capacity; (3) to enhance the competitiveness of research by keeping abreast of international trends and developments; (4) to improve institutional governance by restructuring and reorganizing the university; (5) to improve faculty expertise by reforming human resource (personnel) systems; (6) to increase internationalization by strengthening and expanding university exchange and cooperation with worldwide counterparts and expanding support for faculty and staff foreign engagement; and (7) to modernize facilities by adding and strengthening infrastructure, library facilities, national key labs, and so on.[3]

Most observers are likely to agree that the quality of a university's professorate is a key element in determining whether a university is world-class or not. After all, the critical three-fold mission of research universities involves professors performing at high levels across the teaching, research, and service functions. At Beida, as has been the case with other Project 985 universities, efforts to strengthen the faculty focused on reshaping the nature of faculty work, especially in terms of elevating scholarly productivity. This was manifested in an administration-backed effort to reform the academic personnel system.

The goal of fostering greater productivity among the faculty, mainly through the implementation of more competitive processes, led to widespread debate at Beida during the early 2000s. The "culture war," as one professor described it, actually pitted different groups of faculty and administrators against one another, based on divergent perceptions about what was needed to elevate the productivity of Beida's faculty. Given its role as a national leader, Beida was seen as a test case for raising critical issues about faculty work and workload at the Chinese university.

Before the 1990s, Chinese colleges and universities generally operated under the model of a socialist planned economy. In such a context, many higher education institutions were more like government agencies than true academic communities. For instance, all universities functioned directly under the guidelines and directives of government officials at multiple levels. Relatedly, all academics were regarded as governmental workers, akin to civil servants. Even the most basic operations of academic programs often had to be approved by government authorities. Generally speaking, faculty believed there was far too much government intrusion, even at the nation's more elite universities, such as Beida and Tsinghua.

Although the 1990s witnessed major changes throughout Chinese society, especially in terms of increased marketization, the changes relating to heightened emphasis on competition and markets was not as influential within the walls of the Chinese academy, especially in terms of the highly government-subsidized national universities. While many of the nation's social and economic institutions, including hundreds of colleges and universities cut loose by the national government in terms of funding, adapted to more competitive, market-oriented mechanisms,[4] systems relating to academic appointments and promotions at the national universities were somewhat resistant.

Critical analysis of university-government relations led to the identification of two major problems with university operations at elite universities such as Beida. One was that a lack of autonomy tended to stifle academic life and high-level academic achievements. The second was that the basic structures of faculty life lacked competitive processes, thus perpetuating a model of professional work that at times was ridiculed as offering professors an "iron rice bowl," or *tie fan wan*, essentially implying that professors had excessive security, decent pay, and a minimal workload. To put it another way, some believed professors had too much comfort to encourage high levels of scholarly productivity. And so the argument went that if universities, especially Beida, as the nation's higher education leader, hoped to attain world-class standing, they must alter the fundamental personnel structure. This involved nothing less than rejecting the idea of faculty as cadre in favor of a new model more similar to that of Western universities that would favor market forces, create greater competition, and pressure faculty to produce more research and publications. This was no small challenge.

In January 2003, Beida's administration undertook a reform of the personnel system, promulgating a scheme first announced on the university's website. The proposed measures included the following objectives: (1) to break away from the "all-tenure"[5] system with its "iron rice bowl" syndrome; (2) to remove a rigid structure linking particular posts or jobs to certain titles, so that qualified people, regardless of title, could be considered for them; (3) to link one's salary with one's post, thus widening the gap between different salary scales and encouraging faculty competition for such posts and (4) to downsize the faculty by reassigning surplus personnel to different jobs (Chen 2003, 118).

The president of Beida at the time, Xu Zhihong, offered his take on the matter, noting, "Peking University must maintain innovation. Reform is not a revolution, but a tool for innovation. It is not breaking the 'iron rice bowl,' but changing people's expectations." He went on to add, "Reform must be conducted at Peking University, because there will be no hope for China's higher education without reforms. I do it not for my own benefit. I would not be the president if I were working for my own interests" ("Xu Zhihong" 2010, 1). Another high-ranking official pointed out that the widespread reform of the university had to begin with systemic reform of the personnel system, as people are the critical link in transforming the university to an elite enterprise.

As he explained, you cannot hope to develop world-class teaching and research practices without implementing a reformed system for recruiting and retaining top faculty.

The central administration of Beida organized a task force to draft a framework for change. A key member of the team was Zhang Weiying, an economist and former dean of Beida's Guanghua School of Management and one of the assistants to the president. Zhang Weiying assumed a key role in advancing personnel reform, but controversy followed much of his effort, given great resistance on the part of many Beida faculty. Zhang, who earned his doctorate in economics from Oxford, was a liberal with great faith in the ideas and models associated with Western universities. As one of the primary authors of the personnel reform proposal, he drew extensively from what he had experienced in the United Kingdom. Many of his thoughts about university reform at Beida and Chinese universities in general appeared in his 2004 book *Daxue de Luoji* (*The Logic of the University*). His perspective about how universities ought to operate, including a discussion of the working lives of academics, catapulted him into the center of the university reform debate; for example, he often was a participant in major media events where the pros and cons of proposed reforms were discussed.

Zhang's view centered on de-emphasizing and downsizing the role of the government in university life and operations while inducing more competitive, market-oriented forces. This included introducing greater competition for academic appointments, following typically Western practices such as advertising faculty vacancies widely, requiring formal applications, and employing extensive review of qualifications, including face-to-face interviews and the delivery of an academic lecture or "job talk" (Zhang 2004, 46–49). He saw these as basic steps in making more sound decisions about faculty appointments. Further, he also favored revisions in faculty promotion processes, such as placing greater pressure on faculty to publish in a manner typically associated with the Western notion of "publish or perish," and the adoption of a "tenure-type" promotion system in which faculty had to earn their promotions or leave the university. He also argued that even after faculty earn tenure they should continually have to prove themselves by undergoing annual reviews. Frankly, it is not hard to understand why many Beida faculty opposed Zhang's position.

After the proposed reforms became public, they drew wide attention from both inside and outside of the university. Opposition to the reforms was widespread, especially from within the Chinese academy, where many professors welcomed reduced government interference but preferred to maintain high levels of public funding. University presidents, senior-level administrators, chairs of university councils, and academic administrators tended to support the reform measures, while the majority of faculty tended to oppose them. The first group described the reforms in glowing terms, using such phrases as, "comprehensive and systematic," "transformative," and "innovative." A senior-level Beida administrator, for example, commented, "I was excited when I first read the proposal drafted by economist Zhang. I realized that it was not easy to develop such a plan, although I had given some thought to similar kinds of ideas in my own head. I appreciated Professor Zhang for providing us with such a great proposal. For many years we had been waiting to develop such a proposal—we saw the necessity to reform the personnel system."

Many faculty members, of course, were less thrilled with the proposal. Critical voices came both from within Beida and from faculty working at other universities, given that the implications of reform were likely to extend well beyond Beida. A leading opponent emerged in the figure of Gan Yang, professor and founding dean of the College of General Education at Sun Yat-sen University (*Zhongshan Daxue*) in Guangzhou. Gan, a graduate of the Committee on Social Thought program at the University of Chicago, travelled and spoke extensively about his opposition, putting his thoughts in writing in the form of his book (co-authored with Li Meng) *Zhongguo Daxue Gaige Zhidao* (*A Road to Chinese University Reform*) (2004). Gan argued that the Chinese university context, and the broader cultural context in general, may not be well suited to the kinds of ideas and models Zhang wanted to import from Western universities. Gan acknowledged that the Chinese university had already been shaped to a great extent by, for example, the Soviet Union in the 1950s but nonetheless still had strong roots in Chinese culture. Hence, adopting norms as proposed by Zhang could be detrimental to the university. But Zhang Weiying disagreed with this point of view, arguing that modern universities originated in the West and consequently that the ideas and models related to them should be available for Chinese universities to draw from in pursuing modern governance systems. Adopting advanced ideas and university models from beyond China's borders does not necessarily amount to sacrificing the society's own academic traditions or abandoning China's own university culture. To the contrary, Zhang argued that China could undertake efforts to combine the best of the West with Chinese customs and practices and in turn produce an integrated system (2004, 46–49).

Both sides of the great culture war had legitimate points of view, but the reformists were not able to weaken faculty opposition in any significant way. Consequently, faculty members were able to stem the tide of reform and maintain key aspects of the security they coveted; they felt strongly that a certain degree of security was warranted, given the challenges of university life, including lower salaries than are typically seen by similarly educated professionals, such as those working in business arenas. Additionally, there were elements of the proposed reforms that many faculty did not oppose, including borrowing some norms and practices from outside the Chinese academy, but they preferred to have a say in how such changes were to be implemented. Some professors believed they had an obligation to protect the legacy of the university. Zhang actually summed up this position quite nicely when he argued that the most important concern should be how to reform modern-day Chinese universities and at the same time protect the valued academic traditions and legacy of the nation's universities. Without such a cautious approach, revolution and damage to the heart of the university would likely result. In light of such an outcome, nothing valuable would be left as the basis for the future development of the university (Zhang 2004, 46–49).

To date, the vast majority of the ideas advanced by the reform proposal have not taken root, although they appeal to the administration. Too many of the ideas drawn from Western university norms and practices were judged as questionable for Chinese soil. Zhang's career suffered from the failed attempt; he gave up his post as dean of the Guanghua School of Management, although he remained highly regarded as a professor and an expert speaker.

Enhancing Scholarly Productivity

Although the complete and systematic reform of the Beida academic personnel system did not succeed, some changes nonetheless slowly worked their way into various faculty hiring and promotion processes. For example, faculty hiring has to a great extent become rather formalized. Recruitment of new faculty at today's Chinese universities involves much more extensive processes, and the practice of hiring one's own doctoral graduates is increasingly discouraged. Indeed, it is often said that Beida now only wants to hire new faculty holding foreign doctorates.

An institutionalized procedure has been established for appointments to an academic post, including several formalized steps for recruiting and appointing new faculty members. First, formal application plans are now required from the heads of academic units seeking an additional faculty member. Second, the academic unit is now responsible for advertising openings and recruiting applicants, and announcements must be public. Third, academic units are encouraged to establish a working committee to assist in the review of applications; such committees are likely to include deans or department chairs and the chair of the unit's academic council. The goal is to select one or two final candidates. Fourth, a campus visit is required, including a face-to-face interview, job talk, and/or teaching a seminar. Fifth, the working committee is charged with drafting a final report or recommendation based on the campus visit to be sent to the human resource office. Finally, the human resource office is expected to approve or reject the recommendation or send the report to a meeting of the executive or governance board to make a final decision (typically only in the case of high-level appointments). These procedures were generally well received by the faculty, and most believed that making the recruitment and hiring process more transparent was a good idea.

Changes also have been implemented in the faculty promotion process. For one, the basic faculty ranks were clarified. The initial rank is assistant professorship (*zhu jiao*), which is granted to newly hired faculty members. Two years later, assistant professors are eligible to be promoted to the rank of lecturer (*jiang shi*). Promotion to the next rank—that of associate professor (*fu jiaoshou*)—takes at least five years. The final rank is full professor (*zheng jiaoshou*), and once again a minimum of five years is required at the previous rank to be eligible.

Additionally, the steps involved in submitting an application to be promoted to the next rank were also clarified, including codifying the various campus players and committees involved in reviewing materials and making determinations. The promotion procedure begins at the level of the basic academic unit—a department or a school. Candidates who receive positive votes present their materials before an academic committee or a special disciplinary committee. If approved, a candidate goes before a campus-wide interdisciplinary committee and once again presents the application materials in an interview format. This committee makes the final decision as to whether or not the candidate's application will be included among the eligible list of candidates for consideration at a special academic promotion meeting involving deans and academic committee members. Eventually, an official appointment document is announced publicly at the university's website. If no objections are filed within fifteen days, the appointments become valid.

Generally speaking, faculty have been open to such formalized processes and tend to appreciate the increased transparency. The biggest change, however, and that which has generated the most resentment among faculty members, relates to the way in which competition has been forced upon the academic ladder system. This was accomplished by government officials, in conjunction with university administrators, simply limiting the number of faculty posts at the full and associate professor ranks. Adopting limits—or "quotas," as faculty often described them—has served to create a highly competitive process for faculty seeking promotions. Even a faculty candidate who meets minimum standards for promotion may not receive a promotion if another candidate has a more exceptional record. This shortage of positions produces great competition among colleagues at the same rank. This fact is discussed in negative terms by the majority of faculty members.

A result of the increased competition among faculty has been an increase in faculty publishing, although some openly wonder if quality has kept pace with quantity. This change, combined with increased funding for research from Project 985, has contributed to greater and greater emphasis on the research mission.

Furthermore, increased efforts to further internationalize the university have added new expectations for faculty to publish in international arenas, in many cases having to write in English.

There are differing views on the elevation of promotion standards, including greater pressure on faculty to publish in international journals. Many faculty members see the increased competition within their own academic units as a negative force because such conditions have the potential to stifle collaboration and collegiality. However, university administrators tend to be more sanguine about the changes. For example, a senior academic administrator spoke to these issues, noting that he was fairly satisfied with how faculty in his school had responded to the new expectations: "Our academics and scholars have performed greatly. Meanwhile we also encourage and reward them for publishing in top international journals such as *Nature* and *Science*, as well as in indexed journals such as those included in SCI [Science Citation Index], SSCI [Social Sciences Citation Index], and EI [Engineering Index]. . . . Therefore, the knowledge generated by them is an important component of popular databases, home and abroad."

A second academic administrator and full professor noted similar points, offering, "We very much attach importance to high-level publications, mainly because we believe that a higher quality article is more important than ten or even a hundred qualitatively weak ones. Therefore, we do not push our faculty members to publish as many articles as possible in a short time. We often remind them to slow down their production of papers unless they are producing articles based on empirical studies."

The preceding individuals spoke to the emphasis placed on publishing quality, with one also alluding to expectations for faculty to publish in international outlets. But there is also pressure on Beida's faculty to be engaged internationally in a variety of ways, not simply in terms of their research and publishing. Consequently, in what follows we discuss some of the increasingly important international facets of faculty life.

Internationalization of Faculty Life

In the context of increased funding from Projects 211 and 985, faculty and academic staff at Beida have experienced increased opportunities for a variety of forms of international engagement during the past decade and a half. These opportunities include spending a year or semester abroad as a visiting faculty member at another university, visiting foreign universities for short periods of time to advance one's research or teaching, or simply attending short-term academic events, including international conferences.

Many faculty with whom we spoke discussed their international experiences and opportunities in favorable terms. They saw such opportunities as critical to Beida's effort to earn legitimate standing as a world-class university. For example, a senior professor highlighted how her international experiences had led her to collaborate and publish with numerous foreign colleagues. As she explained, "I can easily get opportunities of setting up academic networks with counterparts worldwide. . . . For instance, I have succeeded in applying for some international collaborative programs, such as the Fulbright New Century Scholars program, Erasmus Mundus, which enabled me to conduct my research at many top universities worldwide." Similarly, another faculty member talked about how over the past ten years he had been very successful in applying for international fellowships and scholarships, including the European Union's Erasmus Mundus program and grant programs in Canada. He also talked about how the university had supported his work in Australia, Finland, India, Japan, the Netherlands, and the United States, among other countries. In the minds of these two faculty members, the university's support for professors gaining international experience had increased dramatically over the past decade or so. Statistics at Beida tend to reinforce such a perspective, revealing that in recent years the university has on average supported roughly five thousand foreign trips per year for its faculty.

Several factors increased international opportunities for Beida's academics. One was a change in policy that emphasized faculty and staff traveling and working abroad. In part, this represented a shift among institutional leaders and their recognition that in order for Beida to compete at a global level, the academic community needed a deeper understanding of higher education worldwide. Of course, part of the shift here reflected increased funding from the government in support of enhanced internationalization. As a high-ranking administrator noted, "We believe that internationalization is the right way to go and that we should adopt relevant regulations to encourage the long-term development of the university. . . . And, we also should encourage all the schools to make use of relevant policies and programs, such as Project 985, the Chang Jiang Scholars program, and the China Scholarship Council to carry on the internationalization of the academic staff." The Chang Jiang Scholars program is a national initiative that offers support for foreign scholars to work at Chinese universities, and the China Scholarship Council (CSC) provides funding to students and faculty to study and work abroad.

In addition to supporting international experiences for faculty, staff, and students, the university also served as a host for thousands of students and scholars on short- and long-term visits. Many of the visitors who came to campus in recent years were part of the two hundred or so higher education institutions (involving over fifty nations) that had formed official partnerships with the university. Foreign professors participated in several capacities, including officially recognized formal visits, conference or workshop participation, jointly organized forums, scholar exchange programs, and temporary visiting appointments. A key mechanism for encouraging the participation of foreign faculty was the development and implementation of the Beijing Forum, initiated in 2004 and jointly sponsored by Beida, Beijing Municipal Commission on Education, and the Korea Foundation for Advanced Studies (KFAS). The forum's basic theme is "Harmony of Civilizations and Prosperity for All," with each year offering a relevant subtheme as the organizing structure. For example, in 2012 the subtheme was "Challenges and Opportunities: New Thinking in New Reality," and "Tradition and Modernity, Transition and Transformation" was the subtheme for 2011. As of 2012, the forum had welcomed over 3,300 participants, including well-known politicians and noted scholars from more than seventy countries and regions of the world. A senior university administrator saw the forum as a crucial component of Beida's internationalization efforts, noting that, "The forum had set a good example for international collaboration and exchange."

Increased internationalization also was reflected in greater emphasis placed on hiring new faculty members who earned their doctorates abroad, most notably in Western nations such as Germany, the United Kingdom, and the United States. The implementation of such strategies was based on a belief that in order to attain world-class standing, Beida's schools and departments ought to search for and appoint the best scientists and scholars worldwide. Consequently, over the past ten-plus years Beida attracted hundreds of excellent scientists and humanists who contributed in significant ways to the university's development. According to recent data, the university has been host to between seven and eight hundred international scholars in the past few years, working under either short- or long-term contracts. Among them are about two hundred who serve at the university as permanent faculty members. Such data signify the seriousness with which the university approaches its quest for world-class ranking.

University Transformation and the Road Ahead

Although the personnel reform efforts at Beida led by Zhang Weiying were mostly unsuccessful, the fact that debates about university reform drew such broad interest, both inside the bowels of the university and beyond its gates, served to raise fundamental questions about the university ideal and what was fitting for Chinese society. In this regard, the reform initiative, in the words of one faculty member, seemed "fresh and innovative" to large segments of the population. This professor went on to add that in light of "the problems relating to the Cultural Revolution and the limitations of Mao's thought," the reform debates "stimulated people in the academic community and in public circles" in intellectual ways not often seen. The reform debates were significant enough, as the preceding professor noted, to turn Zhang and Gan into media stars, "popular beyond their identities as academics." Along these lines, a senior professor noted that the reform effort touched on some very critical issues, which partially explained the popularity of the public debates.

The personnel reform movement at Beida contributed in significant ways to discussions of what kinds of universities China ought to develop and support and in this regard informed the national discourse surrounding efforts to build world-class universities. As advocates for personnel reform pushed the Chinese professorate to embrace new ideas and models, there was pushback as well from many academics. This tension furthered the discussion of what it means for China to build highly competitive research universities, as faculty advocates raised important concerns relating to the need to strengthen academic freedom and institutional autonomy. According to one professor from nearby Beijing Institute of Technology, Yang Dongping, recognized by some as an important public intellectual, "It will be helpful to convince academics and administrators to believe that academic freedom and institutional autonomy are two basic principles in constructing modern universities" (2004).

As part of the quest to strengthen the university, institutional challenges are to be expected. In the words of former Beida President Xu Zhihong, there is still much room for growth: "China still does not have a world-class university, but we must strive for one. And not just Beida and Qinghua [Tsinghua]. More Chinese universities should have a place in the world. There is no hard and fast definition for a 'world-class university,' but everyone has a common understanding that [such a university] should be very well known in the world. Why should it be well known? Because it would have a large number of outstanding scholars and research results and exert a huge influence on developments in such aspects as science, technology, and economics. And it also would generate many new thoughts and concepts and have a great effect on social development and human civilization" (Long 2004, 51). Xu's words offer some insight into how key leaders such as China's university presidents define what it means to be a leading university. What is fairly clear from our case study, and emphasized to some extent by Xu, is that Beida still has much to accomplish in its quest for world-class academic excellence. There is also some concern that its competitive advantage over other Chinese universities may be declining, given the intense national competition and advances by a host of leading universities.

Internationalization is one area where the gap between Beida and other Chinese universities has closed to some extent. This facet of university life has always been stressed at Beida. Indeed, in her discussion of Peking University during its first few years of existence, Xiaoqing Lin highlighted the great influence Zhang Zhidong, scholar, politician, and reformer, had on the curriculum, based on his synthesis of Chinese and Western thought (Lin 2005, 9). As Lin noted, "Zhang tried to integrate an expanded definition of Chinese learning from the past—history, literature, philosophy, philology—with Western learning and practical knowledge" (2005, 10). This openness to the West came to characterize Beida throughout its history, situating the university at the vanguard of internationalization. But owing to the broad national effort to upgrade the nation's top universities through extensive MoE funding, other universities internationalized at an incredibly rapid pace. Thus, at the end of 2012 the difference between Beida and universities such as Renmin or Beijing Normal in terms of internationalization had decreased substantially. This is fairly evident in the other case studies presented in this book.

Competition among the nation's leading universities has grown increasingly intense, with many, once again, closing the gap in terms of various academic and research operations. This is especially true with regard to recent efforts by strong universities such as Renmin to develop and strengthen certain disciplines, some of which have long been dominated by Beida, such as history and sociology. But while the gap may be smaller than it once was, the Beida academic community still takes solace in the reality that it is the only Chinese university consistently considered among the world's best in a variety of arts and humanities fields, including history, linguistics, sociology, and philosophy. In the 2012 QS World University Rankings by Subject, Beida ranked among the top twenty-two universities in the world for all four disciplines.

Another challenge facing Beida, in terms of the national higher education landscape, is the further integration of Hong Kong's and Macau's universities into the competitive student recruitment arena. Since the implementation of the *Gaokao*, at the end of the Cultural Revolution, the very best Chinese high school students have been likely to attend either Beida or Tsinghua. This is no longer the case. As a professor in education explained, "In the past the most promising graduates, including the *Gaokao* champions in many provinces, chose to attend Beida or Tsinghua. But the situation has begun to change with many of the most promising students now selecting higher education institutions in Hong Kong or Macau." This professor went on to note that even in the Chinese media there was some discussion of how Beida and Tsinghua "are kind of at a disadvantage" in terms of "competing for the best talent." Related to this, more and more Chinese high school students are opting to study abroad, increasing the competition universities such as Beida face in the hyper-competitive higher education marketplace.

Another difficult situation the university has had to face is finding adequate financial support for its faculty in light of the incredibly high cost of living in Beijing, most specifically in terms of the real estate market. One professor speculated that Beida was likely to face "brain drain" in the coming years if the problem was not addressed. A junior faculty member expressed similar concern: "Even buying a flat with two bedrooms and a living room in the suburb might cost me at least 1.5 to 2 million RMB. Every month, after paying all my bills for rent, food, telephone, Internet, I will have little money left to save. Nobody knows how long it will take me to save enough money to buy a flat of my own. I am feeling a huge amount of pressure and anxiety having to live in Beijing." Another professor noted that a recent study had shown that people living in Beijing and Shanghai reported being less happy than those living in other parts of the country. This professor attributed the discrepancy to the cost of living. A senior professor and former dean of the Graduate School of Education, Min Weifang, added his take on the situation while addressing the faculty in PKU's Graduate School of Education: "We are very much concerned about the issue and need to consider how to tackle the problem. What we can do though is to continuously improve the conditions for working here at the university. We can improve the environment through professional development for the faculty. But this is a really tough and challenging endeavor."[6]

Concluding Remarks

Beida's special place among the nation's cultural institutions, and especially its leadership role within the higher education community, establish the university as a beacon toward which others look for direction. Weston noted as much when he wrote, "As the country's best known center for 'national learning' (*guoxue*), Beida is viewed as a guardian of the splendor of Chinese civilization" (2004, 2). He went on to highlight an expression shared with him, while conducting his research into the intellectual and political history of the university: "All China looks to Beijing and all Beijing looks to Beida" (2004, 5).

Beida's faculty and students do not necessarily serve as an anchor for existing political and cultural views, further securing the relevance of such perspectives for the society writ large; instead, the university often challenges the status quo by raising important questions about Chinese values, beliefs, and practices. Of course, this is in keeping with Beida's own culture—a culture containing a healthy degree of skepticism. Such norms, though, also present challenges for the university—challenges captured by a well-known Chinese pun, shared by Hayhoe in a 2005 *Comparative Education Review* essay,

> Chinese people love puns, and the Chinese language, with its many homophones, lends itself to punning. In a recent conversation that I had with one of the vice presidents of Zhejiang University, he remarked to me on how the graduates of China's top universities are known for certain defining characteristics of their institution. He started with Beida and Tsinghua and repeated a joke current in Chinese university circles: Tsinghua graduates are known for being likely to 'zuo-guan' (become officials), while Beida graduates, by contrast, are likely to 'zuolao' (sit in prison). The first 'zuo' means to 'do or be,' the second 'to sit,' and the joke's

import is clear. Up to the present, Beida has been viewed with considerable suspicion by the government for its intellectual liberalism and passionate preoccupa-
tion with issues relating to democracy. (577)

Although sitting in prison is hardly the norm when it comes to Beida's faculty and students, the hyperbole employed here is simply meant to convey the
critical quality of the culture of Beida, especially in contrast to Tsinghua's oft-
expressed loyalism; here, we use the word *critical* to mean the predisposition or
tendency to offer cutting analyses of society and social systems—analyses that
at times may contradict dominant values, beliefs, and practices. A historical
example offered earlier in this chapter was the case of Beida professor Liang
Shu-ming, who challenged common interpretations of Marxist class theory and
Chinese social structure during Mao's leadership.

This critical facet of the culture of Beida tends to be seen around the world as
a defining quality of world-class universities. Robert Rhoads and Katalin Szelényi,
in their book *Global Citizenship and the University*, captured this aspect of modern
universities, arguing that they have a responsibility to serve as a "social conscience
for society," offering criticism of societal practices. They went on to add, "Universities have an obligation to use their knowledge capacities to advance social
life and to better the human condition" (Rhoads and Szelényi 2011, 7–8). At
Beida, such responsibilities are taken quite seriously by many faculty and students. An obvious case in point is the leadership role Beida faculty and students
played in the May Fourth Movement. A less popular example in China is, of
course, the role Beida students played in the Tiananmen Square democracy
demonstrations.

But to simply assume that Beida is a bastion of academic freedom is to over-
state the matter. The reality is that while Beida faculty and students may experience forms of academic freedom beyond those typically associated with Chinese
universities, there are still significant differences between Beida and the Oxfords
and Harvards of the world. A case in point is offered by the *Guardian*, which
reported in March 2011 that the university's administration had proposed a new
policy to "screen" students with "radical thoughts" or "independent lifestyles"
(Branigan 2011). The article noted that the proposed policy had drawn a good
deal of criticism, "provoking angry reactions from undergraduates and comparisons to the Cultural Revolution." Zhang Ming, a professor of politics at neighboring Renmin University, also criticized the proposed policy, stating, "For a
university to see a student having radical thoughts or independent thinking as
a bad thing that has to be punished, is terrible" (Branigan 2011). Of course, we
want to stress that this policy was not proposed by Beida's faculty but by the
administration.

The critical quality of Beida's institutional culture was captured to some extent by our discussion of the emphasis the university places on the pursuit of knowledge combined with a healthy dose of skepticism. We also described other key facets of the cultural ethos and identity of the university, including its emphasis on inclusiveness, the loyalty of its faculty to their profession and to the university, and the strong spirit of individualism. Examples were offered to support such assertions, but a myriad of others could have been introduced as well. The point is that Beida has a very unusual culture compared to other universities in China.

As arguably the nation's preeminent institution of higher learning, Beida not only serves as a model for emulation but is also a target for other universities seeking to climb to the top of the nation's university system. Given recent national initiatives, including most notably Projects 211 and 985, the distance between Beida and other top universities has closed considerably over the past decade and a half. This is of concern to some Beida faculty who relish the university's preeminent standing and seek to join the elite universities of the world. Relatedly, some evidence suggests that Beida already stands out as a world-class university, such as the Times Higher Education (THE) World University Rankings, where in 2013–2014 Beida was ranked number forty-five, five places ahead of Tsinghua, and in the QS World University Rankings by Subject, where the university was ranked among the world's elites in terms of several disciplines in the arts and humanities.

But the university has much still to achieve in its quest for elite standing, and the challenge of reforming the university's personnel policies in the early 2000s served to bring several issues into focus. Such issues include divergent views about faculty promotion processes, including differences of opinion about the degree of job security Beida's professors ought to have, the amount of publishing and research they should do, and the extent to which internationalization is to be expected. Additionally, the faculty raised some important concerns about the financial challenges of living in Beijing, particularly pointing to the high cost of owning or renting an apartment. All of this suggests that while the Beida faithful have reasons to be proud of the university's historical and contemporary accomplishments, including its role as a national model for other top universities, it still seeks a higher place in the increasingly globalized higher education landscape. Only time will tell if the university succeeds or not, but if the past is any indication of its potentiality, guarded optimism seems a reasonable posture to assume.

Internationalization of Academic Life and the Changing Face of Renmin University

When significant international economic and political matters related to China arise, it is quite common for news media to turn to the many leading international experts at Renmin University of China (RUC), also known as the People's University and, colloquially, RenDa. For example, when the United States and Japan signed a September 2012 accord to deploy a second advanced missile-defense radar system on Japanese territory, RUC's Shi Yinhong, a highly respected professor of international studies, was asked by the *New York Times* to comment on the situation: "The joint missile defense system objectively encourages Japan to keep an aggressive position in the Diaoyu Islands dispute, which sends China a very negative message. . . . Japan would not have been so aggressive without the support and actions of the U.S." (Shanker and Johnson 2012). Similarly, when Brazil, China, India, and Russia condemned the March 2011 United Nations authorized air strikes against Muammar Gaddafi's military forces in Libya, the same professor again was questioned by the media and noted that, "Many developing nations see a dangerous precedent in the Western attacks and intervention in what is fundamentally a civil war" (Scrutton and Buckley 2011). And RUC professor Jin Canrong, also a highly regarded expert of international relations, is frequently asked to comment on global affairs, such as when the *New York Times* sought his opinion in November 2012 about then-presumptive leader Xi Jinping's close ties to China's increasingly "robust military." As Jin noted, "China should shoulder some responsibility for the United States and the United States should share power with China. . . . The United States elites won't like it, but they will have to [accept it]." He went on to predict that future growth of the Chinese economy will necessitate Americans sharing power with their Chinese counterparts (Perlez 2012a).

Other Renmin professors also play key roles as public intellectuals, providing critical commentary regarding important international developments. For example, when China's state-run media Xinhua and the *People's Daily* announced their intent to move into the Internet search arena, competing with such giants as Baidu and Google, a matter clearly of global significance, Renmin journalism professor Yu Guoming expressed skepticism to the *Wall Street Journal* about state-run media being able to "keep up with private companies" (Chao 2011). When the *BBC News* ran a January 2011 story about rising tensions between China and the United States, linked in part to China's growing economic strength and perceptions of U.S. financial failings, Renmin professor Kang Xiaoguang pointed to rising nationalism and a sense among the Chinese citizenry that the Western world was in decline: "People are now looking down on the West, from leadership circles, to academia, to everyday folks" (Nye 2011).

Academic meetings of international significance also have drawn on the intellectual expertise of Renmin professors. When Columbia University organized international colloquia as part of its ongoing forum "A Free Press for a Global Society," the 2010 East Asian panel offered perspectives from key Renmin faculty members, including scholars from economics, international relations, and journalism. Such international events in fact often are hosted at the Renmin campus, as was the case in May 2013 when the university sponsored a major meeting to address global disasters, including floods and droughts. The university consistently seeks to bring together real-world problems and research-based insights, and many of its leading professors seem committed to the ideal of the engaged public intellectual with, of course, a uniquely Chinese twist.

The university also is a hub for important international visitors, serving as a key site for promoting economic exchange and development as well as working to enhance global political affairs and international stability. For example, U.S. Navy Admiral Michael Mullen, chairman of the Joint Chiefs of Staff, visited Renmin in July 2011 and delivered a speech about furthering stability in Asia through international cooperation and exchange between China and the United States. Further, heads of state regularly visit Renmin to give key addresses, such as when South African President Jacob Zuma visited in August 2010, leading a delegation of business executives; he affirmed Renmin's important role in fostering international trade and relations. Likewise, in August 2011, Republic of Bolivia President Juan Evo Morales delivered an important address aimed at furthering economic ties between his nation and China.

The university has become a vital resource for advancing the nation's economic, political, and legal interests. Further, Renmin's faculty members are at the center of such initiatives, whether speaking at a conference, responding to interview requests from a major news agency, hosting important dignitaries, or forging international ties through shared research interests, such as when a delegation of legal scholars from Renmin's School of Law visited Strasbourg, Geneva, Copenhagen, and Amsterdam in 2010 as part of a transnational collaboration to curb torture. Indeed, there is much evidence that Renmin professors take seriously their role as public intellectuals acting in an increasingly interdependent world. As global public intellectuals, their actions are representative of a university with deep roots in the people's concerns.

None too surprisingly, our interactions with faculty members at Renmin stressed several central themes, but no single issue was more important than internationalization.[1] By internationalization, we mean growing transnational ties and multinational economic, political, legal, and cultural interpenetrations. The Renmin faculty with whom we spoke consistently raised the importance of internationalization, including the ways in which global trends were influencing their working lives.[2] More times than not, internationalization was discussed in terms of changing expectations associated with faculty life, including research and publishing, teaching practices, cultural exchange and communication, and the background and training of faculty members. To succeed at Renmin in these times, faculty members find that they increasingly must engage international arenas. Such a trend also is consistent with changes advanced by China's educational leaders and policy makers, as is evident by the goals and objectives of Projects 211 and 985. Furthermore, the forms of internationalization highlighted by the case of Renmin University shed light on a broad trend evident throughout much of Chinese higher education (R. Yang 2000, 2002).

The Quest for World-Class Standing

Internationalization is deeply implicated in the quest by the Chinese Ministry of Education (MoE) to build world-class universities. Cutting-edge academic science demands international engagement, a reality clearly recognized by Chinese officials and evidenced by the nation's educational policies of the past decade or so. Such a conclusion is supported by remarks from Xu Zhihong, a member of the Chinese Academy of Sciences and former president of Beijing University, who argued in a 2010 lecture given at Huazhong University of Science and Technology that global, high-ranking universities must have well-known professors who conduct high-level research ("China Lacks" 2010). This perspective appears to be widely shared among administrators and policy makers engaged in refashioning China's top universities. The connection between world-class standing as a university and academic research is made clear in Philip Altbach's discussion of research universities in developing countries. For example, in describing the challenges nations face in building research universities, Altbach elaborated on the connections between academic science and the global environment: "Research is increasingly competitive, with researchers and universities rushing to present results and patent or license potentially useful discoveries or inventions. Science, in short, has become a 'high-stakes' and intensely competitive international endeavor" (2009, 21). Altbach went on to add, "Scientific globalization means that participants are linked to the norms of the disciplines of scholarship that are established by the leaders of research, located in the major universities in the United States and other Western nations" (2009, 21). Altbach's remarks foreshadow some problems uncovered through our inquiry at Renmin, specifically in terms of the reality that the push to build world-class universities is in part defined by the nature of the world's leading universities and the nations in which they reside. And although China does not exactly fit the description of a developing nation—it is more accurately described as both developed and developing, especially when one compares urban and rural life—it nonetheless faces some of the same pressures as other developing nations in the quest to build top research universities.

The realities of globalization have firmly resituated the contemporary research university as an international enterprise tied to global markets of students, staffing, technologies, and ideas. This reality was reinforced at the 2010 "Going Global" conference hosted in London, where keynote speaker Simon Marginson (2010b) argued that today's world-class universities have moved beyond Clark Kerr's (1963) vision of the multiversity: "The university with multiple constituencies that did everything, has given way to the Global Research University or GRU. The GRU is the multiversity, plus more research, much more mobility, global systems and ranking." The "ranking" to which Marginson referred, of course, alludes to the growing influence of global ranking schemes, such as those deriving from Jiao Tong University in Shanghai (Academic Ranking of World Universities or ARWU) and the Times Higher Education rankings from London (World University Rankings).

Given the national push by the Chinese government to build world-class universities as well as broader global impulses influencing higher education in China, the goal of this chapter is to better understand the impact of such dynamic forces on faculty life at one of China's top universities—Renmin University. As one of the nation's very best universities, Renmin is a major recipient of both Project 211 and 985 funds. Additionally, former Renmin president Ji Baocheng made the elevation of Renmin to world-class standing his primary goal after his appointment as president in 2000 and throughout his decade-long term.[3] This goal was captured by President Ji's threefold vision: "*da lou, da shi, da qi,*" which literally may be translated as "big buildings, big masters, big environment" but perhaps is best understood as improving facilities, building a great faculty, and embracing a broad vision. The latter two facets of his vision—big masters and big environment—directly implicate internationalization. Consequently, the basic question we seek to address in this chapter may be expressed in the following manner: With efforts underway at Renmin throughout the twenty-first century to advance the university to world-class status, how has faculty life changed? And more specifically, in what ways is the internationalization of the university revealed through the experiences of professors? Here, our focus primarily is on changes taking place during the first decade of the twenty-first century, given that Project 985 was initially implemented during the latter part of the final decade of the twentieth century (Project 211 was implemented a few years earlier).

The People's University: Institutional Background

Like all four universities in our project, Renmin is located within the university district of Beijing known as Haidian. The density of the student population in this part of Beijing is one reason why the student-led Tiananmen protests in 1989 were so large; there are so many universities within the same district that students can collect en masse quite rapidly. As one might imagine, this is a major concern of the national and municipal governments, hence the frequent appearance of Chinese police and military personnel at the gates of the campuses during periods of heightened sensitivity, such as when governmental officials host a major political or economic meeting. Indeed, Renmin's weekly English corner—generally recognized as the largest English corner in Beijing, if not all of China—takes place just inside the university's East Gate and attracts such large crowds of students that government officials regularly attend just to keep an eye on things. They are known to interact with and actively engage students and visitors, perhaps improving their English skills at the same time.

Renmin was founded in 1937 during the war against Japan, and then in 1950 it acquired its official name under the newly established, Mao-led communist state. As the People's University of China, as it was named by the Chinese Communist Party (CCP), the university's primary purpose was to train communist cadre for service to the society. Today, Renmin is a comprehensive research university, as the term is typically used in China, meaning that it offers a comprehensive array of majors and disciplines and emphasizes high-level research. It is considered one of China's top research universities and is generally ranked in the top ten, depending on the criteria used in developing the ranking. Renmin is strongest in the social sciences and humanities, with its degree programs in economics, finance, law, management, Marxism, and sociology among the very best in the nation. Renmin's physical and natural sciences are not nearly as strong, with few actual departments in these areas.

Renmin serves over 22,000 regular students, including nearly 11,000 undergraduates, close to 10,000 graduate students (often described as postgraduate students in China), and some 1,500 international students. Of the graduate students, over 3,000 are at the doctoral level. The university also lists roughly 43,000 online student learners and another 13,000 adult learners, with both groups predominantly studying part-time. The university faculty is close to 1,800 in number, constituting a student-faculty ratio of approximately 13 to 1. Of the overall faculty, some five hundred are at the rank of full professor (*zheng jiaoshou*), and roughly six hundred are associate professors (*fu jiaoshou*). The remaining faculty are divided among the ranks of lecturer (*jiang shi*) and assistant professor (*zhu jiao*).

The university awards bachelor's degrees in over sixty subject areas, master's degrees in over 150 areas, and PhDs in some one hundred fields. Renmin's website lists twenty-six schools and faculties, including schools devoted to agricultural economics and rural development, arts, business, economics, education, finance, history, journalism, law, literary studies, sociology and population studies, and statistics, among others. The university's mission is "to educate for the People, to conduct scholarship for the country," and its motto is "to seek truth from facts." The president's welcome message, posted online, describes Renmin's mission in the following manner: "to take culture and humanity into account when giving primary consideration to the people," meaning, "we should strive to build a world-renowned university that is approved by and which satisfies the people." The statement goes on to add, "RUC has been continuously adapting itself to meeting the needs of China's modernization construction process, and has achieved new accomplishments in Party development and consolidation, in political and ideological work, in the reconstruction of its branches of learning, in syllabus remodeling, in scientific research, in academic exchanges, and in campus planning and construction."

The university's website reports that since 1996 Renmin has conducted 422 social science projects funded by the Ministry of Education and seventy-nine philosophy and social science projects funded by the Beijing municipal government. It further notes that Renmin is home to more than fifty significant research centers, including the Chinese Economic Reform and Development Institute, China's Financial Policy Research Center, the International Affairs Institute of RUC, and the Research Center of American Affairs. Between 1996 and 2009 Renmin faculty members published over 15,000 academic papers and over 4,700 research reports; of this total, 232 publications won ministry or provincial-level prizes for their contributions to a wide array of social science and humanities disciplines.

The campus as a physical space has been improved dramatically in recent years and now is marked by many modern buildings and facilities, including a large recreation building and sports stadium in the heart of campus; the track in particular draws large crowds, especially in the evenings when multigenerational walking parties go for their after-dinner workout. The large and modern main administration building marks the west entrance to the campus and houses some of the university's key schools, including business, economics, finance, and law. Small landscaped parks and lawns adorn the campus here and there, giving the grounds a peaceful ambience despite their location in a bustling area quite close to Beijing's high-tech center, Zhongguancun.

A Vision for Change: *"Da Lou, Da Shi, Da Qi"*

The contemporary rendition of Renmin University reflects the historic influences of its roots as a product of the Chinese Communist Party in combination with more recent forces acting on the university. These recent pressures include major reform initiatives to revise the undergraduate curriculum by incorporating *tongshi* education (a form of general education) (D. Zhang 2012) and, most notably for our purposes, widespread efforts to dramatically strengthen internationalization and research capacity. These more recent trends are well captured by Zhang Donghui in her analysis of curricular reform at Renmin and the challenges of such efforts in light of great pressure on faculty to increase their research productivity. In essence, Renmin has gone from what Zheng described as a "cadre cradle" to a legitimate research university (D. Zhang 2012).

To understand the changes taking place at Renmin, especially its present-day efforts to expand internationalization and strengthen research capacity, the influence of former president Ji Baocheng must be addressed. As we previously noted, President Ji introduced a vision for the university, captured by the motto: *"da lou, da shi, da qi,"* which basically stressed upgrading campus infrastructure, building a great faculty, and embracing a more international vision. President Ji's emphasis on elevating standards at Renmin went hand in hand with national efforts to raise the quality and performance of China's top universities. The importance of Ji's vision was captured in several of our interviews with Renmin professors. For example, one faculty member in history summarized the essence of President Ji's goals: "When President Ji came he had a slogan that included three parts: Big buildings, big masters, and big heart [or vision]. There was a sense that the university and its situation needed to change, that the university needed to revitalize, that it lacked a revolutionary spirit."

Big Buildings (Da Lou)

Much emphasis has been placed on upgrading Renmin's facilities, especially in light of additional funding from the central government and the push by President Ji. Several faculty members noted physical changes on campus over the past decade or so. One faculty member put it this way: "If you came here ten years ago it was quite shabby—it was like the slums in some places on campus. But now everything is getting rebuilt. Before President Ji came to power there was only one big building—now there are many. . . . The changes over the past ten years have been significant. . . . Things have been quite improved since then." A second professor reinforced such thoughts: "You can really see the improved buildings. You know, the campus has changed dramatically; it's a very big change in terms of the material aspects. . . . The physical environment is much improved. . . . Now, maybe ten, maybe just five years ago, we didn't have separate offices for professors. We didn't have them. We just moved into this building and now every professor in this school has a separate office."

But improvements go beyond simply the size and quality of the buildings. Basic equipment for teaching and research also has been upgraded. For example, faculty members noted improvements in terms of classroom support, including improved Internet access, new projectors and PowerPoint equipment, better air conditioning and heating, and so forth. Others pointed to an upgraded library with far more databases available for research and more copyrighted materials, including important foreign works across a variety of fields.

Big Masters (Da Shi)

President Ji's vision also emphasized improving the overall quality and performance of professors. A faculty member highlighted this facet of Ji's vision, noting that having famous professors is part of "the issue of globalization and becoming a world-class university. We want to have great professors and be known around the world." This has involved both developing faculty already employed at Renmin and "recruiting high quality professors" from around the world. Change also involved elevating expectations in terms of faculty productivity, particularly with regard to scholarship. A business professor summarized some of these changes:

> It's easy to talk about academic standards. I remember clearly participating in an international meeting to discuss research in China. I remember the remarks were very interesting. Someone basically said there was no real research in China—that what the Chinese scholars call research is really teaching development. I think that was an accurate statement of the status of Chinese research at that moment. That was the late 1980s. . . . In business, there was very little research in terms of the scientific definition of research, in terms of discovering knowledge. Research to lots of people in China was simply preparing or writing textbooks, translating materials from overseas.

This professor went on to note that today things are quite different in his field, with many Chinese scholars emphasizing empirical work, especially advanced quantitative research.

Whereas in the past, faculty members at Renmin and at most Chinese universities focused primarily on their teaching, now they must also develop and advance their research and scholarship. Along these lines, a history professor noted changes in expectations relative to research and teaching: "Faculty definitely spend more time on research now than they used to. It used to be just teaching. Most professors like me now have to do both teaching and research . . . we have to do extensive research and publishing. We still have to be good teachers as well." Other faculty members offered similar remarks, pointing to how difficult it is now to be promoted at Renmin and the high levels of stress that many Chinese academics face. Several pointed out that even though research and publishing expectations have increased dramatically, they have not seen much of a change in terms of the teaching load, and in fact, student enrollments have increased dramatically.

Additionally, expectations regarding new faculty hires are also changing. In the past, holding a PhD was typically not necessary to be appointed as a faculty member. But in the new, more competitive context of rising Chinese universities, a PhD often is required at universities comparable in quality to Renmin. For example, a professor in sociology and population studies noted that in the present context, hiring new faculty almost always involves looking for recent PhD graduates: "I think it's getting more similar to Western universities. Not just Renmin, but also other universities in China. The universities now expect you to have a PhD to become a faculty member, even a lecturer. And they want you to have international publications and international experience." A faculty member in history added,

> Before this president [President Ji] came, many graduates got jobs here as faculty members. But that has mostly ended. Now we look for PhDs from outside Renmin University. We no longer hire our own except in rare exceptions. So before this president came many of the teachers were relatives and their children and grandparents worked here, but that has changed. Now many of our faculty have their PhDs from abroad . . . If they don't have degrees from abroad, they may have had a postdoc or a teaching experience abroad. We have many kinds of programs that encourage this kind of experience as well. This is very much tied to globalization.

Big Environment (Da Qi)

Changes in the university's environment (sometimes best understood as vision) relate to several issues but tend to revolve around the idea of elevating Renmin to world-class standing. Many faculty members noted that Renmin was moving toward a more international model of the modern university and that such a trend was considered key to elevating the university's status. A professor of business pointed out that Renmin "is changing in terms of internationalization, in terms of the subtle ways it operates and the kinds of things it's engaged in." A professor of sociology also explained that the top Chinese universities are shifting to an international model of the research university, a model that largely is driven by what one sees in the United States. He went on to add, "I think you can see this from the structure of the students. Like ten years ago, or twenty years ago, the majority of the students were undergraduates and now about half of the students are graduate students, half undergraduates. The top universities are shifting to a research university model, and you have to have so many graduate students for your research projects. That's a big change."

The idea of globalization often was raised by Renmin faculty in describing various forces or pressures acting on the university. Indeed, globalization typically was described as the key factor in pushing university reform throughout China and in leading Renmin to embrace a broader vision of its place in the world. A faculty member in business and management said it this way: "The fundamental impact of globalization has been monumental. . . . I see globalization as the most important factor influencing the evolution of Chinese universities. In globalization, we have faculty exchange, student exchange. . . . If you look around this university, at the vice president level, I think pretty much most of them can conduct themselves in English, except maybe one or two . . . so most of them are able to speak English. The executive vice president has been a Fulbright Scholar. . . . The younger vice presidents, they all have experience overseas." Other faculty members offered similar comments, including the following:

> Universities are adapting to the global environment in a very strong way. Globalization is greatly influencing the research university. [professor of finance]

> The global market is operating here now and it's influencing the university. There are multinational companies operating here and more English-speaking talent is needed by the business world. We are responding. [professor of business]

> I think globalization really influences the university. First in terms of what we are teaching. We pay more attention to the whole world. At the beginning, for example, when I was teaching here the first year, second year, at that time, China was not so open to the world. It was the middle of the 1980s. We had a few books and journals that were good, but we were more focused on ourselves, on the history of China. But that has changed. Chinese professors, they see the issues more globally; and they also have a lot of very close relations with foreign professors and we get a lot of the textbooks from the West. [professor of public administration]

> We have a lot of scholars who now focus on globalization and global issues. For example, here at Renmin we have a School of Environment and Natural

Resources. The faculty mostly focus on global environmental change and also global treaties and the top consultant of the Chinese government is from our school. [professor of sociology]

The preceding comments call attention to a perspective held by most of the faculty members with whom we spoke: That Renmin was changing to meet the challenges of an increasingly global environment. In what follows we highlight some of the central changes related to internationalization and uncovered by our empirical work at Renmin.

Internationalization at Renmin: Key Findings

Internationalization is a key facet of the push to develop world-class universities in China. The importance of internationalization is evident in policy documents developed over the past decade or so by the Ministry of Education in Beijing and is part of a larger vision of Chinese educational and cultural institutions playing a bigger role on the world's stage. What we see in Chinese universities, though, is taking place in other parts of the world as well; in this regard, university transformation reflects the globalization of higher education and the growing concern by many nations to develop high-level research universities (Salmi 2009). Seen in this light, the Chinese MoE and its university leaders are simply responding to the necessities of an increasingly globalized, knowledge-based, high-tech economy and perceptions of the key role universities must play in support of such an economy (Peters and Besley 2006; Slaughter and Leslie 1997; Slaughter and Rhoades 2004).

Internationalization and globalization are not new trends, but their nature certainly has been altered in recent decades, and hence their power and force seem magnified in contemporary times. Although Philip Altbach and Ulrich Teichler (2001) argued that the first universities in Europe in the thirteenth century were by their nature international, in that they adopted a common language (Latin) to educate students from a range of countries, thus contending that internationalization is hardly a new trend, it is difficult to compare the nature of internationalization then with more modern manifestations. The point made by Altbach and Teichler is akin to arguing that transportation is hardly a new trend, given that in the thirteenth century people used horses and buggies with four wheels and today we still make use of vehicles having four wheels—such as a BYD, Ford, or Toyota. Our point is that universities are changing in dramatic ways as a consequence of globalization, and although globalization may not be a new idea, its present form and functioning certainly is. As Ka Ho Mok contended, "What is really new today is the intensity and extent of internationalization activities taking place in contemporary universities. Globalization forces have accelerated the pace of internationalization of higher education, especially when contemporary universities are influenced by diversification, expansion, privatization, marketization, and other trends" (Mok 2007, 435).

Jane Knight defined internationalization as "the process of integrating an international, intercultural, or global dimension into the purpose, functions or delivery of post-secondary education" (2004, 11). Along these lines, John Levin (1999) delineated twelve basic ways in which global processes are fundamentally altering colleges and universities around the world: internationalization of students and curricula, public sector funding constraints, private sector interaction, electronic technology and real-time communications, productivity and efficiency, external competition, restructuring, labor alterations, state intervention, partnerships, workforce training, and commodification. Several of the basic global changes highlighted in Levin's work were present in our case study of Renmin. Furthermore, we see changes related to internationalization as key to understanding the growth and development of Renmin as a comprehensive research university, including the ways in which the working lives of faculty members are evolving. Thus, in what follows we further explore key facets of the internationalization of faculty life at Renmin, revealed through the following themes: (1) impact of international standards on scholarship, (2) relevance of experiences abroad, (3) collaboration and partnerships with foreign scholars and organizations, (4) hosting foreign faculty and students, and (5) pedagogical and curriculum implications of internationalization.

Impact of International Standards on Scholarship

A consistent theme of discussions with faculty about present-day changes in faculty life focused on the growing impact of international standards on scholarship, typically expressed in terms of three major issues: closing the gap between Chinese scholarship and that of the West, the importance of publishing in international journals, and issues of academic freedom.

Faculty consistently discussed the challenge China faces in closing the "scholarly gap." For example, a professor working in the social sciences discussed his growing engagement and collaboration with foreign scholars in his field and commented on what he had learned: "I realized that there is a big gap between Western social science and Chinese social science. It is a big difference that is not easy to be resolved. I mean Western education or Western ways of thinking about social science are different." Most faculty members discussed the scholarly gap in terms of the lack of empirical or scientific focus of Chinese scholarship compared to that of Western nations such as Germany, the United Kingdom, and the United States. A professor of business explained that in the past scientific methodology was not always important to social science research in China, but this was now changing. Some faculty members noted that with increased pressure to publish internationally, Renmin professors must more thoroughly embrace Western notions of empiricism, given the expectations of many international journals and their editors. It was pointed out that international journal editors tend to want articles offering new empirical findings, not simply essays that synthesize aspects of one's field.

A few faculty members focused on what they saw as a theoretical gap between Western scholarship and that typically found in China. For example, a professor of business offered the following comments: "The main limitation at the moment is the capability to theorize. In our country theorizing is not so strong. So theorizing, or making theoretical contributions through our research, is a two-stage thing. First, we adopt the Western empirical research methodology and we apply Western theory to Chinese practice. We use Chinese data to expand and test Western theories and models but the next stage must be theory development." This professor was optimistic about the potential for Chinese scholars in the social sciences to develop their own theories: "And so we are, I think, near the threshold—we are still doubting, learning, applying, but not necessarily theorizing. . . . We're on the verge of this. I think it's going to happen maybe five years or so from now. We're still in the learning stage now." Other scholars also pointed to the tendency for Chinese scholars to draw on theories from the West, while a few argued for the need to develop theories based on the uniqueness of the Chinese context. We highlight some of these perspectives in a later section of this chapter focused on debates about internationalization and colonialism.

An additional aspect of closing the scholarly gap focused on changes in publishing expectations. For example, a professor working in history alluded to greater demands placed on Chinese scholars as the nation sought to enhance the quality of academic science. This historian pointed to great pressure on Chinese scholars not only to publish but to publish in the top journals: "I don't know, maybe six years ago we began to evaluate professors by where they publish their papers. Now it matters very much in the evaluation of the professors. That means, you know, you have to publish in the right places, based on the phase of your career." Publishing in the "right places" often is defined as publishing in international journals. One law professor alluded to various scoring systems used to evaluate faculty, noting that publishing in an international journal may lead to more points: "Such kinds of trends exist in law. So, let me say, for the university, if you publish an article in this international journal you will have, for example, ten points. And if you publish an article in another journal, maybe you only get one or two points, so there is a big difference depending on where you publish." A professor in finance reinforced this trend, noting that previously, "Research results . . . the academic papers . . . were published in domestic journals . . . and now, more and more, the research results are published in wider areas, including foreign academic journals. And professors, they are trying more and more to publish their research results in international academic journals. This is the trend to internationalize academic research in China." Institutional data collected during two consecutive four-year periods, the latter ending in 2009, revealed nearly a 500-percent increase in international publications, thus confirming what was reported to us by faculty members.[4]

An area where many faculty wanted to see greater progress concerned perceived levels of academic freedom, with most believing that great differences still exist when comparing Chinese universities with those of Western nations. One professor recalled his experiences in the United States and offered his impression that "professors abroad have more freedom." Specifically, this professor noted that U.S. professors are freer to study controversial social movements and political topics. Although several faculty raised the issue of academic freedom, relative to the scholarly gap between China and the West, for the most part they did not expand much on their point of view, preferring to move on to other topics. This is hardly surprising given the sensitivity of this issue. However, in discussions with a high-ranking Renmin official, expanding academic freedom for faculty was mentioned as one of the two or three major challenges facing the university.

Relevance of Experiences Abroad

Renmin administrative leaders place much emphasis on faculty having international experience and have in fact cosponsored many faculty abroad experiences in combination with the Beijing Ministry of Education. This push is part of President Ji's vision of developing world-class professors (as conveyed by his idea of "big masters" or "*da shi*"). A faculty member at the lecturer rank explained that developing highly successful and well-known professors was part of the central vision implemented by the president: "He started first by traveling to the U.S. and making contacts with lots of universities around the world. He then encouraged the faculty to make international contacts and go abroad. Now we have more and more international programs and are increasingly known around the world."

A professor of social science added, "I can say that it wasn't like this before, so much international emphasis. . . . You know, Renmin University could be a first-class university and so the president encouraged staff to go abroad, professors to go abroad, to study and to learn, and try to have a significant international experience." Institutional data also revealed a growing emphasis on faculty members (and students) going abroad: For example, in 2001 the university reported that 327 faculty members and students went abroad, but by 2009 that number had increased to 1,346.[5]

Several faculty members pointed to recent trends in some of the university's schools to seek new faculty who are trained abroad, particularly those who earned their PhDs in Western countries. A faculty member in public policy had this to say: "In the most recent years, in the past five years, things have changed in terms of hiring. When I came to Renmin I was the only person in my school that had a PhD from the U.S. But now we have about five in my school. In faculty hiring, in my school now, we don't hire domestic PhDs anymore." A business professor specializing in organization and human resources noted that the next step for the School of Business is "to recruit an overseas PhD as a full professor." This of course is a challenging goal given significant differences in salary structure between Chinese and Western universities, in part tied to vast differences in the value of currencies. But Chinese universities have had some success nonetheless, and they are supported through policies and funding from the MoE. In recent years, Tsinghua University, for example, recruited Princeton biologist Shi Yigong. But such practices also have come under attack from Chinese scholars, who point to inequities in terms of the salaries offered to overseas scholars by comparison to their own pay scales (Qiu 2009). Furthermore, some Chinese scientists have questioned whether Shi should be allowed to receive national research funding in China, given his status as a foreigner.

Despite potential internal problems, Renmin has been fairly successful in hiring faculty members holding foreign PhDs. Institutional data, for example, show that for the academic year 2010–2011, 205 academic employees had received their PhD at overseas universities, accounting for over 11 percent of the total faculty. This number had increased from 179 for the previous year.[6] A Renmin University internal report on promoting internationalization lists a target of 20 percent for the year 2020; based on the university's recent success, this target seems reasonable. Once again, institutional data tend to support comments offered by faculty members during interviews.

International experience is also an added plus when faculty members are considered for promotions, and more and more such experience is expected. In fact, numerous schools and departments have created partnerships with universities in the West so that Renmin faculty can easily travel abroad to participate in exchange opportunities. The School of Public Administration, for example, has a program in which faculty can teach at the University of Michigan for a semester and vice versa. Faculty explained that participating in such programs is looked at quite favorably during the promotion process.

Collaboration and Partnerships with Foreign Scholars and Organizations

In terms of international collaboration and partnerships, Renmin faculty tended to focus on international conferencing, writing and research collaboration, and seeking foreign funding opportunities. A history professor offered the following: "Another way that internationalization is advanced is that we just have more international conferences and engagement with international colleagues. . . . We have more chances to communicate with scholars in other countries." Related to this point, several professors described very specific experiences at conferences abroad and the positive outcomes evolving from their participation. One described an invitation to write a chapter in an edited book. Another became a participant in a larger international research project. A third was invited to be a discussant at a future international conference. Another was included in a major U.S.-based initiative to improve foreign language teaching involving fifteen countries. These are the sort of benefits most Chinese professors hope to attain through their expanding participation in the international conferencing stage.

Writing and research collaboration with foreign scholars and organizations was also stressed as an aspect of international collaboration. In fact, faculty members at Renmin often are expected to report on such activities as part of their department promotion meetings. As one faculty member explained, "Every year we have a meeting where we present what we are doing—it's like a small seminar where the junior professors present their work and what they are working on, what they've published, if they have any grants or not. They talk about whether they are collaborating with other international colleagues or working on stuff internationally." Faculty spoke of their international collaborations as adding a great deal to their overall academic experiences and as enhancing the quality and impact of their research. Many also noted the important friendships that evolved from such contacts.

A handful of faculty discussed opportunities to tap into foreign sources of research funds. A professor in public policy explained, "One thing I should mention is also that Chinese professors use international funding to do research. . . . They actually are able to get funds from sources outside of China. This is definitely a new development. . . . For example, we have some who participate in the Fulbright program. We get some funding from the World Bank, and international labor organizations and foundations. That's never happened before. . . . That's new. . . . For the last ten years, we've been getting funding from abroad." This professor was particularly enthusiastic about his university's participation in the Fulbright program, noting that his school had "hosted three Fulbright Scholars over the past eight years" and had sent two to the United States. Institutional data shared with us revealed that foreign-based grants had increased significantly in recent years, reaching 5.72 million *yuan* in 2010. This represented nearly a tenfold increase from 2008 funding levels.[7]

Hosting Foreign Faculty and Students

Faculty at Renmin also talked about the importance of hosting foreign faculty and students, raising two primary points: the benefits and opportunities of hosting and the role English proliferation has played in making it easier to receive students and faculty. A faculty member in education stressed the enhanced learning opportunities associated with bringing foreign scholars to Renmin to give talks: "International scholars and visiting professors do have some influence here. . . . The visiting professors, no matter how long they are here, maybe one week, maybe one semester, most of them are from good universities around the world. . . . And almost every time, from the lectures, we learn much from them. It's what we really want to continue, such a system, to invite more visiting professors to come here. It's our goal to have more and more come."

A second professor spoke of Renmin's collaboration with MIT to host a conference in Beijing and the benefits of numerous foreign scholars coming to campus. A third noted the frequency of foreign visitors giving talks on campus and reinforced the benefits of such exchanges: "Almost every week professors from abroad visit us, and every month there is a lecture from foreign professors given to our students. . . . There are lots of big changes related to foreign faculty coming here and ours going abroad. That's part of globalization, of internationalization."

Still other professors spoke of the influence of international students and the benefits such diversity brings to the classroom. As one professor of business explained, "The classroom composition in my school is quite diverse, internationally speaking. . . . The student composition, we think, is important because the mixed student composition gives our students the opportunity to experience many cultures and international experiences . . . and dispels many myths about foreigners, foreign cultures, and gives the students confidence in speaking English. It's really important."

The Renmin Higher Education Studies Office provided institutional data revealing that the number of enrolled international students increased from 768 in 2002 to 1640 in 2010. Foreign experts teaching at the university went from twelve in 2001 to forty-five in 2009, but these figures do not include short-term visits, which occur quite frequently at different schools throughout the campus. Additionally, with the addition of an international summer term, more than fifty courses were taught by foreign professors during the most recent summer, and it was anticipated that more than seventy would be offered by foreign professors in the coming summer term.[8]

Another point raised with regard to hosting foreign scholars and students is that the proliferation of English throughout the university has made it much easier to be a host. A professor of sociology and population studies elaborated, "Also, one phenomenon you may notice is that twenty years ago or fifteen years ago, no maybe ten years ago, if we had lecturers or foreign scholars come to lecture here, we had to translate for them. Now you don't need to; they can go ahead and speak English and the faculty members and the students can easily understand. Maybe not fully understand, but at least we don't need a translator now." A faculty member in public policy reinforced such comments: "Foreign scholars who cannot speak Chinese don't have to worry. English is so widespread here, at many universities throughout China. . . . A lot of professors know English quite well so it's okay. We can talk about anything and communicate fairly well."

Pedagogical and Curriculum Implications of Internationalization

Several faculty spoke of how teaching and the nature of classrooms at Renmin had changed as a consequence of international influences. One faculty member discussed how her experiences as a postdoctoral scholar in the United Kingdom helped her to better understand Western styles of education and how useful that was for her own teaching: "For me, that was very new, very interesting. For example, they rarely just gave lectures, from the beginning of class to the end. They allow students to speak more in class. They just asked them questions and the students answered. The relations were more equal. But in China the relations between professors and students are not so equal."

This faculty member went on to note that when she asks her students questions in class they do not always answer her, mainly because they are afraid to be wrong. As she explained, "They will be afraid to get a lower grade or something like that. So, how do you get real equal interaction? How do you build that kind of atmosphere in the classroom? I just did not know how to do that, but the experience helped to teach me how to get there, how to develop that kind of atmosphere in the classroom." A history professor added similar remarks: "We learned from Western teachers. . . . I think many Western educators like to ask whether the students have questions during their teaching. The traditional Chinese method did not realize the importance of encouraging students to ask questions in class. The students are less creative under the traditional Chinese method. Many Chinese educators now are talking about the different ways of approaching teaching. Western teachers have showed us some good experiences." Additionally, several faculty members discussed the formalized course evaluation processes used in the West, pointing out that such processes were being adopted in China and that overall they seemed beneficial to improving teaching and classroom management. And a handful noted how technological influences were leading to different teaching tools, such as the use of laptops and PowerPoint in Renmin's classrooms.

Although several Renmin professors saw advantages to what they perceived to be Western styles of teaching, at least one faculty member noted some value in preserving certain aspects of traditional Chinese educational practice, as described by this professor of law: "Traditional factors exist also and have much strength. For example, for students, when they talk with the professors, I think they really respect the professors. Yeah, and they are naturally inclined to be more obedient to the professors. So, in the matter of asking professors this or that question, their manner, their demeanor shows that it is a very Chinese style, not a European or American style." Generally speaking, many Renmin professors hoped that the respect that Chinese students typically show for faculty members would be retained, despite the sizeable changes taking place.

In addition to teaching and classroom management, Renmin faculty also discussed programmatic and curriculum changes reflective of increased international influence. A change in teaching materials was commonly identified as a major outcome of internationalization. One professor noted that in economics many of the textbooks now used are the same as those used in Western countries. Others echoed this point, noting that things started changing in the mid-1980s as Chinese universities became more open to the West. Some faculty described programmatic changes, such as the development of an English-based international MBA program and the adoption of a summer term offering numerous revenue-generating international programs. The latter example calls attention to the increasing importance marketization plays in Chinese higher education, as universities face greater and greater pressure to generate their own sources of revenue (Mok 1997c, 2000).

The findings from this section support the central thesis of this chapter—that vast changes are taking place at Renmin and that many of these changes are linked to internationalization. The shift toward greater internationalization tended to be discussed in terms of two broad forces: (1) national pressure from the Ministry of Education to elevate top Chinese universities to world-class standing, evidenced both by institutional decision making and increased funding; and (2) forces linked to the globalization of higher education and a general recognition of the important role research universities must play in a more knowledge-based, high-tech economy.

Broader Internationalization Findings

Several themes more tangentially connected to internationalization also emerged from our case study of Renmin. Hence, in this section we briefly discuss these secondary themes: recognition of gender differences, elevation of scholarly productivity, and increased competition and stress. These additional themes also raise a variety of internationalization issues and are important to consider as part of Renmin's quest to achieve world-class status.

Recognition of Gender Differences

Our study revealed differences in terms of how female and male professors defined the general challenges confronting academics, especially with regard to their pursuit of faculty promotions. Male professors generally did not see any difference between the academic lives of men and women, but women often pointed to additional obstacles that they believed limited their scholarly achievement and promotion opportunities. The biggest challenge the women noted was their additional family responsibilities, most specifically, having and raising a child. For instance, one female faculty member discussed the challenges she faced in trying to balance work and family life: "I have no time. I have to find time for work. Especially for the past year I felt very tired because I needed to take care of my child and I had to finish my work. I also needed to write many articles and books for my research." A second female faculty member echoed this point of view: "My son is three years old now. I think I had a difficult time in my first two or three years, after I started at the university. I was a new faculty member then . . . and then I had a baby. So it was very difficult. I was a new mom and a new faculty member. So it was a big challenge." A third stated, "As a woman professor, sometimes we can face more problems than male professors. . . . We have to balance family and work. . . . It's been very hard. That means I have to do more work without complaints. . . . My son is about ten years old now. In China, our child's education is very hard. So I have to spend more time helping him."

Of course, the idea that women faculty members at Renmin might face additional barriers in their career pursuits should not come as a major surprise, given that women academics around the world have been described as dealing with a variety of challenges different from their male counterparts (Bagilhole 2002, 2007; DesRoches et al. 2010; Gregory 2006; Ismail and Rasdi 2006; Jones and Lovejoy 1980; Normile 2001a, 2001b; Ozkanli and White 2008; Probert 2005; Skachkova 2007). This is clearly a global phenomenon requiring an international discourse. Study after study, from developed and developing nations and from women across a range of disciplines, reveals extra challenges assumed by female faculty members. The struggle to find balance between family responsibilities and faculty work seems most troublesome for women at research universities, where developing and maintaining a research agenda while also having and raising a child is overwhelming at times. One woman specifically spoke to research pressures: "Maybe some of the male professors' wives are not faculty members and so they don't have to work in the evening. So the research work for the male professors has no time limit. Maybe the wife is a housewife so the husband can focus on his work. But I can't! My husband is not a househusband. So I have to do research work and have some family responsibilities at the same time."

The issues raised here are not necessarily unique to women working at universities. One female faculty member noted as much, explaining, "I just think the tension between family and work is common to any woman with a career. I had a baby three years ago and when my child was born I had to spend more time with him and take care of him. I didn't want to lose my job just because

I had a baby and so I tried to maintain a balance between family and work. But sometimes I felt exhausted. Before I had a child, I didn't feel any tension between family and work." Clearly, the nature of society and the structure of male-female relations play a major role in shaping the working lives of women academics. And, in general, universities such as Renmin pride themselves on being fair and equitable; after all, Renmin was founded on the basis of the communist ideal of equality among women and men, an idea consistent with Mao's notion that "women hold up half the sky." Most women with whom we spoke saw the issues as being deeply rooted in cultural norms, even biology, and were not necessarily blaming the university. As one woman maintained, "The university treats us all the same, but at home we're not the same . . . and so the women have more work to do at home." But even though universities such as Renmin may not be the primary source of gender-related inequities, taking proactive steps to develop support structures for women and their academic pursuits seems a reasonable strategy. Also, universities can assume vital leadership roles in advancing global dialogues concerned with the ongoing challenges of women in the world of work.

Elevation of Scholarly Productivity

In part, our discussion in this subsection is tied to previous points related to closing the scholarly gap between China and other nations, mostly those in the Western world. But here we focus more on scholarly *productivity* and less on the *nature* of the scholarly work. We also look at these issues from the perspective of individual faculty members and the challenges posed by such changes, which leads into the next subsection focusing on increased competition and stress.

MoE officials and university leaders recognize that for Chinese universities such as Beijing, Tsinghua, and Renmin to someday join the ranks of Harvard, Oxford, and Stanford, faculty productivity must be elevated to higher and higher standards. These rising expectations are evident in commentary from numerous Renmin faculty members. The following are just a sample:

> Let me say that we attach much more importance here to research than before. For example, for me, each year, I am expected to publish three or four articles in the most prestigious journals in my field. [professor of law]

> The higher expectations are mainly linked with the promotion process. If you want to be promoted to associate professor, for example, you need to have vertically sponsored funds, such as from the National Science Foundation, National Social Science Foundation, National Graduate Education Foundation, or the Ministry of Education; funding from these types of foundations or government agencies is critical. Then you must successfully carry out the research, and then you can get credit for it toward promotion. And then if the papers you publish

are in the top journals in your specialization, in your field, then you can get more credit. If there are not enough accomplishments, then it is hard to pass the evaluation for promotion. [professor of agricultural economics and rural development]

One change is that the pressure has become greater and the professors must survive by publishing more papers, because the number of papers is a key indicator to measure the performance of the professors. [professor of sociology]

You should publish at least one book. For example, if you want to be promoted to professor, then you should publish one book. That's the minimum to be eligible, but in actuality two is probably not enough. . . . Because it's very competitive. You know, other professors may publish more than the two and if you only publish two you may not be competitive. If you can publish three or four then maybe you have a better chance of getting promoted to professor. [professor of history]

Comments like the preceding were widely expressed by interview subjects and revealed a consistent and powerful trend at Renmin—the push toward higher institutional attainment. This trend was seen to be reflective of broader changes taking place at China's top universities. Although many faculty members described this trend with a touch of trepidation, given the added workload they faced, at the same time they welcomed the push toward world-class recognition and tended to relish being part of the Chinese academy at such a historic moment in its development.

But problems are associated with the great pressure placed on faculty to publish more and more, and several faculty members alluded to various concerns. Some noted that professors, not just at Renmin but throughout China, may write too many essay-type publications just to meet expectations; they maintained that such forms of scholarship are likely to "come up short" in terms of meeting the empirical standards of international scholarly communities. A professor of education commented on some of these concerns: "Nowadays, we just see emphasis on the numbers and do not pay enough attention to the quality of the research of publications. . . . Consequently, China, as a whole, may have huge numbers of publications, but that does not mean there is a major impact. So publications of low quality should not be counted the same as high quality ones. . . . In my view, the most important thing is not to emphasize the number of publications in the promotion process." This professor argued that "low-level essays" lacking "deep content" are not likely to improve Chinese educational reform. She went on to suggest that perhaps the government could take the lead by placing less emphasis on quantity and giving more consideration to quality.

In terms of a potential shift toward focusing on publication quality, several faculty members noted that evaluations must involve more than simply gauging the impact of the journal through citation index measures. They preferred some type of rigorous peer review when assessing the quality of publications. One faculty member pointed out that it is difficult for administrators or government officials to make judgments of scholarly quality, particularly in fairly specialized fields of study. Forms of peer review are in fact built into most Chinese university systems for evaluating faculty members, but the role of peer review needs to be strengthened, especially in terms of evaluating the quality of scholarly work.

Increased Competition and Stress

The tremendous pressure placed on faculty members to increase their scholarly productivity has served to increase internal competition within departments and added stress to the professors' working lives. In some ways, stress is built into the structure of faculty life in China: many departments and schools are limited in terms of the number of promotions they get each year, thus requiring faculty to compete for them (we discuss this structural facet of academic units in terms of a "quota system" for faculty positions in chapter 4). For example, a department or academic unit may have a regular allocation of eight full professor positions, and so if an opening occurs for a full professor, such as when one retires, there may be five, six, seven, or more associate professors waiting to apply for such an opening. They all may meet the minimum requirements, so the ultimate decision will be based on overall achievement as well as other considerations such as politics or personal connections and relationships (sometimes described as *guanxi* in China). Of course, the latter considerations—politics or connections —are not unique to Renmin, or to China for that matter, but are found at just about any university around the world.

The fact that faculty members face great competition and stress was a consistent point expressed by many interview participants, especially those at the rank of lecturer and associate professor. A professor of history addressed these matters: "For example, if a lecturer wants to become an associate professor, a department may only have one opening each year. But there may be many lecturers who want to move up, to get promoted. But the positions for associate professor are limited. . . . It's the same situation in other departments, not just history." And a professor of sociology offered similar comments: "One thing is that the pressure has become greater and the professors must survive by publishing more papers, because the number of papers is the indicator in checking the performance of the professors. So this is one form of pressure. . . . Another thing is that the competition between the professors has become more intense, more serious."

Faculty members also talked about the growth of Renmin and Chinese universities in general and how the number of students on campus also adds to their workload. A professor of history talked about how the size of the student population had "exploded over the years" and described how much time must go into working with master's and doctoral students in terms of thesis and dissertation work. As he stated, "Suddenly, China has many graduate students and many people getting their PhD. But if we spend too much time on teaching, or working with students, then we do not have enough time to do research. . . . So, the pressure on the young teachers is increasing. It's getting harder." Add the growing research expectations to these additional forms of teaching and it is fairly easy to understand the sense among Renmin faculty members, particularly the more junior ones, that the challenges and related stress have increased substantially.

The issues discussed in this section relating to recognition of gender differences, elevated scholarly expectations, and increased competition and stress are reflective of broader trends at top Chinese research universities. For example, recognition of the issues women faculty face in China is increasingly tied to global movements to enhance women's rights and opportunities. China, as a global economic leader, is not immune to the pressures brought about by international forces and movements concerned with gender equity and working to redefine the place of women and men in societies. Similarly, China's changing scholarly expectations are partially tied to what it means to be a world-class university, and such notions are not entirely under the control of China's economic, political, and cultural leaders. Likewise, as faculty around the world come under higher levels of competition, especially in light of the increasing flow of scholars transnationally and the internationalization of scholarship, it is not surprising that stress levels would be rising. In this regard, Renmin faculty members are reflective of faculty members at top universities around the world. These indirect changes linked to internationalization, combined with those more direct internationalization findings discussed earlier in this chapter, all call into question the degree to which Chinese universities are shaping their own destiny or being shaped by forces beyond their control. Here, there is meaningful debate concerning the transformation of Chinese universities and whether or not university leaders and faculty members ought to take a more reflective, perhaps more cautious, approach. In what follows, we highlight aspects of this debate.

Internationalization or New Forms of Colonialism?

Despite the many positive results of internationalization professors identified, some skeptics questioned the degree to which China and Chinese universities are fully in control of the nature of higher education reform. These more critical voices tend to believe that China may be following international higher education leaders such as the United States without complete awareness. For example, several critics raised concerns about changes in publishing expectations and over-reliance on Western ways. Along these lines, a professor in finance pointed out that international pressures are likely to alter the fundamental direction of scholarly work in China: "The foreign readers, foreign professors, their interests may be different from those of Chinese scholars. So, the Chinese scholars, the professors, when they want to publish their articles, they have to adapt to the interests of those foreign scholars. Otherwise, they lose their opportunity to publish their articles or papers in those international journals." A specific example was noted with regard to rural studies and the need for Chinese scholars to direct their attention inward, in light of national concerns about significant urban-rural economic inequalities. A professor working in this area explained, "International experience is important and publishing internationally is good for some scholars. But it's not good for others, especially for the rural studies field. Do you really need a foreign editor, a foreign journal, to understand what you are doing in terms of local issues in China?" The two preceding professors focused their concern on the possibility that pressure to publish internationally may redirect Chinese scholars toward lines of study that are less beneficial to national interests; essentially, they argued that pressures to elevate scholarly productivity and world ranking may at times work in opposition to other important national interests.

One senior faculty member linked the quest to follow Western models of scholarship with the immense pressure on Chinese scholars to publish in journals listed in the Social Sciences Citation Index (SSCI) and Chinese Social Sciences Citation Index (CSSCI), noting some of the problems this raises: "I think the pursuit to follow the Western model creates some problems. That means the universities must encourage people to publish in SSCI journals. . . . But for many Chinese scholars they may not want to publish in those journals, to be limited in that way. So it's more influential if you publish in some SSCI journal, but now many scholars they say, 'Why should I do that? I'm not American.' So for some faculty, they would rather publish in more local journals. They may want to research Chinese philosophy or maybe Chinese economic reforms and these may not be key topics for some international journals. So that's maybe another kind of problem—internationalization may negatively impact the topics and issues studied by Chinese scholars."

Another faculty member likened the pressure to publish internationally to a "serious competition . . . a kind of business competition," replete with behaviors not necessarily indicative of serious scholarship: "Even if you are not capable of publishing an English paper in an American or British journal, you can possibly have some kind of joint project . . . and then ask a foreign colleague or assistant to help you to publish. And then if you publish in English, you have a better chance for promotion. But how does this help to advance knowledge in China?"

A few faculty members focused not so much on the publication process as on how Western norms might limit Chinese scholars in terms of theory and methodology. As one skeptical professor opined, "Social science is mostly created based on the experiences of Western economic development processes. I mean, that is the historical reality. Based on that, you create knowledge of social science but it is rooted in Western economic assumptions. Do you really believe this is universal knowledge? And that it should be universally applied to any country?" This professor went on to describe the internationalization of social science as a form of "soft power"—part of the propaganda and ideological system of the West. "It's a kind of strategy."

Critical professors argued that the more China borrows social science knowledge, theories, and textbooks from Western powers, "then the more cultural colonization . . . can take place at the university." The preceding professor elaborated on this point: "And then it's worse. Originally, the Chinese university was colonized by Russian culture and the Russian social sciences in the 1950s and 1960s. Now it changes to the United States. It's not progressive. It's backward." The view expressed here is that as Chinese scholars employ more theories and frameworks from the West, as part of gaining acceptance at an international level and credibility with Western organizations, including funding agencies, Chinese research and scholarship becomes increasingly colonized.

Some professors talked about shifts in scholarly practice in China as a form of business strategy. As one senior professor explained: "Research has become a business. . . . Yes, it's a business now. . . . Everybody may have similar ideas, but it's become part of the business—because that is the way to have more Western foundations sponsor you—by using Western theories and ideas. Yes? The IMF, World Bank, UN, Ford Foundation, Rockefeller Foundation. So, many foundations they sponsor what? They sponsor colonized culture." This professor tended to embrace a "very critical attitude" when it comes to what he described as "the Western centralist knowledge system," arguing that "the Chinese university needs to build up a new knowledge system," one more capable of understanding and explaining the unique aspects of contemporary China, given its unique history, size, and rapid growth.

The ideas expressed in this section tend to see China's university reform as more or less an adjustment to the dictates of a global knowledge system dominated by Western universities and Western ways of thinking. Although most Renmin faculty members with whom we spoke saw internationalization generally in positive terms, the faculty voices highlighted in this section had serious reservations about the future of China's top universities and the nation's system of knowledge production.

The criticism of a minority of Renmin faculty resonates with some of the work deriving from postcolonial studies, as reflected in the writing of the likes of Edward Said (1993) and David Harvey (2003). From Said's perspective, the colonialism of earlier periods of human history has passed to a new stage. No longer do countries build and extend their empires primarily through military force and violent occupation; it's not that such methodologies are entirely of the past, a point highlighted by Robert Rhoads and Katalin Szelényi (2011), but that such methods are now surpassed by new forms of imperialism operating in more subtle and ubiquitous global forms. As Said argued, modern forms of empire building largely depend on ideological penetrations: "For reasons that are partly embedded in the imperial experience, the old divisions between the colonizer and colonized have reemerged in . . . various kinds of rhetorical and ideological combat" (1993, 17).

Ideology is advanced in complex ways; as the world economy becomes more fully integrated across nations, Western powers such as the United States and the United Kingdom have the potential to shape the operations of key nongovernmental and intergovernmental organizations, including the World Trade Organization (WTO), the International Monetary Fund (IMF), the World Bank, the Organisation for Economic Co-Operation and Development (OECD), and the United States Agency for International Development (USAID) (Calderone and Rhoads 2005; Collins and Rhoads 2010). These organizations shape global economic and cultural arenas, including educational policy, and they often act in terms of the interests of the most powerful global players—the wealthiest nations. David Harvey is insightful here: "If, for example, the US forces open capital markets around the world through operations of the IMF (International Monetary Fund) and the WTO (World Trade Organization), it is because specific advantages are thought to accrue to US financial institutions" (2003, 32). In terms of shaping the policy directives of NGOs and IGOs, Christopher Collins and Rhoads noted, "Decision making at the World Bank, for example, is tied to the financial contributions of donor countries, with the nations that give the most thus gaining greater control over loan programs and their conditions" (2010, 184). Many NGOs and IGOs are of course actively involved in shaping the nature and content of national higher education policies, as the research of Collins and Rhoads (2010), as well as Boaventura de Sousa Santos (2006), highlighted in the case of the IMF and World Bank.

In terms of higher education policy and particularly university reform, as China increasingly moves toward an internationalized notion of the research university, one can legitimately ask: To what degree is China simply following the U.S. model of the university, and is it certain that adopting such a model will fully benefit national interests? Certainly, the quest for world-class ranking seems to be driven to a great extent by the U.S. version of the research university, a point supported by Kathryn Mohrman, Wanhua Ma, and David Baker in their elaboration of the Emerging Global Model (EGM); they delineated eight fundamental features, which, not coincidentally, look quite similar to characteristics of top U.S. research universities: "global mission, research intensity, new roles for professors, diversified funding, worldwide recruitment, increasing complexity, new relations with government and industry, and global collaboration with similar institutions" (Mohrman, Ma, and Baker 2008, 5). They acknowledged the influence of the U.S. university model: "At this particular stage in the development of the university, many of these features of the EGM are rooted in the American experience of the past four decades" (6). Additionally, the U.S. research university tends to dominate the global university rankings, further supporting its worldwide influence and potential hegemony (Rhoads 2011).

Although one might easily argue that university rankings have reached an absurd level of influence on higher education policy, resisting their impact is easier said than done. Furthermore, policy makers and educational leaders are under great pressure to promote stronger ties between higher education and economic development. In today's world, developing research universities capable of playing a vital role in the knowledge economy is seen as crucial. The world rankings of universities simply reflect quick and easy score cards by which to gauge national and institutional success (or failure), even though the calibration of such score cards is lacking in serious ways; for example, most if not all global ranking schemes lack good measures indicative of a university's commitment to social justice or service to low-income and working-class students.

A major facet to various university ranking schemes is the importance placed on research expenditures—in essence, the generation of capital for the research enterprise. The central role that capital plays at U.S. research universities is readily apparent and highlighted in the work of Sheila Slaughter, Larry Leslie, and Gary Rhoades and captured nicely by their concept of academic capitalism (Slaughter and Leslie 1997; Slaughter and Rhoades 2004). The capitalization of universities is most evident by the commodification of university outputs (e.g., research findings, inventions, and patents) and their eventual marketization. The heavy focus on marketization is in part a response to the reality that public funds cannot adequately support the size and scope of the modern academic enterprise, especially the research enterprise. This is true not only in the United States but in China as well, where, as Ka Ho Mok and Yat Wai Lo highlighted, we have witnessed a shift from state reliance for higher education funding to "diversification of education finance," necessitated to a large degree by the need to "meet the challenges of the rapidly changing socio-economic environments wrought by the rise of the knowledge-based economy" (Mok and Lo 2007).

In today's global higher education context, it is hard to imagine a major nation adopting a university development strategy that rejects marketization, given the importance of generating research revenue and the fact that governments likely cannot fund research alone. And if global university rankings matter, then marketization and capitalization are that much more important, given that research revenue is such a large factor in the ranking schemes. There is some circularity at work here: the wealthier the university, the greater its status and rank; the greater the status and rank of the university, the greater its likelihood of generating more revenue (and wealth). Thus in the global ranking schemes, having one Fields Medal winner may be far more significant than having five hundred superb teachers.

The preceding discussion of the research literature raises some important questions relative to Renmin University and the broader Chinese higher education context. Is the internationalization of the Chinese university, such as Renmin, simply a pathway to restructuring top Chinese universities along the lines of an emerging global model reflective of the U.S. research university? Does a highly commercialized and marketized model of the university best fit the needs of Chinese society? Does China's quest to establish world-class universities necessarily require that it follow the existing schemas rewarded in the worldwide university ranking systems? Finally, are there alternative choices and pathways to success that Chinese policy makers and institutional leaders might follow in their quest to build world-class universities? These may be interesting questions to ponder, but the bigger issue is this: Just how much resistance can a nation offer to a host of powerful global forces operating in today's world, including the expanding role of the new-knowledge, high-tech economy and the role universities play as producers of knowledge? The questions presented here, and highlighted in this section both explicitly and implicitly by several Renmin professors, point to the challenges of internationalization and the difficulties nations face in charting their own course. They also call to mind the degree to which globalization—including the globalization of the research university—may at times further forms of domination.

Internationalization: Ready or Not!

The findings presented in this chapter, and especially in the preceding section, offer a great deal to consider as we ponder the changes taking place at Chinese universities. Faculty life and the norms of scholarly work are undergoing a significant restructuring at Renmin. In considering this basic point, one must keep in mind that Renmin is not just any Chinese university; it was founded by the CCP and holds a special place in Chinese society as the People's University. Given this reality, combined with the fact that the CCP fills a key administrative role as part of the dual authority structure of the Chinese university, it is hard to imagine change at Renmin as an isolated case. Instead, the internationalization of Renmin indicates patterns at other Project 985 universities, as our case study research at Beijing, Tsinghua, and Minzu confirms; the widespread nature of this phenomenon also was emphasized in our interviews with Renmin faculty members, who often spoke of internationalization as systemic, not as a unique feature of Renmin. Clearly, China's top universities are internationalizing at a rapid pace and on a grand scale. Furthermore, policy makers and institutional leaders, including key faculty members, cannot fully control the re-norming of scholarly practices.

Renmin faces major challenges in building a more internationally oriented faculty. Scholarly expectations at Renmin today differ significantly from those of a decade or so ago. A question that arises is whether or not the university is fully committed to and prepared to accept the far-reaching implications of building a world-class faculty. For example, although the university places great pressure on faculty members' international engagement and increased research productivity, the teaching load has not been dramatically altered as a consequence of increased scholarly expectations. Lecturers and associate professors at Renmin tend to advise high numbers of master's students in their thesis work and also teach a rather hefty course load, by comparison to faculty of similar rank at many Western research universities. The workload of Renmin's full professors (*zheng jiaoshou*) is more likely to resemble that of research professors (of all ranks) at leading Western universities, both in terms of heavy doctoral student advising and smaller teaching loads. Expectations and pressures for lecturers and associate professors may be quite high, given their combined teaching, advising, and research responsibilities. This point was reinforced in our interviews, with high levels of stress often noted by faculty members in the lower and middle ranks.

Furthermore, the internationalization of faculty life is likely to lead to greater numbers of Renmin professors embracing more cosmopolitan forms of academic citizenship. Burton Clark (1987a, 1987b), building on the work of Alvin Gouldner (1957, 1958), pointed out that cosmopolitan professors are more likely to be tied to their disciplines and professional associations and less likely to engage in localized institutional concerns. This raises the question: Is Renmin prepared for a campus of cosmopolitan jet setters? And, will the broader system of Chinese higher education be able to accommodate shifting priorities among its faculty? Given the traditional conception of the Chinese faculty member as highly committed to and engaged in the education of the next generation, how will cosmopolitanism be accommodated through institutional policies and practices? Certainly, there is evidence that Renmin's policies support travel to international conferences as well as lengthy foreign visits focused on faculty development in either teaching or research, but cosmopolitanism suggests a fundamental shift in professional identity that may have deleterious effects for faculty engagement in more localized concerns. As Rhoads and Szelényi (2009, 2011) highlighted in their work on global citizenship and university life, there are serious implications for faculty becoming increasingly engaged at an international level.

Related to the potential shift toward cosmopolitanism are some concerns raised by several Renmin faculty about what is actually in the best interest of Chinese society when it comes to the forms of knowledge production to be advanced by China's top universities and professors. Are there social, cultural, and economic issues important to China and its scholars that may not appeal to international scholarly venues—venues in which Chinese faculty are under great pressure to join and perhaps lead? Put another way, do the norms and practices associated with international scholarly practices operate in a manner beneficial to China's national interests? Do, for example, the heavy reliance on English as the language of international scholarship and the dominance of Western theories and ideas limit the potential of Chinese scholars to address the nation's internal needs? Some faculty members at Renmin believe the answer to this question is yes. Although the latter group of faculty members is a minority, their concerns nonetheless are important.

A few skeptical Renmin professors recalled that not so long ago Chinese authorities and university officials spent valuable resources reforming their system of higher education, as the nation turned away from the highly specialized university model previously adopted under Soviet influence. For example, many highly specialized campuses were merged in order to build more comprehensive universities (Mok 2005a). Presently, China once again looks beyond its own borders, to foreign models of research and scholarly activity oriented toward internationalization, and yet pitfalls once again are likely. Implementing the positive facets of internationalization, while limiting the negative, may prove quite difficult. Indeed, cosmopolitanism as a form of academic citizenship in many ways contradicts the idea of a university managed and controlled through strong administrative and governmental policies. Indeed, the idea of cosmopolitanism, as advanced by Gouldner and then later taken up by Clark, suggests a type of faculty identity characterized by high levels of autonomy and relatively resistant to administrative control.

Changing Times, Changing Expectations

Certainly, the working lives of faculty members at Renmin University are rapidly changing under the influence of internationalization. In this regard, Renmin is simply a reflection of the broader Chinese landscape; globalization increasingly influences the overall society, including its economy, politics, and culture. Beyond our empirical analysis, evidence of social change is widespread and touches life at Renmin in many ways. For example, when a nineteen-year-old female student exhibited her nude photos on campus as a part of a "body art" exhibition in order, by her account, to pay school fees, the university was relatively powerless to stop her (Dasgupta 2011). Increased freedom of expression obviously poses new challenges in a society where traditionalism still holds much sway. But freedom of expression also becomes highly contentious, politically speaking, in these changing times, as the son of the famous Renmin-affiliated poet Ai Qing, the activist and avant-garde artist Ai Weiwei, found out in 2011 when he was detained and charged with economic crimes. Isabel Hilton, writing for the *Guardian* (2011), speculated that Ai Weiwei may have been held because of his activism and the fact that "he was treading on sensitive toes." The boundaries of acceptable and unacceptable forms of civic and social engagement obviously are being defined and redefined every day in China. What is increasingly clear, though, is that the norms of Chinese life, including daily life at its top universities, are being refashioned under the weight of global pressures.

The global pulse increasingly shaping Chinese society is readily apparent at Renmin, most notably through the ways in which Renmin scholars offer critical analysis of sensitive social and political matters. For example, Renmin professor and dean Wen Tiejun, who specializes in agriculture and rural development, reported in 2005 that about "90 percent of CCP officials' spending exceeded their income. The more power the officials hold, the more serious the problem is, and this includes officials from the regime's own discipline department" (Zitan 2011). Such critical comments have been publicly offered even by China's political leaders, including former premier Wen Jiaboa, who was quoted by the BBC in 2011: "Without political restructuring, economic restructuring will not succeed and the achievements we have made in economic restructuring may be lost" (Bristow 2011). The former premier went on to add, "If we are to address the people's grievances we must allow the people to supervise and criticise the government." Along these lines, Renmin professor Kang Xiaoguang, who specializes in regional economics and politics, criticized the CCP for mostly serving China's urban elite: "It is an alliance whereby the elites collude to pillage the masses" with the result being "political corruption, social inequality, financial risks, rampant evil forces, and moral degeneration." Commenting in the *Economist* in May 2007, Kang argued for a wedding of sorts between Confucianism and communism. His proposed solution at the time was to "Confucianise the Chinese Communist Party at the top and society at the lower level" ("Confucius Makes a Comeback" 2007).

Although critical voices are encouraged to some extent, there are still lines that Chinese professors must negotiate carefully. For example, in the spring of 2007, Renmin political scientist Zhang Ming was removed from his post as department chair in part because of his biting criticism of university bureaucracy ("Three Outspoken Academics" 2011). The reality of professors needing to tread softly in their criticism of university administrations, or public officials for that matter, is of course not unique to China. However, our empirical findings revealed serious concerns that Renmin faculty members have about the need for expanding academic freedom, not only at Renmin but throughout Chinese higher education.

Expanding academic freedom for its professors is not the only challenge for Renmin as it seeks to join the elite research universities of the world. A major barrier to Renmin's ranking is the fact that it is primarily oriented to the social sciences and humanities, while the largest sources of research revenue typically flow to the natural and applied sciences (e.g., engineering, medical research, and applied physics). Consequently, in any global ranking model stressing research expenditures Renmin faces serious limitations. Even in the United States—home to the world's biggest university spenders in terms of research—universities that lack medical centers rarely appear among the very top universities in terms of research spending. Renmin, having only a few natural and hard science departments, has little chance of capitalizing on research growth linked to the advance of "big science" and its growing importance to new knowledge, high-tech economic activity. Nonetheless, Renmin still has the opportunity to be a leading voice in advancing the importance and prominence of the social sciences and humanities in a world where, arguably, the lack of such critical voices has contributed to significant global problems (Rhoads 2011).

But there are dangers in applying Western notions of internationalization and norms associated with Western models of the research university. Most prominently, the cultural and historical development of universities in the West, and particularly in the United States, follows a rather unique trajectory. For example, the U.S. research university was targeted by political leaders in Washington, DC, around the time of World Wars I and II for the specific purpose of connecting academic science to war initiatives, such as the Manhattan Project. Massive support for university research tied U.S. professors to the nation's expansive military-industrial complex, resulting in major fields focusing almost entirely on military application and hence neglecting many important areas of knowledge production and application (Rhoads 2011). Adopting such a strategy may not be best for China's needs or match its cultural orientation and values. Along these lines, Mok warned of Asian nations uncritically following Western university norms, especially with regard to internationalization:

> We should not simply understand internationalization merely as following the American or Anglo-Saxon standards and practices. Although the academic communities in Europe and the United States have been regarded as more advanced than their Asian counterparts, higher education institutions in general and academics in particular must critically reflect to what extent and in what way good practices identified from the West could really integrate well with their education systems (2007, 438).

Mok's cautionary remarks must be taken seriously, as cultural differences may limit the adoption of various facets of Western universities in nations such as China and, worse yet, could potentially produce negative or even devastating outcomes. Surely there are dangers in uncritically adopting Western scholarly norms, as several faculty members at Renmin noted in their critique of internationalization. Mok also reinforced such criticism: "The introduction of English as the medium of instruction . . . and the quest for world-class universities as predominantly defined by the Anglo-Saxon world have not only created a new dependency culture but also reinforced the American-dominated hegemony" (2007, 438). Writing for *University World News*, Hans de Wit raised a similar concern, pointing out that the proliferation of English as the international language of instruction "has gone too far in some respects. For instance, it can encourage those who have English as their mother tongue to further abandon the idea of learning foreign languages and lead to preferred treatment for native speakers" (2011).

Cautionary points offered as part of our concluding remarks are presented only as additional fodder for the many exciting international advances evident at Renmin, as reported by faculty members during our case study inquiry. The overall findings presented in this chapter offer evidence of important changes in faculty life at Renmin and are suggestive of a broad transformation of higher education at China's top universities. As the nation moves to strengthen the quality and capacity if its top universities, particularly in terms of internationalization and research productivity, faculty members are positioned as central players in the shifting academic landscape. Because their working lives and daily activities reportedly are changing, initiatives such as Projects 211 and 985 appear to be having a significant impact in modifying the very nature of the Chinese university. Many challenges and obstacles to achieving world-class university status remain, but the path to internationalization appears to be well established.

China's Ethnic Diversity and the Critical Role of Minzu University

A striking feature of campus life at Minzu University of China (MUC), also known as Central University for Nationalities (*Zhongyang Minzu Daxue* in Chinese), is the obvious commitment of the university to ethnic affairs. In addition to the vast diversity of the student body, where roughly 60 percent of the students come from ethnic minority backgrounds (approximately 70 percent of the undergraduates are ethnic minorities), cultural signposts around the campus point to the university's commitment. For example, MUC is host to one of the nation's largest ethnic minority museums. Also, the main entrance to the university is marked by one of its most treasured buildings—a concert hall known for high-quality musical productions reflecting the cultural diversity of the nation's many ethnic groups. The university also offers separate dining facilities to accommodate the culinary needs and preferences of both Muslim and non-Muslim students, staff, and faculty. At MUC's Chinese Corner, foreigners can mingle with native speakers and practice their Mandarin Chinese (*Hanyu Putonghua*), and some may be surprised to meet MUC students also working to improve their Mandarin. Such students may come from the autonomous regions of Tibet or Xinjiang, where their schooling quite likely was conducted in the dominant language of the region—such as Tibetan or Uyghur.

The university's embracing of ethnic diversity is also evident in its academic programs and curricular offerings. For example, the following academic programs at MUC are all highly regarded, with some being classified as "national level," meaning they are considered to be among the very best in the nation (a few are also well known within certain international circles): the School of Ethnology and Sociology, the Kazakh Language and Literature Department, the Korean Language and Literature Department, the Mongolian Language and Literature Department, the Tibetology Research College, and the Uyghur Language and Literature Department. Additionally, MUC's programs in the performing arts, in the areas of ethnic minority music and dance, are renowned for their expert faculty and high-quality student productions. Although it is difficult to compare the overall academic quality and research capacity of MUC to that of nearby top research universities such as Beijing, Beijing Normal, Renmin, and Tsinghua, when it comes to ethnic affairs and related academic activities, including teaching and research, MUC is perhaps the most advanced and comprehensive university in China.

Minzu University, along with fourteen other minority-serving universities (six at the national level and nine at the provincial or municipal level) scattered throughout China and known as *minzu* universities (the term *minzu* typically is translated as *national ethnic group*), plays a key role in Chinese society. Indeed, one of the most pressing challenges confronting the present-day Chinese nation-state is that of advancing a common sense of national identity in the face of widespread ethnic and linguistic differences (Clothey 2005; Gladney 2004; Hansen 1999; He 2008; Ma 2004, 2007a, 2007b, 2010; Mackerras 1994, 2004; Oakes 2000; Postiglione 2009). Given that the breakup of the Soviet Union was in large part attributed to its inability to reconcile ethnic tension (Rupesinghe, King, and Vorkunova 1992), the Chinese Communist Party (CCP) is ever mindful of the potential calamity of unresolved ethnic problems. And although China's fifty-five ethnic minority groups, known as *shaoshu minzu* (national minority ethnic groups), officially account for only about 8.5 percent of the overall population, in a nation of close to 1.3 billion people this amounts to over 110 million.

Differences between the Han majority and the nation's ethnic minority populations contribute to regional tensions, most notably in the autonomous regions of Inner Mongolia, Tibet, and Xinjiang, where ethnic-based protests are not uncommon (Mackerras 2004). Much of the tension is tied to economic inequalities, but irredentist movements in some of the borderlands also contribute to regional instability (Zhu and Blachford 2006). Consequently, national policies have sought to address the social, economic and demographic issues of ethnic minorities, with a primary goal "to maintain unity and internal cohesion" (Zhu and Blachford 2006, 330). A particular area of policy development has been to look to higher education as a source of economic opportunity and social mobility for economically disenfranchised minorities (Clothey 2005). In this regard, a vital component of the nation's higher education system has been the development of the *minzu* college and university system.

Although their original mission was to train administrators and cadre for minority regions (Tang 1996), today the *minzu* colleges and universities, often termed "Universities for Nationalities" or "Institutes for Nationalities," have the primary function of serving the diverse needs of the nation's ethnic minority population; this includes providing higher education access for ethnic minority students and serving as centers for research and training in the areas of minority culture, language, and history. The *minzu* system forms a critical component of the nation's preferential policies (*youhui zhengce*) to address economic inequalities among ethnic minorities.[1] Arguably the most important university in the *minzu* system is Minzu University of China in Beijing.

The vast majority of MUC faculty and staff recognize the importance of the university's longstanding mission to serve the nation's ethnic affairs, but pressures arising over the past decade or so pose new challenges to the university's mission. These pressures relate primarily to national initiatives to build stronger, more comprehensive universities but also connect to broader changes taking place in Chinese society, including transformation of the nation's economic structure. In using the term *comprehensive university*, we draw from the term commonly used in China, *zonghexing daxue*, conveying that a university has a relatively broad array of academic programs but also implying a degree of importance placed on research and scholarly inquiry. This differs from the usage of the term *comprehensive university* in the United States, for example, where it often delineates a type of university limited to offering baccalaureate and master's degrees (and having limited research capacity). Accordingly, we focus on the ways in which key organizational actors—namely, MUC faculty members—make sense of the contemporary challenges faced by their university in light of its historic mission to serve the nation's ethnic affairs. More specifically, we analyze various interpretations—what we call "narratives of change"—employed by faculty members as part of their effort to make sense of the present-day organizational context.[2] We delineate three such narratives: internationalization, marketization, and ethnocultural development. We go on to discuss how changes at the university are impacting the working lives of MUC faculty members, especially in terms of the promotion process and relative to rising expectations for faculty research productivity. But first, we explore ethnic diversity in China.

An Overview of Ethnic Diversity in China

There are fifty-six officially recognized *minzu* (national ethnic groups) in China, with the largest group—the Han people—accounting for roughly 90.5 percent of the total population. The ten largest *minzu* are the Zhuang, Manchu, Hui,

Miao, Uyghur, Tujia, Yi, Mongol, Tibetan, and Buyei peoples. China's ethnic minorities account for over 110 million people, roughly the size of one-third the U.S. total population, about the same size of the population of Japan, and larger than the national populations of France, Germany, and the United Kingdom.

Although ethnic minorities constitute roughly 8.5 percent of the overall national population, in higher education they only account for about 6 percent of the enrollment, and since both 1990 and 1997 (two years for which data are available) ethnic minorities have actually declined in their representation at the nation's colleges and universities (Zhu 2010). Furthermore, given their low enrollment at the most prestigious universities, ethnic minorities have less access to the many advantages and opportunity structures associated with elite higher education.

Although there are fifty-six officially recognized ethnic groups delineated by the Chinese government, the very concept of ethnicity and ethnic group is rather contentious, and not everyone agrees that the official list is inclusive of all groups. The great Chinese ethnologist Fei Xiaotong noted, for example, that "when Sun Yat-sen founded the Republic of China in 1912, he defined it as a 'Republic of Five Nationalities,' meaning the Hans, the Manchus, the Mongolians, the Huis [Chinese Muslims], and the Tibetans," and yet some four hundred groups registered with the government in the early post-liberation years as part of the nation's massive effort to accurately classify ethnic groups as *minzu* (again, this term refers to officially recognized national ethnic groups) (Fei 1980, 94). Along these lines, Zhenzhou Zhao and Gerard Postiglione noted, "Although around 400 groups applied for registration as a nationality in the ethnic identification program initiated in the early 1950s, only 55 minority groups (Han as a majority is excluded) are recognized based on the criteria formed by Stalin in 1913" (Zhao and Postiglione 2010, 2). The reference here to Stalin relates to a "four-part definition of nationality—common language, common territory, common economic life and common culture" (Leibold 2010). Classification as a *minzu* involves a range of complex decisions requiring extensive data collection and analysis. Problems and disagreements are likely.

An MUC faculty member specializing in ethnology and sociology elaborated: "The complexity of the matter is that *minzu* is a special kind of ethnic group. They are confirmed by the central government. We just have fifty-six *minzu*, not more, not less. But if we use the term 'ethnic group,' we can see, for example, that in Xinjiang Province, there is another ethnic group called Tuwa. You can't say it's a *minzu*, but you can say it's an ethnic group. Because they have their own names, their own language, especially their own culture." This faculty member also offered a second example, noting the Guang Fu Ren people near Guangzhou. "They have their own culture. And they also have a unique identity. They call themselves Guang Fu Ren. They think that they are Guangzhou ancestors." He went on to add that even in Beijing there are areas in which a particular group of people may constitute a unique ethnic group.

Another MUC ethnologist pointed to the problems of actually quantifying the number of ethnic groups. He maintained that the category of the Yi people may in fact represent many different ethnic groups: "I think the government put nearly 70 different titles of people together to make the Yi category. But among them, the Liangshan Yi—or Cold Mountain Yi—is the biggest group." Whether a group is or is not recognized as an official nationality is not a minor point, given that the central government uses such classifications to grant privileges and extend opportunities as part of the national effort to address ethnic inequality. Additionally, Lin Yi made the point that simply being recognized as a unique cultural group by the broader society influences the group's social mobility and standing (Yi 2008).

There are other complexities to China's ethnic context. As Fei Xiaotong stresses, China's ethnic minorities, many of whom represent indigenous populations, are characterized by extensive contact with the Han majority and thus share significant cultural forms (Fei 1989, 1992). Additionally, not all of the nation's minority groups are likely to be classified as "marginalized" minorities. A case in point is the ethnic group known as the Manzu (commonly known as Manchu or Manchurians in the Western world), mostly of northeast China, who actually ruled the country during the Qing Dynasty, China's final imperial period. Furthermore, there is much debate in China about the best policy approach toward the nation's ethnic affairs, with some scholars, such as Ma Rong, arguing for a policy of "de-politicization" in combination with "culturalization"—essentially rejecting the idea of *minzu* as political groups and instead emphasizing them as cultural or ethnic groups—*zuqun* (Ma 2007a, 2007b, 2010). Related to this point, some of China's leading ethnic scholars have advocated a policy of "pluralist unity" or *duoyuan yiti*, arguing that the nation should seek unity by recognizing and accommodating its diversity (Fei 1989; Ma 2007a). In some sense, the *duoyuan yiti* policy is similar to the notion of "unity in diversity" commonly associated with multicultural perspectives in the United States (Bloemraad 2007).

Another important facet to ethnic diversity in China is its regional quality, a fact that exacerbates the challenges facing the central government and efforts to strengthen national unity. The regionalization of China's ethnic minority populations, of course, has been well established by scholars working across a variety of fields, including anthropology, ethnology, sociology, and genetics.[3] And although recent decades have seen greater and greater numbers of ethnic minorities migrating from the more rural border regions to urban centers such as Beijing, Guangzhou, and Shanghai, coastal China continues to be dominated by the Han majority, while the western, southwestern, and northern borderlands are more likely to be home to the nation's sizeable ethnic minority population.[4]

Among the professorate of MUC are some of China's leading scholars of ethnic affairs. They are to be taken seriously both in terms of their knowledge of the nation's ethnic populations and with regard to their understanding of historical trends in policy development for ethnic minorities. A leading MUC ethnologist noted that he points to three phases in the development of the nation's more recent ethnic minority policies:

> The first phase is from the beginning of 1950 to 1957. At that time a formal system of ethnic minority recognition was established by Mao. . . . But after 1957 there was a shift, a change—Mao no longer talked about ethnicity; before this second phase he had talked about ethnicity a lot, but then he stopped. And we can examine why he stopped talking about ethnic diversity and so it seems that his mind had been changed. Something likely changed in the way he thought about ethnicity. And so from the end of the 1950s to Mao's death, this constituted the second phrase. During this phrase ethnic minority policies were mostly suspended; it was a revolutionary period and included of course the Cultural Revolution. . . . After Deng Xiaoping assumed power, there was a restoration—a restoration of the 1950's policies and their application to the Deng regime and the formal system. For example, our law of ethnic regional autonomy was issued by the state in 1984.

Not everyone believes that ethnic classification schemes benefit ethnic minority populations. Indeed, scholars have argued that ethnic classification may push toward modernization and the integration of ethnic minorities into mainstream society while relegating their unique cultural forms to marginal status. For example, the classification of Chinese nationalities, as Stevan Harrell argued, was a primary product of the communist movement and part of the civilizing project of the dominant group. As he opined,

> The communist project has been the most explicit and systematic in its process of definition. It has classified the population within China's political borders into fifty-six *minzu*, or 'nationalities,' so that every citizen of the People's Republic is defined as belonging to a group that is more civilized or less so. This scaling of groups, in turn, is based on an avowedly scientific scale of material stages of social process (derived from Morgan and Engels, refined by Lenin and Stalin), that tells each group exactly how far it needs to go to catch up with the civilizers (1995b, 9).

Although we can debate the basic thesis of Harrell—that the objectification and classification of ethnic groups has served a form of cultural and political hegemony—it is much more difficult to debate the overall importance ethnic minority groups have come to play in shaping Chinese social and cultural policies, including those policies giving form and function to the nation's higher education system. And, of course, MUC is a key component of the national educational approach to better serving ethnic minority populations.

MUC in Historical Perspective

MUC was officially established in Beijing in 1951 and opened for students in 1952. The early mission of MUC was primarily to train administrators and cadre for the nation's minority regions, given that such areas historically lacked the capacity and wherewithal to provide advanced education and training suitable for governmental service. Of course, MUC is not the only minority-serving university in China, but is part of a national endeavor involving a group of fifteen colleges and universities all geared toward serving ethnic minority affairs. Thus, in addition to their original mission of training administrators and cadre, all *minzu* colleges and universities play a critical role in providing college access to ethnic minority students as part of China's national policy to address social and economic inequality. In this regard, *minzu* colleges and universities are a critical link in the nation's affirmative action strategies for ethnic minorities.

Minzu colleges and universities are regionally dispersed but tend to be located in the western and northern provinces where minority populations are the largest. Six of the *minzu* universities (including MUC in Beijing) are coordinated at the national level by the State Ethnic Affairs Commission, although the national Ministry of Education (MoE) also provides special funding, especially to MUC. These six national *minzu* universities are in Beijing, Chengdu, Dalian, Lanzhou, Wuhan, and Yingchuan. Another nine *minzu* universities are associated with provincial governments and are located in the following provinces: Guangxi, Guizhou, Hubei, Inner Mongolia (2), Qinghai, Shanxi, Sichuan, and Yunnan.

In addition to its basic funding from the State Ethnic Affairs Commission, MUC also receives funds from two national initiatives run by the MoE, Projects 211 and 985 (discussed in the introduction). In essence, then, MUC has two supervising national agencies to which it is accountable, adding a layer of complexity and at times confusion to its operations.

For the purposes of this chapter, we pay much greater attention to Project 985 than to Project 211, given that a large portion of this funding is to be used to strengthen research capacity and further develop MUC as a more comprehensive university. As a so-called Project 985 University, MUC received extensive funding, approximately 230 million RMB (roughly 38 million U.S. dollars), over the last funding cycle, from 2010 to 2013. MUC, of course, also receives Project 211 funds, mainly to support the development of key disciplines such as anthropology, ethnology, sociology, and minority language and culture. But Project 211 funds cover a range of activities, including teaching and classroom support, and are not as focused on research development as Project 985 funding.

As a university founded during the era of Soviet influence, MUC's particular focus on ethnic minority populations reflects the specialized nature of Chinese universities in a manner consistent with the Russian model. And just as other universities were mostly closed during the Cultural Revolution, MUC also had limited activity during this period. Many of the campuses were not entirely closed but were used to train peasant workers and cadre as part of the educational programs of the Cultural Revolution. This was true of MUC as well. Interestingly, a senior faculty member recalled his time as a "peasant student" beginning in 1972: "At that time the curriculum was very simple; it mainly involved reciting Mao Zedong's works—his four volumes of textbooks. It was helpful for us to study Chinese too. We studied Chinese versions of those works. Our main purpose as minority students was to study Chinese. . . . We just recited Mao's works and slogans every day for three years." This faculty member pointed out that the university was only open for "workers, peasants, and soldiers." It was not until 1977 that MUC, along with other colleges and universities around the country, opened their doors for regular student enrollment, with the national college entrance exams being reinstituted in 1977.

The late 1970s through the mid-1990s marked a new chapter in Chinese higher education and in the experiences of faculty and students at MUC. The nation's Open Door policies, under the leadership of Deng Xiaoping, resulted in vast changes in academic life. This era marked the beginning of the internationalization of university life and a growing openness to Western notions of science (Hayhoe 1989). Many MUC faculty worked or studied abroad during this period, increasingly drawing from their experiences in countries such as Japan, the United Kingdom, and the United States. Some were deeply influenced by what they saw of the working lives of Western professors and returned to MUC with new notions about teaching and conducting research. Such ideas contributed to modifications of more traditional Chinese views of knowledge, grounded primarily in Confucianism; today Chinese higher education practices may be best characterized as a fusion of East and West, incorporating diverse philosophical traditions and influences.

The later 1990s and early years of the twenty-first century saw MUC's inclusion in key national higher education initiatives—namely, Projects 211 and 985—launching a new era for the university as part of the national quest to expand the quality and number of comprehensive universities. Today, MUC continues to anchor its institutional identity in service to ethnic minority affairs, but the challenge of further developing as a more comprehensive university, based to a great extent on conducting high-level research, adds another layer of complexity to the university's mission. The national effort to build and strengthen universities is in part tied to erasing the highly specialized curricular focus of Chinese universities, as was stressed under the influence of the Soviet model.

For example, many Chinese universities that were once developed as highly specialized agricultural, forestry, geological, or chemical universities may still carry such descriptors in their official names, but most of these universities today are much more comprehensive in terms of their curricula. Beijing alone has many examples, including universities such as Beijing University of Chemical Technology, China University of Geosciences, China Agricultural University, and Beijing Institute of Technology. Although China's universities are mostly shrugging off their once particularized academic focus in favor of comprehensive status, MUC instead seeks to develop in more comprehensive ways while retaining its particular focus on ethnic affairs. This is not a simple task and hence forms the thrust of our concern in this chapter.

Contemporary Life at MUC

MUC is located on the west side of Beijing, in the university district known as Haidian, not far from the city's famous high-tech center Zhongguangcun. Its main entrance, the east gate (*dong men*), sits along the busy Zhongguangcun Boulevard, only a couple of blocks from the landmark National Library of China (*Guoji Tushuguan*). To the north is Beijing Institute of Technology, and to the west is Beijing University of Foreign Languages. The area surrounding the university is known for its many small ethnic restaurants and student-focused shops and food stands; for example, just a couple blocks from campus one can find restaurants specializing in Dai, Mongolian, Sichuan, and Tibetan cuisine, and adjacent to MUC's west gate there are several Uyghur restaurants specializing in Muslim cuisine and attracting many MUC students from Xinjiang Province. The dining facilities on campus also are known for their diverse ethnic selections and have been known to attract college students from other universities in Haidian District.

As a growing comprehensive university, MUC has twenty-three colleges and five departments offering fifty-five baccalaureate-level, sixty-four master's-level, and twenty-five doctoral-level degree programs. The university enrolls some 16,000 students, with approximately 60 percent coming from ethnic minority backgrounds. Of the total student population, there are roughly 11,800 undergraduate students, 3,750 graduate students, and about 450 international students. The university employs over two thousand faculty members, including just over five hundred professors and associate professors. It is estimated that more than 40 percent of the faculty and staff come from ethnic minority backgrounds.

In 2008, the university officially changed its English name from Central University for Nationalities to Minzu University of China. Part of the rationale was that the term *central* might be understood as referring to the central region of China. Today, references to the university appear in many forms, including the formal title noted above but also Minzu, Minzu University, MUC, and the colloquial MinDa (derived from *Minzu Daxue*). This of course poses potential name recognition and branding problems for the university.

In terms of campus life, MUC is one of the busiest universities one will find in China, in part because its actual campus space is quite small compared to the expansive campuses of Peking and Tsinghua universities. For example, it is quite commonplace for the campus to be packed on Saturday and Sunday evenings not only with students, faculty, and staff but additionally with outside visitors flocking to the university's musical and dance performances. Given the high-level student talent and the well-regarded advanced training offered by its faculty members, tickets for performances at MUC are hot commodities.

Recreational facilities are rather limited at MUC, but students tend to take advantage of the outdoor stadium facilities, including a track, multiple soccer fields, and volleyball and basketball courts. The basketball courts are particularly popular with the male students, and on any given evening one can easily count close to two hundred students playing or waiting to play (as is commonly the case in China, given the popularity of basketball and the size of the population); even in the winter, on subzero, snowy days, one will find students playing basketball on the outdoor courts. Sports Day draws student excitement at MUC as cohorts of student classes (first-year, second-year, etc.) in various majors hold a friendly competition, including such events as the 400-meter run, long jump, and shot put. The day is marked less by competiveness than by camaraderie, evidenced by the smiles and laughter among the student participants and their class leaders. Sports Day is one example of organized student life at MUC, but for the most part, MUC students, and students generally throughout China, organize much of their own out-of-class life by socializing with friends and roommates. This is quite a contrast to the highly organized extracurricular activities that students at universities in the United States, for example, often experience.

Of course, what MUC is best known for is its service to ethnic minority populations. A senior MUC faculty member spoke to this basic facet of the university's identity and culture: "Minzu is a special higher education institution in China. It's special for minorities. Minzu University includes the students from different minority ethnic groups and also the majority people. It reflects the diversity of China, which is the special point of Minzu. Diversity is colorful! It can add to the peace, creativity, and harmony of the culture and of the university. The fact that our teachers and students come from diverse ethnic groups is a very special point for us." The ethnic and cultural diversity at MUC is certainly a highlight of campus life. On any given day, in the late afternoon or evening, one can walk around the campus and possibly observe fifty or sixty college students practicing a traditional Xinjiang dance, or another smaller group dressed in traditional clothing practicing a special Mongolian dance, or perhaps meet several Bai[5] women visiting the campus in their bright and colorful traditional garb and selling skillfully crafted folk art.

Although for the most part, MUC may be accurately portrayed as an environment of peace and harmony among all of China's ethnic populations, there nonetheless are times when tensions among ethnically diverse students arise. Faculty discussed student problems they had heard about in terms of the dormitories but for the most part felt that students generally learned to get along with one another at MUC. As one faculty member in education explained, "I think there are cultural differences here. For example, several years ago in one of my classes, some minority students from Xinjiang and some Han students quarreled over the smell of the food in the dormitories." However, this same faculty member went on to add, "There are different cultural conflicts that happen from time to time at Minzu because of the great cultural diversity, but I think it's fewer and fewer. We understand each other more and more." A second faculty member specializing in minority language and literature reinforced this more positive interpretation of the benefits of campus life at MUC: "The university is really good at witnessing the harmonious society and the advantages of cultural diversity. . . . Learning from the books is just one thing. Living together for four to five years is another thing. The university is the very place to train students in integrity and respect for their nation and for one another."

As a center of ethnic diversity in Beijing, the campus is at times a flashpoint for ethnic tensions arising in other parts of the country. For example, it is not uncommon for Tibetan and Xinjiang supporters to gather for protests at the MUC campus when problems arise in those regions. During these periods of high tension and during other politically sensitive times, such as June 4,[6] there often are additional guards at the campus gates in what is termed a "lockdown." During such periods, one must show a MUC identification card to gain access to the campus.

Finally, of central importance to this chapter is the fact that MUC is included among China's top universities as a participant in both Projects 211 and 985. In this sense, MUC is part of the national push to build world-class universities, with *world-class* being a rather nebulous term but generally meant to convey that a university is academically comprehensive and has high-level research capacity (Salmi 2009). Such an investment by the national government has altered life at the university, as was noted by every faculty member with whom we spoke. Accordingly, a senior professor said, "We can feel those changes. For example, the investment that the government gave to this university increased our research work in several major fields, including minority language and literature, anthropology, ethnology and traditional minority medicine. These are special fields at Minzu—they receive the most funding." Furthermore, faculty interpretations of the present-day challenges facing the university revealed both points of convergence and divergence, although most seemed to agree that the university's mission was becoming broader or "more obscure," in the words of one senior professor. Changes confronting MUC faculty members, tied to contemporary challenges faced by the university, form the thrust of the remainder of this chapter. We begin with our discussion of the three narratives of change: internationalization, marketization, and ethnocultural development.

Internationalization as a Narrative of Change

A key narrative of change at MUC focused on efforts to expand the university's engagement internationally. Aspects of this narrative were voiced by every faculty member with whom we spoke, and in general, efforts to internationalize the university were not seen to be in conflict with the other two narratives of change: marketization and ethnocultural development. A faculty member in education captured aspects of internationalization at MUC:

> We want the university to be known internationally, to have international prestige; we want to be the top *minzu* university in the world. We want to move into the top 50 university rankings [in China]. People think of the development of our university from a global perspective. And you see we are trying to get more international students, and we also have started to send more students, even undergraduate students, to foreign universities. And more and more journal papers in English are required to be read by our students. And faculty members are encouraged to publish or work in foreign countries.

The preceding comments also speak to some of the pressures on MUC to advance as a comprehensive university, in line with the goals of Project 985. In this regard, international strategies were seen as central to the overall strategic vision to elevate the university's standing, both in terms of national and international recognition.

Faculty spoke of a multitude of international partnerships and initiatives relating both to the educational and research missions of the university. One frequently highlighted aspect of internationalization was the dramatic expansion of English usage on campus over the past decade or so. Several noted that faculty members can receive extra rewards for teaching in English and that MUC has adopted a program to specially prepare faculty for teaching in English. As one faculty member explained, "We have such a program and some of our young teachers are selected to be trained abroad for one year as a bilingual teacher. And bilingual teachers are supposed to teach their classroom lessons in English." This faculty member went on to add, "Faculty members are also encouraged to use original edition textbooks in English from abroad." In part, the increasing adoption of English was aimed at strengthening the university's appeal to foreign students who might otherwise shy away from courses taught in Chinese or in one of the minority languages.

Faculty at MUC commonly go abroad for scholarly work. Indeed, nearly every faculty member who participated in the semistructured interviews described the importance of their experiences at a foreign university, often as part of multiple and extended visits. Several formed close relationships with colleagues during their time abroad and continued to stay in touch with and sometimes collaborate with them. For example, a faculty member specializing in minority anthropology described how his experiences in Canada, studying indigenous populations and Canadian bilingual policy, helped him to develop a more comparative analytical framework for thinking about ethnic affairs and bilingualism in China. This faculty member went on to note: "We have much more communications with professors from abroad. . . . And we have many projects that involve collaboration between Western scholars and our university." A professor specializing in English language and literature added, "Our faculty are more and more aware of the issue of internationalization and globalization. We think that if you are not involved with the international scholarly community, it is difficult for you to advance academically. Not only in terms of promotion, but I mean to advance in your knowledge and understanding."

Faculty tended to see the push to internationalize as being strongly aligned with MUC's commitment to ethnic affairs. Three reasons generally were offered. First, MUC students need experience with cross-cultural interaction to work in an increasingly global environment. This was true whether students planned to remain in China or work abroad. Although certainly the national cultural differences that are so much a part of campus life at MUC support forms of cross-cultural learning and exchange, having students engaged with students and scholars from abroad also was seen as critical.

Second, although many faculty members believed that governmental funds were important to building research capacity at MUC, they also increasingly turned to international organizations as sources for research funding. International funding was seen as significant to strengthening both applied and theoretical research in ethnic minority regions. Relatedly, a faculty member specializing in minority education spoke of the importance of expanding research opportunities by tapping into international funding sources, "like UNESCO, Ford, some NGOs from Hong Kong, many NGOs, and from the World Bank and the Asian Development Bank."

Third, faculty believed that their own experiences in the international realm, including collaboration with foreign scholars, only served to strengthen their understanding of minority affairs and public policies. For example, several faculty members talked about their extended visits to Canadian, U.K., and U.S.

universities to interact and collaborate with scholars working in the areas of ethnic and racial diversity, bilingualism, and multiculturalism. They discussed how such experiences helped to inform their thinking about possible policy solutions to China's many ethnic challenges, including issues relating to urban migration and bilingual education.

Marketization as a Narrative of Change

A second narrative of change tended to focus on the need to marketize the university. For a group of faculty members, definitely in the minority, the national push to expand research—roughly beginning in the mid-1990s with the adoption of Project 211 but then accelerating with the launch of Project 985 in the late 1990s (MUC did not actually participate until a few years later)—suggested a rationale for broadening the university's focus, both in terms of academic programs and its research orientation. These faculty linked programs such as 211 and 985 to the broader national push, coming from the very top of the Chinese government, to build world-class universities. This effort to strengthen the nation's top universities included transforming MUC into a more comprehensive university as well as elevating certain departments and programs to world-class status. Along these lines, a faculty member in education related efforts to improve the university to the national goal of competing in the global higher education market: "The whole higher education system is trying to improve education quality now. Because the government wants to improve the level of Chinese higher education, they want to improve higher education quality, its competitiveness, to help Chinese universities to better compete in the global arena." And a professor in history noted efforts to improve the university's academic programs "and learn from world-class universities. . . . We can't just rely on the money [Projects 211 and 985], but the real key for us is to study the structures, policies, and systems of the world-class universities. We need to study what it is they do to compete at a global level."

Most faculty members agreed that a certain level of marketization already was well underway, and in fact, the majority pointed to the late 1990s as the key period during which it began to take firmer root at MUC. A faculty member in minority language and literature explained it this way: "Since the end of last century, I think the mission of MUC has changed . . . [the university] started to engage more in the market economy. So we have to meet the needs of society, to match the economy, to match the society. So we have many new schools, such as the School of Management, School of Education, School of Law, and the School of Computer Science."

MUC faculty members who supported greater emphasis on marketization tended to be just as concerned as other faculty with further developing the university as a comprehensive university, and they cared deeply about serving minority ethnic groups, but they viewed the market as the ultimate source for shaping and directing the university's activities, including its research priorities. They questioned the value of supporting minority research programs and curricula that were not connected to the market and the broader economic needs of Chinese society. A faculty member in history displayed these sentiments: "Minzu University should do something for national development. Especially I think the university itself and the scholars should do some research to support the constitution, the basic law, to help develop the ethnic minority groups and to help them succeed in the market economy."

Faculty members who believed the university should stress marketization to a greater extent, including in terms of MUC's research focus, generally were less satisfied with how Project 985 monies were disbursed. This group of faculty tended to work in fields somewhat removed from ethnic minority affairs, such as biology, computer science, mathematics, or foreign languages. From the time of Minzu's initial involvement in Project 985, the funds had been used to support the university's historic mission of serving ethnic affairs; hence, for faculty working in such areas as computer science and engineering, obtaining research funds was not a simple endeavor. A professor of ethnology and sociology supported this assertion, noting that in the past research proposals had to be connected to ethnic affairs, "Otherwise it would be difficult to get 985 or 211 funding."

Those faculty in support of increased marketization saw Project 985 funding as critical to advancing the university as a comprehensive university, yet they argued that by focusing a good deal of such funds on ethnic affairs, the university was limiting its research scope and hence undermining the goal to become more comprehensive. Accordingly, these faculty members felt the university should place less emphasis on ethnic affairs and related academic disciplines and pay greater attention to connecting the university's research mission to a variety of revenue streams, including the possibility of MUC building stronger ties with business and industry. This group of professors tended to favor what one described as "more marketable research," meaning research that might appeal to China's growing private sector as well as diverse funding agencies. We interpret these points as not simply a matter of adopting a self-serving point of view, as these faculty members tended to believe that a more market-oriented research enterprise ultimately would better serve the needs of ethnic minority students. An economics professor offered support for such a view: "Research ought to connect to the market, to the needs of business and industry, to the companies that are likely to hire our students. We should take that obligation more seriously." Similarly, a faculty member in ethnology and sociology stressed the value of connecting students to the labor market: "Students from minority backgrounds need to be integrated and have opportunities in the society, and to be integrated into the national market and to higher education. So you need to take some special measures to help them to benefit from the opportunities and integrate into the economy." Additionally, several faculty members noted, for example, that many build personal relationships with various companies as a way to add to their annual income while also potentially furthering employment options for their students. Many such arrangements are private in nature and not shared with university administrative personnel.

Although several faculty members voiced support for the marketization narrative, others who were opposed to such a perspective nonetheless acknowledged its growing influence. For example, a senior faculty member specializing in minority language and literature described the marketization position of his colleagues: "Some people say that as a modern university Minzu should meet society's needs by connecting more to the market economy. We should train people to work for a market society. We should have computer science, engineering, and management—those are more important than the traditional disciplines relating to [an ethnic group's] language and culture." Similarly, a professor of history added, "Some question the legitimacy of developing nationalities [ethnic groups] . . . that we should focus on marketization or better connecting students and research to more economic concerns, better encourage job opportunities for students. . . . They see the American university as more connected to the marketplace and think we should also do the same." The most recent decision regarding Project 985 funding at Minzu reflected the growing influence of the marketization position, with the greatest portion of 985 funds going to science and engineering programs. This indicated a significant shift from past emphasis on academic programs oriented toward advancing ethnic affairs.

Faculty who supported the marketization narrative were at odds to some extent with the majority of MUC faculty members, most of whom vigorously defended a mission focused on further developing ethnic minority cultures. Although the faculty group in support of ethnocultural development included many leading scholars at the university working in fields related to ethnic affairs, even they were quick to acknowledge the growing influence of marketization.

Ethnocultural Development as a Narrative of Change

A third narrative of change tended to tie the university's traditional mission of service to ethnic affairs with more recent efforts to expand research capacity. The alignment of the two goals was typically discussed in terms of research efforts to strengthen ethnic minority cultures. Indeed, faculty expressing such a narrative saw increased funding from Projects 211 and 985 as a vehicle for expanding their involvement with ethnic minority populations. Whereas faculty members who advocated marketization tended to define success in terms of ethnic minority graduates assuming positions within the mainstream economy, ethnocultural development advocates instead put greater stress on strengthening local ethnic cultures. A faculty member specializing in minority education argued that the university's research focus, including the use of Project 985 funds, should "apply culturally-responsive ways instead of copying the development models of Han regions." This professor went on to explain:

> We should value the interests and agency of local ethnic groups. . . . It is quite necessary to work to preserve and strengthen minority cultures. The different ethnic cultures offer indigenous knowledge and wisdom. This is a key resource of the ethnic group members and one of their primary strengths. This is the basis for their local development and innovation, instead of stressing cultural assimilation.

Similarly, a faculty member in ethnology and sociology added, "Preserving cultural diversity can keep people's dignity and promote being an active member in such a big country like China." For faculty espousing an ethnocultural development perspective, national harmony and economic integration are unlikely to be achieved if students' cultural roots are severed along the way. As a professor of minority language and literature explained, "Cultural diversity is really good for harmony. Look at the Soviet Union's model—with efforts to eliminate cultural diversity it collapsed. Respecting everyone's culture, language, and customs is the way to create a harmonious society."

Faculty subscribing to an ethnocultural development narrative rejected any idea that tension necessarily exists between expanding the university's research capacity and serving ethnic minority affairs. These faculty members acknowledged the national push to build high-ranking, global universities, with a professor of history noting, "Nowadays, the Chinese government is saying that we should develop our universities into world-class universities." But at the same time, they were quite realistic, with most pointing out that a "great distance exists between MUC and top research universities, especially Western universities." From their perspective, the real goal at MUC is to build a handful of world-class academic programs among those focused on the nation's ethnic affairs.

For faculty aligned with the ethnocultural development narrative, advancing the university's research capacity was not so much an end goal but was viewed as a means of better serving the needs of ethnic minority populations. While those subscribing to a more market-oriented narrative saw the market as a form of barometer for guiding academic and research development, faculty expressing an ethnocultural development perspective tended to see marketized forces as potentially undermining the social obligations of the university; hence, they expected the university to be supported to a great extent by governmental funding. A professor of minority language and literature captured the essence of this point of view:

> A country needs to be well enough financially to support the university and the traditional disciplines relating to ethnic minority affairs. The university can then

eliminate all the disciplines that focus on meeting the economic needs of society. Then you do not have to care about the needs of the market society—you can just train students to be specialists who work in minority regions and with ethnic minority populations, focusing on history, literature, the many unique languages.

This professor's comments are not out of line with several others who seemed most committed to ethnocultural development. For some of these faculty members, it made little sense for MUC to be overly invested in fields tied more directly to the marketplace, given that other universities are likely to address those fields better than MUC. This group of professors did not see the market as irrelevant, but they tended to define the university's ethnic affairs charge as a public good dependent to a great extent on popular support.

Faculty members who discussed the mission of the university in a manner consistent with an ethnocultrual development perspective were actively engaged in ethnic affairs research and worked in fields that easily intersected with minority issues. These faculty members had an easier time tying their scholarly interests to increased funding for research, especially in terms of university funding sources such as Project 985. For some, funded research resulted in the development of key reports designed to inform government decision makers. For example, a faculty member in education talked about how his data—"the facts uncovered and the research conclusions"—were to be used "to develop some policies for the central or local governments. . . . [Such] policies can be developed to benefit all the minority peoples and help to meet their needs." For others, research objectives were less about informing public policy and more about strengthening ethnic minority cultures. Along these lines, a faculty member in music talked about how his research was aimed at preserving aspects of folk music among certain ethnic minority groups. And an anthropologist highlighted how his research helped to preserve the teaching materials used in remote ethnic minority schools, in part, to better understand the complexities of localized knowledge as well as the views particular ethnic groups hold about schooling.

Faculty members specializing in ethnic minority history also reported ways of connecting what they do to the growing research thrust of the university. For example, a faculty member discussed his research on diverse populations of nomadic peoples and "how they lived together in the past." He explained the importance of such inquiry: "Though there are some problems among minority peoples, like the Uyghurs and Tibetans, I'm interested in how they lived together in the past. . . . I think it's very interesting . . . so I study in this field because today in China the Uyghurs and Tibetan people have their own strong identities. Today we have some conflict but in the ancient times, how did they live in one country together?" He went on to add, "For me, it is just history itself. The relations between different kinds of ethnic groups in China are important simply for understanding our history." For professors such as this one, increased research funding from the national government was key both to furthering service to ethnic affairs and to advancing MUC as a comprehensive university. This, to reiterate, contrasted with the perspective of those faculty members advocating increased marketization, who saw the university's heavy focus on ethnic affairs as limited in scope.

Reconciling Tension among Narratives of Change

This chapter centers on efforts of MUC to advance as a stronger, more research-oriented, comprehensive university. Such an initiative is rooted in the national government's desire to further develop the nation's top universities. This national objective may be understood in terms of broad forces acting on higher education at a global level, including the growth and impact of global rankings (Marginson 2010a) and potentially the influence of institutional isomorphism (DiMaggio and Powell 1983), but also in terms of a growing recognition that universities, especially research universities, are increasingly vital to a nation's economic development (Etzkowitz and Webster 1998; Peters and Besley 2006; Slaughter and Rhoades 2004).

In thinking about the contemporary challenges facing MUC, research in comparative higher education is particularly relevant. Some of the key issues at MUC are strikingly consistent with those taking place at other universities around the world. For example, Philip Altbach described the widespread push by universities to become top-tier research universities in spite of the vast resources required to attain top-tier status. As he argued, universities lacking deep financial resources will find it "virtually impossible to join the ranks of the top academic institutions" (Altbach 2004, 8). MUC certainly has benefitted from strong governmental funding, but it does not compare favorably with the wealthier research universities around the world or even those just a few miles away in the form of Beijing Normal, Peking, Renmin, and Tsinghua. Along these lines, most of the faculty interviewed for this study recognized the university's research limitations, and thus when they spoke of "world standing" or "world-class status," they typically focused on a handful of academic departments or centers focused on ethnic affairs. These academic programs are the institution's most highly regarded, with some already enjoying an international reputation.

A key aspect to the development of top-tier universities is the emphasis often placed on internationalization. Indeed, of the eight key indicators of the Emerging Global Model of the university delineated by Kathryn Mohrman, Wanhua Ma, and David Baker (2008), three relate directly to forms of internationalization: global mission, worldwide recruitment, and global collaboration with similar institutions. And a fourth, research intensity, as Altbach (2009) noted, is unlikely to be achieved without extensive international engagement. Additionally, recent studies of university transformation in China also revealed a great deal of emphasis on internationalization (Mohrman 2008; Mohrman, Geng, and Wang 2011; Mok 2007; Rhoads and Hu 2012; Rhoads and Liang 2006). In light of these global and national trends, the emergence of internationalization as a narrative of change at MUC is hardly surprising. Indeed, there was no disagreement at MUC, in any of the evidence that we uncovered, about the importance of strengthening the university's international engagement, especially for faculty. Internationalization seems deeply entrenched in the vision faculty have of their university, both in terms of what MUC is now and what it might hope to become in the future.

Where some disagreement did exist, however, was with regard to the two narratives of change described in terms of marketization and ethnocultural development. Here, it is necessary to focus mostly on the research goals of Project 985, including most importantly the block-grant funding provided to the university in four-year cycles. Faculty subscribing to the ethnocultural development narrative tended to work in MUC's more highly regarded academic programs, which benefitted greatly from the university's allocation of Project 985 research funds. This is to be expected, given that the development of ethnic minority populations is at the heart of the university's mission statement: to develop as a world-class ethnic university by serving as the cradle for high-level talent development of Chinese ethnic minorities.

MUC faculty identifying with ethnocultural development saw efforts to advance the university's comprehensiveness as strengthening their research commitment to ethnic minority populations. Accordingly, they tended to support efforts to expand the university's research capacity in conjunction with elevating the university's standing. The key from their perspective was to stay focused on ethnic minority affairs, the areas that have long defined the university's strength.

In contrast to faculty focused on ethnocultural development, professors working in fields less connected to ethnic affairs tended to argue for greater marketization of the university, especially in terms of its research mission. Also, they found university research funds less accessible. These professors, who constitute a minority of MUC's faculty, argued that the university was likely to face a difficult road furthering its status as a comprehensive university if it continued to focus too narrowly on ethnic affairs. The fact that university research funds tended to go to ethnic affairs projects left them feeling somewhat marginalized, in contrast to the typical situation in the United States and other Western nations, and at many Chinese universities as well, where professors most closely tied to the market tend to enjoy greater institutional status and influence.

Although faculty advocating either the ethnocultural development or marketization narratives may disagree to some extent about the direction the university ought to go, there is no disagreement about the reality that faculty life is changing at MUC, particularly in terms of increased pressure to engage in more serious and extensive research and to publish accordingly. Hence, in the following section we focus on various pressures faculty reportedly face as a consequence of efforts to elevate the university's standing.

The Quest for Greater Institutional Status and Concomitant Faculty Pressures

During the course of both formal and informal interviews, MUC faculty consistently spoke of having to elevate their productivity in an environment characterized by rising research expectations. A beginning point for exploring this aspect of faculty life is to examine the promotion process at MUC, as it was repeatedly referenced during our interviews.

The Faculty Promotion Process and the Role of Quotas

As at other Chinese universities, new faculty at MUC typically begin as assistant professors (*zhu jiao*) or lecturers (*jiang shi*), depending on the degree they hold and their teaching and research background. From there, they seek to progress to associate professor (*fu jiaoshou*) and then to professor (*zheng jiaoshou*). Typically, five years must be spent at each level before one is considered for the next promotion, but a faculty member can be promoted only if an opening exists, and typically there is great competition for these limited openings. Because the Chinese government sets limits on the number of faculty at the ranks of full or associate professor at most national universities, the institutions are forced to manage the allocations across various schools or departments. Given such a system, the competition among academic units as well as among individual faculty members can be quite intense. Many MUC faculty referred to this as a "quota system."

There is much complexity to the quota system and great room for political maneuvering by universities, academic units, and faculty members. High-status academic units are likely to be allocated more full and associate professor positions, and when additional openings arise at the university, such units are in better position to present faculty candidates for new openings. The decision making typically is handled by an administrative body composed of deans and party officials representing each major academic unit (this body is sometimes described as the university personnel committee). Tradeoffs are common, and no unit gets everything it wants, even the most prestigious ones. In some cases, especially if the department is highly successful in terms of research and student recruitment, the unit may be able to make the case for additional faculty positions.

For low-status academic units, such as those with limited research potential, helping their faculty to be promoted when openings arise can be quite challenging. This means that lecturers and associate professors in these units may be stuck at a particular rank for much longer than the usual five-year period. A foreign language faculty member shed some light on this aspect of university operations: "The staffing of the university is decided by the Ministry of Personnel in collaboration with some other departments such as the Ministry of Education or the State Ethnic Affairs Commission.[7] . . . The total number of faculty as well as the administrative staff are established. Sometimes the quota given to you is already equal to the current size of your faculty, so there is no room to hire someone new, or to promote someone." In cases where the quota at the full professor level, for example, is already filled, associate professors may need to wait for a colleague to retire, and lecturers may need to wait for an associate professor to be promoted, creating somewhat of a backlog. Another faculty member spoke to this reality: "In the past we could apply for a promotion and as long as our publications and our working hours, I mean our teaching hours, were enough, then we could be granted the promotion. But now even if we have enough publications and enough teaching hours, we have the quota system to face. For example, our department is full at the associate professor level and so our lecturers must wait and see. Unless some associate professors get promoted, they will have to wait to apply to be promoted."

The actual decision-making processes involved in evaluating faculty also are rather confusing. At MUC, university administrators have some authority, but decisions also are influenced by government and party officials. A faculty member in education captured some of this complexity: "First, they start at the department or school level. . . . They will examine one's achievements. Then the promotion materials go to the whole campus, where there is a comprehensive or expert committee, and where all the subjects and disciplines are examined together. There are faculty representatives, mostly deans, from each discipline who will evaluate you. Then once you pass the campus committee's evaluation you need to be evaluated by an academic committee appointed by the education authority of the Beijing municipal government in the case of Minzu since this campus is in Beijing. You see, the faculty from my campus cannot make the final decision, they just make a recommendation." This faculty member went on to explain that the top academic units, such as those specializing in ethnology and sociology or minority languages and literatures, have greater authority in determining who should be promoted, whereas younger or less reputable departments have less authority. This professor also pointed out that more prestigious universities such as Peking or Tsinghua have far greater control over the faculty promotion process. As he observed, "Obviously, Peking University is recognized around the world, and consequently, government officials grant it levels of autonomy less commonly seen or experienced at Minzu."

Although the process is rather formalized, there is still room for social networking and relationships to play a major part in the decision making, as is quite common elsewhere in the world as well. A professor specializing in ethnology and sociology spoke to both the formalized and less formalized facets of the process: "In my opinion, if we observe the academic process, we can easily divide it into two parts: One part is the formal system and the other part is the informal system. For the formal system, your academic title and reputation become less important, but your real qualifications become very important. . . . But in another regard, we can see that faculty also belong to an informal network . . . some private circles that exist in academic life. So, we have some friends and among them we have more opportunities." Along these lines, several faculty members expressed the point of view that formalizing the promotion process is best for the national development of the universities, as they depend on high-quality faculty members being rewarded for their hard work and research success. These faculty members favored limiting the role that social networking or *guanxi* (this commonly used Chinese term roughly equates to *connections* or *relationships*) plays in determining promotion outcomes. A faculty member in history favored adopting some of the promotion methods of Western universities: "We want to develop like the Western countries. So, I'd say that many Chinese scholars including me think that higher education in the West is good and we should follow it in developing our universities. For an associate professor to be promoted to full professor, we should select the best ones, the way it's done in developed countries in the Western world. This can lead our universities to a higher level of development."

Teaching remains a central consideration of the evaluation and promotion process at MUC; faculty are expected to meet certain levels of teaching productivity, typically measured in terms of weekly classroom hours. For most faculty members, the teaching load is approximately five to six classroom hours per week (roughly two to three courses). Junior faculty have slightly lower teaching requirements than their more senior counterparts, although many of the highest-ranking professors are likely to spend less time teaching, as faculty may reduce their teaching load based on research performance. For example, faculty members may earn credit toward their annual teaching requirements (measured in total classroom hours) with a major journal publication, and, of course, senior professors are more likely to attain such accomplishments. Additionally, senior professors tend to devote a greater percentage of their teaching to graduate-level courses and spend a sizeable portion of their time advising master's and doctoral students. Also, faculty in departments with major research endeavors are likely to teach less than faculty working in departments or schools whose primary function is undergraduate education. An example of the latter is MUC's School of Foreign Languages, which in terms of research does not garner much Project

985 funding, giving the difficulty of connecting their research to ethnic minority affairs. Paradoxically, and much to their consternation, foreign language faculty still must publish and produce research results at a comparable level to other faculty in order to be promoted.

As a consequence of limited openings at higher ranks, competitive pressures sometimes arise within particular departments and schools. A junior faculty member discussed this facet of academic life: "Of course there is internal competition. I think the most significant competition is among colleagues within the department. Because the academic title means salary, it means opportunities, it means qualification, it means everything! It is very important for everyone. So I don't think it is a system of fairness."

A more senior professor added, "It's more and more difficult to be promoted nowadays, because the number of posts is limited, and you have more candidates. Therefore, you have to compete with each other in terms of the amount of your publications, the quality of your scholarship, your performance. The pressure is higher." And a faculty member in the field of minority language and literature described the problems in his department: "We have many associate professors who want to be promoted to full professor, but they don't have a chance, because the positions are all filled."

But not everyone saw the quota system as generating excessive competition. As one very senior professor explained, "It depends on the situation. Some of us are very good friends. And in our department we have good relationships. I am a professor and you are a professor. I share ideas with you and I respect you. You are my friend and we have common conditions, similar academic research, similar promotion rules. And so we can still be friends." A junior faculty member supported such a view, noting that faculty stand to benefit from working together and thus should not allow themselves to become too caught up in competition. As she explained, "Collaboration can produce mutual benefits."

A form of market mechanism has been introduced recently as part of determining the number of faculty positions at each level that a department or school can have. One faculty member discussed his department being able to make the case for additional faculty positions because the research productivity of the faculty in his department had increased (namely, the number of faculty publications went up significantly). Student enrollment can also affect the number of allotted positions to a department or school. As a faculty member in education explained, "If you get higher student enrollments, or more doctoral students, then the university may give you more positions. The quota may go up. If you lose students, if your student numbers go down, then it is possible that they may take away one of your professors or one of your associate professor positions." But such a market-oriented mechanism may create a different form of competition in which each university in turn places great pressure on its faculty to accumulate publications and research grants as a means of better positioning the university with regard to national competition for faculty positions and resources. Sometimes this may lend itself to other sorts of problems. A senior faculty member captured the nature of this potential structural problem: "Each university tries to produce more publications to get in a better position. This orientation really reduces if not eliminates creativity. And moral standards may also be lowered."

Rising Levels of Faculty Stress

Faculty at MUC generally described a working environment characterized by increasing levels of stress. Such notions typically were linked to three facets of their work: (1) a growing student population, and consequently, greater pressure to use one's time for teaching and advising responsibilities; (2) increased pressure to publish in top scholarly journals; and (3) increased pressure to obtain and successfully manage funded research projects.

Most faculty talked about the expansion of the Chinese university, including MUC, and the sort of challenges larger numbers of university students presented for the faculty. Faculty members generally did not think that faculty hiring had kept pace with rising student populations. They typically alluded to the fact that China's higher education system had shifted from an elite to a mass system and that such expansion had taken place rather rapidly. Indeed, as we note in the introduction, less than 5 percent of Chinese adults aged 18–22 attended higher education in 1990, but by 2009 that figure had reached close to 25 percent. A consequence of such expansion was addressed by a senior faculty member: "There is too heavy of a workload, including too many classes with too many students. This is part of the bad side of expanding higher education." The reality that teaching pressure is probably on the rise is further supported by data from MUC. The table below reveals the number of MUC students and faculty at two points in time, 2000 and 2010. The student population in 2010 was four times larger than that of 2000, while the size of the faculty increased less than threefold. The data clearly support faculty comments that hiring has not kept pace with student expansion and that teaching responsibilities may be more challenging today than in the past.

	Student Enrollment	Total No. of Faculty
2000	3,603	726
2010	16,000	2,000

In terms of research expectations, a consistent story was told by MUC faculty members: Simply put, faculty are expected to publish much more now than in the past. Consistent with such a perspective, a senior faculty member felt that junior faculty especially faced significant challenges because of higher research expectations: "I think their conditions are not as good as when we were young. When we were young, we felt the material shortage, but now the young people face more pressure in terms of the research and their future looks not as easy as ours was before. When we graduated at that time, we were still the elites who could select a job from many choices. But now one job has so many candidates." A faculty member in education echoed the preceding sentiments: "I think the pressure is much higher than before. Someone said to me that working in the universities as a teacher is very easy, but I don't think so. I think it's very hard for me."

Most faculty associated the pressure to publish with a growing sense that Chinese universities in general and MUC in particular were trying to improve research capacity and catch up to some of the top research universities in the West. Along these lines, faculty spoke of the increased research funds as helpful but also noted that the bar for publishing academic articles was being raised as a consequence of such high levels of research support.

In addition to publishing, obtaining grant money and leading funded projects was discussed as another key source of stress. A senior professor explained, "There is the pressure of writing papers, but that is only one side. There is also pressure to get money. Pressure to get compensation, pressure to get money to support your fieldwork—this is another side of it. . . . Your funded projects and grants also are considered as part of your promotion." Another senior faculty member observed that the focus on funded research is "part of a new trend . . . it is part of the new standard for evaluating faculty members." And a junior faculty member added, "Now they pay more attention to funded projects instead of just publishing . . . before maybe we paid more attention to published articles, to publications, but now there is a focus on research projects. And faculty have more opportunities to apply for projects and funding. And so maybe the weight of the research projects is getting higher."

Faculty also pointed out that funded projects are evaluated in part on the basis of where the monies come from—such as whether they are part of a national- or provincial-level funding source; for example, obtaining a MoE grant garners greater prestige than a provincial- or municipal-level grant. In general, faculty said that being successful at obtaining and leading funded research projects had the potential to offset lack of publications, at least in some cases. As a faculty member in education noted, "If you don't publish, then they must see how much grant money you have, how much money did you bring into the university or to your department." Comments such as the preceding tend to support other scholarly claims of a global trend in higher education in which faculty increasingly are expected to connect their research to revenue streams and market-driven opportunities (Slaughter and Rhoades 2004; Rhoads and

Liang 2006; Rhoads and Torres 2006). China clearly is not immune to this trend, and neither is MUC.

An added element of the pressure for some faculty is their lack of adequate research training, which is problematic in an environment increasingly emphasizing research productivity. Although MUC has several nationally ranked departments, namely those concerned with ethnic language, culture, and literature, other departments are not so highly regarded, and the faculty working in them struggle at times to meet the higher research expectations. Some thought that they lack the kind of research training helpful in developing and maintaining a meaningful line of inquiry. For such faculty, there is little to no opportunity to advance beyond the rank of associate professor. Additionally, several faculty members explained that they were hired because of their teaching ability but more recently had felt pressure to refashion their professional lives to incorporate research. A few questioned the national shift to redefine national universities as comprehensive, rather than teaching oriented; accordingly, they questioned whether academic research is really critical to university operations and the nation's economic development.

A Case of Quantity over Quality?

More than a few faculty complained about the new evaluation and promotion processes placing too much emphasis on the quantity of research contributions without adequately weighing the quality. One senior professor thought that because there was so much more money for research, expectations were too fixated on the number of journal publications. He described the expansion of publications as "polluting the environment" in that many do not seem to offer anything "constructive to the field." As he argued, "They give you money, so you are obliged to intensify your activities and then write things to produce publications." A faculty member in history offered a similar perspective:

> Things have changed since Projects 211 and 985. When I was promoted at this university, you didn't need to focus so much on the number of publications. It didn't matter how many books or articles you published—you were just required to show two things: one article and one book that you were most proud of and that demonstrated your highest level of work. The important evaluation standard was not the quantity but the quality. Personally speaking, I think the academic ecology nowadays is very messed up. Although we get much more money, the evaluation system has made us more uncomfortable. The professors who can publish more will get a lot of things, like more money, better positions, more prizes. But many of the publications are low quality and they don't accomplish anything.

Several faculty members pointed out that because university administrators play such an important role in the evaluation of faculty, and because they often lack the specialized expertise to evaluate the quality of specific publications, they must simply resort to counting. A few professors looked to Western models that stressed peer review and openly wondered if increased emphasis on such models was needed. A senior faculty member captured this sentiment: "I know that in the U.S., the publications first are evaluated by expert peers. But in China, the first thing is to count the number of books and articles, or the research projects. If you have the highest number, then you can be promoted. The quantity does not necessarily stand for quality. In this model, the control is with the administrators, and so it's difficult to have a fair academic evaluation."

One criterion often used in evaluating faculty is the number of publications in key or core journals. A faculty member in minority education noted, "I think most officials think that if the faculty member publishes in core journals then the publication is probably of a higher quality. The journals have a higher rank so then they think the publications will be better." Universities have differing lists of core journals for various fields and for the overall university. More prestigious universities such as Beijing and Tsinghua typically will have more elite standards in terms of which core journals count when compared to lesser research universities. The campus list of core journals is typically determined by administrative personnel with extensive input gathered from faculty members. There often are disagreements about the classification of various journals as well as the inclusion or exclusion of particular journals. Furthermore, looking at publications in international journals is sometimes used as a simple way of measuring quality and evaluating faculty productivity. As one senior professor explained, "Of course the papers published in the international journals are considered best." But publishing in international journals typically demands writing in English, a rather difficult endeavor for many MUC faculty members, given that English is likely to be their third language (Mandarin Chinese is a second language for many of MUC's ethnic minority professors).

Concluding Remarks

This chapter highlights three basic narratives faculty employed in describing the organizational context of MUC: internationalization, marketization, and ethnocultural development. The first narrative—internationalization—was widely accepted by MUC faculty and for the most part did not exist in opposition to the other narratives of change. The second and third narratives—marketization and ethnocultural development—were somewhat divergent at times, suggesting competing views of the university and its organizational strategies. A key point to take from this chapter is that the pressures of marketization are likely to increase in the coming years, given the broader changes taking place in Chinese society. But such a trend should not come at the expense of service to the nation's ethnic affairs. Creative ways of linking ethnocultural development endeavors to markets surely will be needed. But at the same time, it must be recognized that key facets of the contemporary university, whether located in China, the United States, or elsewhere, require a certain degree of public support. Without such support, typically in the form of governmental funding, a good deal of what the modern university has come to signify may be lost, and services addressing forms of inequality associated with racial or ethnic injustice conceivably could suffer irreparable harm. This would be a huge loss for societies and for minority-serving universities such as MUC.

In general, MUC faculty members recognized the importance of China developing its universities by emphasizing expanded research capacity. They also were fully cognizant of the reality that growing the research mission necessarily involves altering their working lives and the way they go about their daily routines. Although the general conviction at MUC was that increased government funding from Projects 211 and 985 had helped to elevate academic and research standards, this facet of institutional change, combined with larger student enrollments, put substantial pressure on faculty members. Junior faculty in particular seemed to be under greater stress than their senior colleagues, although this phenomenon is likely to be the case at universities throughout the world.

Building world-class research universities seems to be a natural progression for a nation that since 1978 has had to play catch-up to the world's most highly developed nations such as Germany, the United Kingdom, and the United States. As one senior faculty member surmised, "If China is going to be one of the world's leading nation's economically speaking, then our leaders see no reason why we shouldn't also have some of the top cultural institutions, including world-class research universities like those in the West." It should come as no surprise then that MUC faculty members often look to universities in the Western world as they seek to improve and expand their own research and scholarly efforts.

For many of MUC's leading faculty who work in the university's top academic programs, placing greater emphasis on research is enthusiastically embraced—many have been committed world-class scholars for years, and so Projects 211 and 985 support their inquiry. Such support is often used for research travel and conducting extensive field work in minority regions, where faculty often engage their undergraduate and graduate students, enabling them to expand their research skills. This facet of increased research support is especially important in that it helps universities such as MUC to advance China's next generation of scholars in fields relating to ethnic culture, language, and literature.

The reality that MUC enjoys strong governmental support for its public good mission of serving ethnic minority populations offers a counternarrative to the usual neoliberal tale, which involves declines in public funding, increased marketization, and a weakening of the public good mission (Marginson and Considine 2000; Rhoads and Szelényi 2011; Rhoads and Torres 2006; Santos 2006; Vaira 2004). The fact that the university's social science and humanities professors enjoy high status also seems counter to the logic of neoliberalism and academic capitalism (Slaughter and Rhoades 2004). In fact, there appears to be strong evidence that Chinese higher education policy, which offers high levels of funding for its top hundred or so universities through Project 211 and then even greater levels of funding for a group of thirty-nine universities in the form of Project 985, runs counter to the neoliberal trend. The heavy involvement of China's central government in managing the nation's university admissions process, as well as the comanagement of universities by the CCP in general, also points to policies and practices diverging from the neoliberal trend of governmental decentralization. This is not necessarily the case, however, for hundreds of Chinese universities not funded by Projects 211 or 985. During the 1990s the nation's decentralization of higher education led to significant marketization, as Ka Ho Mok has well documented (1997c, 1999, 2000); this is especially true of provincial universities largely cut off from funding by the national government. Nonetheless, the case of MUC, and China more broadly speaking, challenges the usual discussion of neoliberalism as a global force in higher education.

The promotion process, of course, is a key structural component of the changing Chinese research university. Promotion processes and the reward structure in general are critical to shaping faculty behavior, and clearly a system is now in place to promote greater engagement in research. However, there appear to be some problems at MUC, at least if we are to believe the faculty members participating in our study. One problem commonly identified relates to the use of quotas at various levels of the faculty ladder and the fact that such a system may limit the ability of a highly qualified faculty member to advance to the next level. This may negatively affect faculty morale. Also, the vast majority of MUC faculty consistently pointed to processes that tend to favor quantity of publications over quality. Most suggested increasing the role faculty play in evaluating the quality of their peers' publications while at the same time minimizing in some manner or form the high level of control held by academic administrators. As was the case with other suggestions from faculty, they believed turning to Western universities as a source for modeling some of MUC's promotion and reward structures would strengthen faculty scholarship and improve the university's research enterprise.

With such rapid changes taking place at universities such as MUC, faculty stress levels appear to be going up, especially for those faculty members whose doctoral training may have been lacking in terms of research preparation. Stress levels also seem to be higher among junior faculty, who must figure out the norms of academic life at a time when they are evolving rapidly. These issues point to the need for implementing or expanding faculty development at universities such as MUC. Such efforts could focus on helping faculty to develop their research skills and better connect streams of inquiry to the basic mission of the university. A few junior faculty went so far as to suggest that simply participating in our study—namely, having the chance to talk about their research and the university's changing expectations—was a helpful activity. This hints that further dialogue among faculty about research and changing academic norms might be a good starting point for assisting junior faculty in their development as scholars. Incorporating research expertise into a faculty development office could also be quite beneficial, especially for junior faculty struggling to find their way but also for middle and senior faculty trained in a different era.

Achievements and Challenges in the Quest to Build Leading Universities

In recent times it seems hardly a day goes by without a new story about one Chinese university or another building academic or research partnerships with foreign universities. At UCLA, home to the lead author of this book, it is virtually impossible to keep track of all the collaborations and partnerships forged between academic departments and related programs at Chinese universities. Indeed, examples of Western universities partnering with their Chinese counterparts are too numerous to count. Just to offer a few examples from one relatively brief time period, in 2012 Fudan University in Shanghai formed a partnership with the University of California to create the Fudan-UC Center to be hosted at UC San Diego. The center was founded to further advance China studies, obviously in recognition of the growing importance China plays in the geopolitical arena. A few months later Carnegie Mellon University in Pittsburgh announced it had agreed to develop the Joint Institute of Engineering (JIE) with Sun Yat-sen University in Guangzhou (also known as Zhongshan University). And a month later, McGill University in Montreal announced it had formed a partnership with Peking University to promote increased collaboration, especially in the fields of law and medicine.[1] The fact that universities all over the world are lining up to formalize relationships with China's leading universities is further evidence that Chinese higher education truly has come of age.

A 2013 story in the *Economist* further highlighted the general trend of Chinese and Western universities building collaborative programs, noting that Britain's Lancaster University, New York's Juilliard School, and Duke University "are just the latest foreign institutions to pile into an already crowded marketplace. Other co-operative and exchange programmes in higher education are being announced almost every month. Some recruit Chinese students to foreign universities, or foreign students to Chinese ones. Others take the form of research facilities or academic-exchange centres. Some offer dual degrees. The most ambitious involve building, staffing and operating satellite campuses in China" ("Campus Collaboration" 2013). However, such partnerships have not been without their problems. The article went on to note that differences in academic "standards and values" have resulted in some failed partnerships, noting that Yale University ended its joint undergraduate program with Peking University. Yale's administrators pointed to various issues, including low enrollment and excessive costs, but early on in the program some of Yale's faculty had complained of "rampant plagiarism" on the part of Chinese students in the program ("Campus Collaboration" 2013). Despite these and other organizational complications, including differences in academic culture, Chinese and Western universities continue to forge collaborative ties at a breakneck pace.

Although one might think that the proliferation of partnerships among Chinese and Western universities reflects the aggressive push of Chinese university faculty and staff in light of vast governmental funding and support for internationalization, the reality is that such collaborations are just as likely to be initiated by Western partners hoping to gain a foothold into China. Western faculty and staff may not be sure about what riches lie in the vast Middle Land,[2] but no university wants to be left behind. As much as MOOC-madness[3] has consumed the world of higher education, it pales in comparison to China-madness. The general attitude is captured to some extent by Amsterdam's Vrije Universiteit (VU) and its rationale for developing the VU China Research Centre:

> One of the more distinguishing news items of 2010 was that China has developed into the second economy in the world. Moreover, the continuing growth of the Chinese economy also made China lead the world out of the recent global recession. This economic growth can be felt far beyond its national borders. In particular in Europe, the rapidly increasing investment of Chinese companies in the region is the talk of the day. This is alternately described in terms of opportunity for European businesses and threat. Surely, when even institutions like Volvo are acquired by Chinese enterprises, that feeling of threat is understandable, though not necessarily justified. Perception of threat is usually caused by a lack of understanding, and the best way to mend such a lack of understanding is research.

In the background of these developments, it makes sense that an academic entity like the Faculty of Economy and Business Administration (FEWEB) of VU University Amsterdam has decided to make the study of the Chinese economy and Chinese enterprises into a core research theme. The mission of the VU China Research Centre is to combine the specific expertise of a number of researchers and focus it on studying the mechanisms that steer China's economic development. Although in this stage it is still basically an effort of our Faculty, contemporary China research conducted at the Faculty of Social Sciences is also included. More faculties may follow soon.[4]

The preceding text from VU's China Research Centre brings us full circle: Recall that we began this work in the introduction by discussing the growing strength and influence of China as a nation-state and noting how its top universities are implicated by its rapid transformation and accelerated rise to power. From international and geopolitical concerns to the advance of high-tech inventions and industries and efforts addressing environmental and cultural challenges, universities such as those highlighted in this work have become critical to China's success.

The reality that universities—especially research universities—have become important to the modern nation-state is of course evident around the world. To affirm this point, all one needs to do is examine the great emphasis placed on today's research universities as sources of economic development. Indeed, few experts—whether working in the areas of technology transfer, economics, higher education, or organizational studies—are likely to dispute the potential of research universities to stimulate economic growth. The cases are just too numerous. For example, research and innovation at Stanford University fueled to a great extent the rise of Silicon Valley as a leading high-tech center (Moore and Davis 2004; Saxenian 1996). MIT was critical to the emergence of the many technology companies lining Boston's Route 128 (Saxenian 1996). And "the Cambridge Phenomenon" is a well-known expression used to describe the development of innovative high-tech companies in close proximity to the University of Cambridge (Kirk and Cotton 2012). The interplay and interconnections among academic scientists, industrial entrepreneurs, and venture capitalists in the many examples of "high-tech clusters" around the world offer resounding evidence of the key role universities play in today's knowledge-centered economies (Bresnahan and Gambardella 2004). With growing emphasis among national leaders and policy makers on increasing investment in high technology and information- and knowledge-based creations and discoveries, research universities, as centers for knowledge production, are a core component of national development strategies. Few examples highlight this trend better than China's Tsinghua University.

But Chinese universities, as is the case with universities around the world, have a much broader mission than simply serving economic development concerns. The modern research university is complex, serving multiple constituents and facing a wide array of pressures. As the cases in this book highlight, universities also are called on to address important social issues, including concerns linked to social inequality, as the case of Minzu University highlights. Furthermore, universities are challenged to interpret, enhance, and preserve important facets of a nation's culture and history, and no university in China takes this more seriously than Peking University. Universities are also expected to offer guiding commentary and research-based insights into the complex terrain of international affairs and politics. Some of the leading professors at Renmin University are known for fulfilling this important role, and scholars at Peking and Tsinghua also serve in such a capacity. As the highest organizational level within complex and stratified educational systems, universities must provide guidance to the lower levels of a nation's most critical institutional enterprise, such as by helping to enhance and modernize rural and urban schools. In this regard, all the universities in this book contribute to such social obligations.

When Peking and Tsinghua celebrated their hundredth years as universities, in 1998 and 2011, respectively, the nation's political leaders appeared front and center. Indeed, it was in conjunction with Peking's centennial celebration that then-president Jiang Zemin introduced the national initiative to build world-class universities in the mold of Peking University. The initiative became known as Project 985, and it marked a change in Chinese higher education that helped to catapult reform efforts from the Open Door era to a new age focused on accelerating development and attaining high-level university standing. It is the age of Chinese higher education reform that we call the Global Ambition Period. In many ways, this book is about capturing facets of this ambitious age of higher education attainment among the nation's leading universities.

The cases highlighted in this book further reinforce the commitment of China's leaders to develop their top research universities across a range of university functions, including most notably their role in economic development as well as their responsibilities as purveyors of a society's cultural forms and commitments. From the academic excellence stressed at Peking University to Tsinghua's economic innovation and entrepreneurialism, Renmin's commitment to international and public engagement, and Minzu's service to ethnic affairs, the cases presented here reinforce the range of university mission and function that has become so critical to China's higher education venture. The cases speak to the "city of infinite variety" we first noted in the introduction.[5]

In what follows, we summarize the major findings deriving from our four cases and contributing to the infinite variety of Chinese university life. We then discuss practical issues linked to our findings. First, we identify eight major highlights pointing to positive changes at China's leading universities—what we see as "achievements." We move on to delineate seven points of concern—what we describe as "challenges." The latter discussion most notably includes the pressing need to strengthen university autonomy and enhance academic freedom for faculty members. We conclude the chapter and the book by stressing facets of China's global ambition that have served to redefine university reform and elevated its university enterprises to the global stage.

Summary of the Four Case Studies

In order to further delineate key achievements as well as additional challenges confronting China's research universities, we believe it is first helpful to review our four cases by highlighting the essential findings. Reviewing the organizational context of the four universities will serve as a starting point for summarizing our empirical findings and their implications.

Tsinghua University

Our chapter about Tsinghua University centered on the innovative and entrepreneurial spirit of the university's academic culture. Founded with payments deriving from the United States through the Boxer Indemnity Fund, Tsinghua from the start was a unique form of higher education institution in China. The university's distinctive characteristics included greater openness to foreign ideas and diverse ways of thinking about knowledge and its discovery and creation, including an embrace of applied science. The unique culture at Tsinghua also reflects the influence of Southwest United University, which incorporated Tsinghua, Peking, and Nankai universities in the city of Kunming in Yunnan province during the Japanese occupation of the late 1930s and early 1940s. The vitality and optimism of what became known as the United University spirit is seen as a key influence in the development of Tsinghua, especially in terms of promoting elements of progressive scientific thought. As evidence, it is often noted that Tsinghua's Nobel laureates in physics—Li Zhendao and Yang Zhenning—graduated from United University. These facets of the university's culture were later refashioned to some extent by the transformation of Tsinghua to an institution more focused on applied science and engineering under Soviet influence in the 1950s. Thus, Tsinghua's distinctive culture today must be understood in light of historical processes that contributed to a convergence of progressive scientific thought and application, combined with a greater openness to international scholarly exchange.

There are many ways of exploring the innovative and applied qualities of Tsinghua, but we chose to focus on two institutional structures: Tsinghua University Science Park, or TusPark, and the University-Industry Cooperation Committee (UICC). These structures focus university resources on the development of close ties with business and industry with the goal of encouraging technology transfer and the marketization of innovative ideas produced by Tsinghua professors and students. As we point out in chapter 1, these types of structures stressing research entrepreneurialism have contributed to the university's status around the world as a leading applied science and engineering university, as evidenced by its position in various global university ranking schemes and its inclusion among the top three hundred organizations in terms of patents granted by the U.S. Patent and Trademark Office; here, it is worth noting that Tsinghua is the only non-U.S. university included among the likes of IBM, Samsung, Sony, and General Electric.

In addition to being recognized for its applied science and innovation, Tsinghua also is known for its loyalist graduates, many of whom have assumed leading positions in Chinese politics. They include the current and previous presidents—Xi Jinping and Hu Jintao—as well as both the former premier and chair of the National People's Congress, Zhu Rongji and Wu Bangguo, respectively. This loyalist facet of Tsinghua has been noted in the sociological literature, specifically in Joel Andreas' 2009 book *Rise of the Red Engineers: The Cultural Revolution and the Origins of China's New Class*. This culture of loyalism to some extent contrasts with Peking University's history of challenging dominant ways of thinking, including most notably its role in the May Fourth Movement of 1919.

Peking University

Our discussion of Peking University in chapter 2 highlights the reality that the nation's development of its preeminent research universities involves more than simply focusing on their role in economic development. Indeed, the goals and objectives of Projects 211 and 985 also stress the development of social and cultural facets of China's leading universities. This is quite evident in the case of Peking University, where academic excellence is pursued across a wide range of fields, including heavy emphasis on the social sciences and humanities. Of course, the university also stresses the development of world-class departments in the areas of the natural and applied sciences. But perhaps what is most important to highlight is the characteristic trait of the university's faculty and students to question societal norms and dominant ways of thinking and promote social progress—a quality recognized throughout China as the "Beida way," or *Beida jingshen*.

Peking was founded under the influence of China's progressive intellectual movements of the late 1890s and was one of the few reforms to survive the eventual conservative backlash (Hayhoe 1996). The progressive vision of Peking was most evident in May of 1919 when students and faculty played a leading role in challenging the government's weak response to concessions to Japan as part of the Treaty of Versailles. In time, the movement came to symbolize a form of Chinese renaissance, and the role of Peking University as an intellectual and cultural leader was cemented in Chinese society. Contributions of university students and faculty at the time included a more powerful emergence of ideals associated with democracy and science. This form of challenge to Chinese traditionalism in part came to define the Beida way, which involved the pursuit of knowledge with a healthy dose of skepticism. An example of this was the way that Professor Liang Shu-ming challenged aspects of traditional Marxist thought under Mao, raising questions about whether or not China's rural social structure could be analyzed along class lines. The fact that he took such intellectual and political risks epitomizes the skepticism and intellectual individualism that has come to characterize Peking University's academic culture.

Peking continues to be recognized as the preeminent academic institution in China while earning status worldwide as well. Still today it is looked to by all of Chinese higher education as a national signpost, as was evident during the culture wars of the 1990s and 2000s, when personnel reform targeting faculty productivity captured the nation's attention. Although widespread reform measures did not entirely succeed, several significant changes related to faculty recruitment, hiring, and promotion practices were adopted. Such changes were seen as critical to fostering increased competition among faculty and furthering academic norms relating to research and scholarship, and they were understood to be characteristic of leading world-class universities. Reforms of the faculty personnel system at Peking eventually percolated throughout the Chinese higher education system, reinforcing once again the university's place as one of nation's most important cultural institutions.

Renmin University

To some extent, Renmin University lacks the historical legacy of its close neighbors to the north, Tsinghua and Peking, having been founded at a different point in the nation's history under the more direct influence of the Chinese Communist Party. Given its roots and ties to the early CCP, Renmin has served an important role in Chinese society as a training ground for many government officials (Tsinghua has as well). Intellectually speaking, though, Renmin has become a key university in terms of developing and promoting China's version of the engaged public intellectual; several of Renmin's leading professors are recognized for their contributions to international politics and law.

As is highlighted in chapter 3, Renmin faculty members are often called on to address key world events. Indeed, commentary from Renmin professors frequently appears in important global news outlets such as the *New York Times*, the *Washington Post*, the *Wall Street Journal*, *BBC News*, and the *Guardian*. The university's economics, law, journalism, and international affairs programs, among others, are some of the very best in China, and so it is not surprising that faculty members working in such areas garner a good deal of media attention. But the public visibility of many of its scholars is also part of the core culture of the university and its embodiment of social responsibility to the people, indicated to some extent by another name by which it is also sometimes known—People's University of China.

A key theme of chapter 3 is the internationalization of the university, a characteristic also present at Peking and Tsinghua and at Minzu University to a lesser extent. The internationalization of Renmin reflects the national drive to build world-class universities, as building partnerships and collaborative ties with foreign universities and scholars is seen to be critical to such an endeavor. Of course, funds from Project 211 and 985 are at the heart of such efforts. Given our focus on faculty life, the discussion of internationalization at Renmin revolved around five key themes: (1) the impact of international standards on scholarship, (2) the relevance of experiences abroad, (3) collaboration and partnerships with foreign scholars and organizations, (4) hosting foreign faculty and students, and (5) the pedagogical and curriculum implications of internationalization. But critical questions relating to internationalization and the potential for Western influences to operate as a form of colonialism were also raised by several Renmin professors; such criticism is relatively consistent with the public intellectualism the university seeks to promote. This critical analysis of internationalization may serve as a helpful guide to other Chinese universities seeking to further develop as world-class universities.

Minzu University

The case studies of Tsinghua, Peking, and Renmin center to a great extent on the quest to further develop as world-class universities, but our inclusion of Minzu University presents a somewhat different perspective. As we note in chapter 4, Minzu generally is not considered among the top research universities in China; its inclusion as a Project 985 university is due mostly to its importance to the nation's ethnic affairs as well as to political sensitivities regarding the inclusion of a minority-serving university among the nation's elite. We included Minzu in our study for similar reasons. In China, there is no more important university when it comes to addressing ethnic minority issues than Minzu. And given the overall importance of the nation's ethnic diversity, this means that Minzu has an extremely important role to play among China's leading universities.

The organizational context of Minzu is best discussed in terms of the diversity of its student and faculty populations, where approximately 60 percent of the students (about 70 percent of the undergraduates) and as much as 40 percent of the faculty come from ethnic minority populations. Further, the university is known for its strong academic programs focused on ethnic minority perspectives, its famous ethnic museum, and its popular folk and ethnic musical and dance productions reflective of the nation's diversity and the talent of the university's students and faculty.

Minzu faculty discussed some of the challenges they faced in the context of a diverse campus environment, increasing internationalization, and relatively recent personnel reform; such challenges are also noted relative to recent pressures on Minzu professors as part of Project 211 and 985 funding. And although the goal of elevating Minzu to the status of a world-class research university, comparable to Tsinghua or Peking, is seen as rather distant if not improbable, there is still great pressure on faculty to advance their research and increase scholarly productivity. This pressure, most often voiced in terms of enhancing Minzu as a comprehensive university, was discussed in light of the institution's historic mission to serve the nation's ethnic affairs. Consequently, faculty operating in fields closely tied to ethnic minority issues found it easier to expand their research commitment using sources of research funding such as Project 985. To the contrary, faculty members working in fields less connected to ethnic affairs, such as the natural sciences and foreign languages, for example, had a more difficult time and often wondered how they fit within the changing landscape of Minzu's development. A few even questioned the traditional mission of the university and openly wondered if the market should play a greater role in shaping the university's priorities.

Summary of Institutional Achievements

Our case studies reveal some important improvements related to elevating the operations of the nation's top universities. We summarize these in terms of institutional achievements in the following eight areas: infrastructure for research and teaching, research capacity, scholarly productivity, university-industry connections, internationalization, academic quality, faculty promotion processes, and faculty recruitment practices. In highlighting these areas of achievement we are not suggesting that more work is not needed. Indeed, in some ways the long march for Chinese research is just beginning. What we report in terms of achievements mostly pertains to how the faculty with whom we spoke assessed the situation of their university's development. Here, it may be helpful to review the basic methodological assumptions framing our analysis.

As we highlight in the introduction, the basic focus of our study was an analysis of organizational culture, particularly academic culture. Such a focus involved extensive interviews, informal conversations, observations, and document analysis. We chose to center our data collection primarily on faculty members, reflecting our belief that professors are crucial to the formation and perpetuation of norms and practices associated with academic culture. Our intent was to better understand how they construct meaning about their working lives at the four universities, especially in light of national initiatives to alter the operations of their universities and increase their status and standing as comprehensive research universities. Our view that the social reality of faculty members is critical to understanding contemporary Chinese universities reflects a basic proposition of the symbolic interactionism wing of sociological thought, captured to a great extent by the Thomas Theorem: Situations defined as real are real in their consequences (Thomas and Thomas 1928, 572). Thus, from our perspective, it is critical to know how faculty understand and describe their realities and how they develop and adjust their lines of action based on their understandings.

Infrastructure for Research and Teaching

Faculty at all four universities consistently noted that increased funds were used to strengthen the infrastructure for research and teaching activities. Examples here included additions to classrooms, such as enhanced technological capabilities in the form of multimedia equipment and lecture rooms with increased seating capacity and comfort; in terms of research infrastructure, faculty noted improvement in computing hardware and software as well as greater access to key resource databases. Faculty also spoke of increased numbers of visiting foreign professors as well as greater availability of higher-quality books, textbooks, and journals, including those of an international variety. All of these changes were described as enhancing the ability of faculty to perform higher-quality teaching and research.

Research Capacity

Since 1998 and with the onset of Project 985, the Chinese government has poured more and more money into the nation's top universities with a particular focus on strengthening and expanding the academic research enterprise. A central concern of our study then focused on whether faculty perceived changes in institutional research capacity as a key facet of their organizational reality and, if so, how such a perception altered their patterns of acting. Our study is less concerned with "objective" measures of research capacity than with faculty beliefs about expanded research capacities. Here again, we stress the point of view that social actors more often than not choose lines of action on the basis of interpretations of their social worlds, whether such interpretations are accurate or not (the Thomas Theorem).

Our findings overwhelmingly pointed to perceptions of a sizeable increase in research capacity, which is hardly surprising given the scope of increased funding from the national government. Accordingly, faculty at all four of the universities expressed the point of view that increased funds for various research-related activities are widely available, including funds for conducting empirical inquiry. Not a single faculty member with whom we spoke suggested that research funds had somehow become scarcer; indeed, a few faculty even noted that at times using up all the money was in itself a new kind of problem.

Scholarly Productivity

In light of improvements in infrastructure and the expansion in research capacity, faculty consistently noted that scholarly productivity at their respective universities had increased over recent years, primarily relative to publishing research and research findings. This also was seen as being linked to changes in faculty promotion processes, which over the past several years increasingly emphasized publishing; most faculty talked about how the present-day promotion process focused on the quantity of a faculty member's scholarly contributions, including such things as the number of A-level publications and, in some cases, the number of publications in international journals. This heavy emphasis on quantifying faculty scholarly productivity also was evidenced at institutional-level assessments conducted by the government (we talk about some of the negative facets of this later in this chapter). Such a reality was highlighted by faculty at all four universities. Most saw the increased scholarly expectations and research output as positive, although more than a few professors pointed to high levels of stress and judged that the pressure to publish was at times excessive. This seemed especially troubling to women (in light of major household responsibilities among other concerns) and junior faculty members. Some faculty openly wondered if the teaching mission of the university was becoming compromised as a consequence of so much emphasis on research and publishing.

Data regarding Chinese scholarly publications shows incredible increases in recent years, suggesting that the assessment offered by the professors in our study is fairly accurate. For example, in *Building Bricks: Exploring the Global Research and Innovation Impact of Brazil, Russia, India, China and South Korea*, a research report produced by Thomson Reuters, it is noted that China moved from very few scholarly publications in the early 1980s to roughly 25,000 in the late 1990s and then, remarkably, to over 150,000 in 2011, based on Web of Knowledge databases comprising some 250 subfields (Adams, Pendlebury, and Stembridge 2013, 10). Furthermore, worldwide data from the Social Sciences Citation Index revealed that in 1996 Chinese scholars accounted for only 1.6 percent of the world's scholarly publications (among the journals and fields indexed), but by 2008, only twelve years later, Chinese scholarship constituted 6.6 percent, moving from fourteenth to fourth place. Ignoring legitimate questions of quality, clearly the production of scholarly publications has dramatically increased since the late 1990s, and commentary from faculty members at the four universities we studied very much supported such a position.

University-Industry Connections

Although Tsinghua drew much of our focus in terms of examining university–industry ties, increased coordination and exchange between universities and various business and industrial enterprises were also noted at the other three case study sites as well. There appears to be a conscious effort among Chinese professors to build stronger ties to companies, and the labor market more broadly speaking, both for the purposes of advancing research partnerships and in terms of connecting students to internships and graduates to potential job opportunities. This was especially true for faculty working in areas more likely to intersect with the needs of business and industry, such as the applied sciences. However, even at Minzu University, where the university's mission largely serves a public mandate to address the nation's ethnic affairs, there was significant attention paid to connecting the student educational experience to career opportunities; further, one of the key institutional narratives of change deriving from the Minzu case study focused on marketization, which included calls for stronger ties to business and industry. Several faculty members noted, for example, that many are involved in building personal relationships with business and industry as a means of supplementing their income and at the same time furthering possibilities for their students.

Internationalization

One of the most compelling narratives coming from our cultural analysis of faculty life was the way in which faculty members consistently and across the board stressed internationalization as a defining feature of their universities. Internationalization encompassed many facets of campus life, influencing scholarship, research collaboration, faculty recruitment, academic programs, student and scholarly exchange, curriculum and teaching, and even structural changes such as adopting an international summer semester, as in the case of Renmin University. Faculty generally discussed internationalization as a broad outcome associated with initial higher education reform under Deng Xiaoping's Open Door policies, mostly during the 1980s and early 1990s, but more recently they associated international trends with focused efforts to strengthen China's top universities as part of Projects 211 and 985, beginning in the mid-1990s. Additionally, Project 111 (also known as the "Thousand Talents" project), implemented jointly in 2006 by the MoE and the State Administration of Foreign Experts Affairs, aimed to recruit up to a thousand scholars from the world's top research universities while offering funding to develop a hundred key research centers. Such programs provided needed financial support toward efforts to recruit and engage leading foreign scholars across a range of fields.

Although we discuss internationalization here in terms of accomplishments, we do not suggest that improvements are not needed. For example, at one level Project III seems highly successful, having attracted more than three thousand Chinese "returnees" with PhDs or extensive research experience, well beyond the program's original goal (Cao 2013). However, as Cong Cao pointed out, many of these "returnees" have minimal research experience and are hardly the kind of "top talent" research stars the program originally had in mind (Cao 2013). In fact, Cao went on to note that "Statistics released by the U.S. National Science Foundation show that, over the past three decades, Chinese have been the top foreign recipients of doctoral degrees in science and engineering from American universities," and yet after "receiving their PhDs, nearly all the students indicated their intention to remain in the United States—more than 90 percent have managed to stay." Cao argued that a fundamental change is needed in China's research culture if the realized goals of internationalization are truly to be achieved. He identified some key barriers to this deeper form of internationalization, including too great an emphasis placed on personal relationships (*guanxi*) as a means to access research resources, too much emphasis on immediate results, and plagiarism.

Academic Quality

Across all four institutions, faculty generally saw increased support from the national government as a source for strengthening academic programs, particularly in terms of enhancing teaching practices and strengthening the overall student experience. Teaching was seen to be improved as a consequence of numerous opportunities for Chinese faculty to go abroad and observe foreign teaching practices and also in terms of equipment upgrades to classroom facilities (as noted in the preceding subsection focused on infrastructure). Increased funding from the national government enabled many departments to create additional opportunities for student engagement, including greater opportunities to gain research experience and acquire research-related skills. Many departments at Minzu could include larger and larger numbers of students in faculty research projects involving extensive field work. This form of achievement by the four universities in this study is consistent with the stress placed on "talent cultivation" by the Chinese government and enacted through its highly funded national initiatives.

Faculty Promotion Processes

At all four universities, faculty consistently spoke of efforts in more recent years to formalize faculty promotion processes while elevating the basic standards for research and publishing (aspects of this were noted in the subsection on scholarly productivity). Many of the changes are linked to tensions at Peking University in the late 1990s and early 2000s, when a culture war of sorts occurred with regard to administrative-led efforts to challenge the nature of academic life, criticized by some as offering faculty members excessive security and expecting too little in return. Some described Chinese faculty life pejoratively as providing an "iron rice bowl"—or *tie fan wan* in Chinese. As we note in chapter 2, such efforts met great resistance on the part of the faculty, but nonetheless significant reform initiatives were passed. These reforms seem to have been critical to altering basic understandings and expectations about the nature of faculty work and workload. Although we interpret these changes largely as achievements, under the premise that clear and more formalized personnel policies are an improvement over ambiguous and unclear ones, many of the faculty members with whom we spoke were not convinced that the changes were necessarily positive (we discuss some related issues later in this chapter when we address the challenges that lie ahead for China's top universities).

From the perspective of building top research universities, it is fairly obvious to us that raising standards for the quality and quantity of research produced by faculty members is a necessity. Without faculty actually altering their day-to-day work activities—and giving greater time and energy to their research—it is hard to imagine the funds from Projects 211 and 985 actually achieving their intended purpose. From this perspective, changes in the faculty personnel policies may be understood in part as an attempt to alter the basic norms of faculty life at the nation's leading universities toward the goal of building truly world-class universities. Based on our discussions with faculty at the four universities in question, changes in faculty personnel policies and practices have in fact elevated faculty research performance.

Faculty Recruitment Practices

Related to the preceding changes, and also reflective of the debates taking place at Peking University involving reform of the academic personnel system, several changes were enacted to formalize faculty recruitment processes. New expectations relating to faculty recruitment included developing more formalized application plans when seeking additional faculty, advertising faculty openings in appropriate public venues, organizing working committees to review candidates, requiring campus visits by leading candidates, and generating a final report to recommend selecting a particular candidate. These new procedures were to challenge longstanding patterns of making hires on the basis of personal connections and ties. Although changes in faculty recruitment and hiring practices initially only applied to Peking University, such changes soon followed at many other universities throughout China, including the other three universities that are part of our study. As a result of more formalized recruitment and hiring practices, combined with an emphasis on internationalization, top universities throughout China increasingly seek to recruit candidates earning their PhD abroad, such as from OECD (the Organisation for Economic Co-Operation and Development) countries.

The preceding eight areas reflect some of the key improvements we uncovered as part of our case study inquiry. Obviously, the Chinese university—as reflected by the four key institutions included in our study—has made significant progress since the mid-1990s. However, institutional change, particularly with regard to academic organizations, can move slowly, and challenges still await the Chinese university and the national quest for world-class standing. Accordingly, in the following section we delineate and discuss some of the most significant challenges that lie ahead.

The Quest Continues: Additional Challenges

The preceding section delineated some of the more positive changes as perceived by the faculty members in our study. In this section, we turn our attention to various challenges faculty pointed to as part of the quest to strengthen the nation's top universities. Although most of the faculty comments were made in the context of discussing their own university, many also referenced the broader arena of higher education in China, specifically considering the nation's research universities and the push for world-class standing. Hence, many of the points we make here are likely to have relevance at other top Chinese universities, especially those included as part of Projects 211 and 985. We organize our discussion around the following seven key areas of concern: institutional autonomy, administrative transparency, diversified funding, faculty empowerment, faculty evaluation and assessment, ethnic affairs and diversity, and questions of colonialism.

Institutional Autonomy

One of the most commonly expressed concerns on the part of faculty related to their perception of the need for universities to have greater autonomy in institutional decision making, including those decisions pertaining to faculty life and work. Their concerns also were expressed relative to academic programs and administrative appointments, suggesting that universities should have greater authority to hire who they see fit (including university presidents), with less involvement from government agencies. Although governmental funding was welcomed, faculty generally saw too much governmental involvement as restrictive and potentially detrimental to the goal of building world-class universities. The general feeling was that if China wanted to truly develop universities comparable to the elite universities of the world, including the likes of Oxford,

Harvard, and Stanford, then Chinese universities should follow some of the administrative practices employed by such institutions. Not to do so means placing China's top universities at a competitive disadvantage.

Administrative Transparency

Another issue raised by faculty related to the lack of transparency of university administrative operations, including decision making and budgetary matters. Obtaining institutional information or data, including budget information, is not an easy task at Chinese universities. Information just does not flow freely. The serious challenge of obtaining institutional information is true not only for outsiders but even for professors working at a particular university. This, of course, contributes to levels of suspicion and mistrust, which may ultimately undermine efforts to elevate the operations of a university. An environment of guarded information does not seem conducive to furthering the development of universities as world-class enterprises. The restricted flow of information, including key institutional data, also places the Chinese research university at a distinct disadvantage when universities are compared across a variety of measures and categories, given that doubts may arise about the authenticity of the data when its collection and storage remain somewhat mysterious.

Diversified Funding

One issue that top Chinese universities likely will be confronted with is their present-day heavy reliance on government support. It is not clear to us whether the national government will be able to sustain such levels of support. Certainly when economic times are good, extensive support seems reasonable. But what is to come if the Chinese economy slows and revenues to the government decline? Will China face some of the same challenges that many national governments around the world are facing? One potential source of revenue—and likely an unpopular one among the nation's rising middle and upper classes—is the adoption of tuition policies that seek to collect a greater share of the costs from upper-income families. Another source of support that Chinese universities have begun to pursue aggressively in recent years is philanthropy. But efforts in this area could potentially be significantly enhanced if universities were to become more transparent about their financial operations, including opening up their budgets, thereby giving prospective philanthropists a greater sense that the money would be put to good use. At least one Chinese businessman, Zhang Lei, chose to pass on giving vast sums of money to Chinese universities and instead funded Yale University in the United States to the tune of 8.88 million USD (Ying 2010). Although Zhang attended Yale's School of Management as a graduate student, he attended Renmin University for his undergraduate studies.

Faculty Empowerment

Consistently, faculty spoke of a broad need to empower professors to a greater extent. The view expressed among many of the faculty in our study was that professors in China do not consistently experience levels of professional independence and autonomy that promote the most serious forms of scholarly engagement. Instead, faculty seemed to define their experiences as under the supervision of the university administration. To support their point of view, many faculty noted that even the positive changes that have come about as a consequence of national initiatives such as Projects 211 and 985, implemented largely through a strong university hierarchy, have more or less been thrust upon faculty members. Some even alluded to modest resistance to various initiatives to expand and strengthen research capacity, given that faculty generally felt somewhat voiceless throughout the reform process. For example, a minority of the faculty in our study seemed to disagree with efforts to elevate research and instead felt that their university ought to put greater stress on the teaching mission. These professors did not fully support the changes associated with building world-class universities.

Perhaps it is worth noting here that a cultural analysis of organizations and of organizational change, as we have stressed in our methodology, centers on the norms, values, and attitudes of key organizational actors—faculty members in the case of our study—and that altering such aspects of everyday culture is not necessarily accomplished through top-down, administratively directed strategies. From our perspective, true grassroots-based change is likely to result when faculty are empowered and engaged in everyday decision making. Reform efforts that take into account the empowerment of key organizational actors have a better chance of succeeding. Making tons of money available and then telling faculty to do more research may simply result in wasted spending; a number of resistant faculty members may simply present the appearance of engaging in more research. The building of a truly deep research culture must at least partially spring up from the everyday work and decisions of professors. Hence, our study suggests a real need to strengthen faculty voice and engagement in institutional decision making as a strategy to improve faculty empowerment.

In terms of some specific challenges relating to faculty empowerment, we see issues of academic freedom as critical. Concerns about academic freedom were raised by many faculty members, although more often than not these and related issues were mentioned in informal settings, as opposed to during the semistructured interviews. Several professors noted that limitations in the area of academic freedom posed one of the most significant barriers to the nation's leading universities joining the elite of the world, although many were also quick to point out that academic freedom had indeed improved over the last decade or so. Faculty specifically discussed limitations relative to their teaching and research. The extent and nature of the limitations, though, were not exactly clear and, in fact, were described by some as "ambiguous and inconsistent." Many examples of the confusing nature of academic freedom were noted, including the case of one social scientist who was able to empirically investigate a sensitive issue but then could not find a Chinese press to publish his work. It was also noted that issues related to academic freedom tended to limit the ability of China's leading universities to recruit top faculty worldwide.

Another issue relating to faculty empowerment concerned salaries. A large percentage of the faculty with whom we met raised concerns about the ability of Chinese faculty members to compete with scholars from the West, pointing to lower salaries and the reality that many Chinese professors had to take on extra work or additional positions to make ends meet. This seemed especially problematic for the faculty in our study, given the high cost of owning an apartment in Beijing. One particular strategy that was noted as a means for earning additional revenue was assuming extra teaching duties, sometimes with weekend training programs. As many professors noted, this seriously cut into their research activities.

A second salary issue related to perceived inequities in the salaries of foreign professors recruited to China. Some faculty noted that their foreign colleagues were being paid three to four times more than faculty in the same departments. This, as they pointed out, was not good for faculty morale.

Another faculty empowerment issue is teaching workload, particularly in terms of the number of courses typically taught per semester. Along these lines, faculty often discussed the challenge they faced in conducting empirical work in light of what they perceived as heavy teaching loads. The general feeling was that although the government had poured more and more money into the research enterprise, the teaching load had stayed relatively stable. Thus, as Chinese universities transitioned from teaching universities to research universities, the teaching load for faculty members tended to limit their time and energy for research. Combined with the aforementioned salary issues and the fact that extra teaching is sometimes taken on as a means to bolster income, this is particularly problematic to the goal of strengthening the research enterprise.

In addition to the teaching load, faculty also talked about the substantial amount of time they spent working with master's students on their theses. A few faculty members described advising some fifteen to twenty such students annually, spending innumerable hours working with students. Other faculty also noted that undergraduates in their senior year often complete a thesis, and this, too, takes up a good deal of advising time. And some noted that unlike at U.S. universities, Chinese professors generally do not get sabbaticals, paid leave, or teaching assistants.

One barrier to furthering faculty salaries is a relatively weak academic marketplace for professors in China, as noted during many of our conversations with professors. It is quite unusual for Chinese professors to move from one university to another. Most remain at the same institution throughout their lifetime, and while top Chinese universities such as Peking and Tsinghua have started offering large salaries to foreign star professors to lure them to China, national competition of a similar variety does not really exist. Personnel files largely are controlled by the government, making it difficult in most cases for professors to leave one university for another. And given that the government provides a large portion of university budgets, at least at the Project 985 universities, creating a national competition for faculty among the leading universities does not align well with the government's overall financial responsibilities.

An additional area of concern was the need to develop support structures for professors, especially at the more junior levels. Many reported high levels of stress and felt that the universities could do a better job of helping them to manage the growing demands that accompany the further development of universities as research enterprises. Faculty around the world, including in China, are largely socialized to the academic profession during their graduate studies, and in particular, as part of their doctoral studies. But the doctoral phase in China is relatively short, and the research training PhD candidates obtain is limited. In fact, this is one reason some top universities such as Peking have started to look to hire more faculty members holding foreign doctorates. Programs could be created to support the further development of research skills, methodological and theoretical understanding, grant writing techniques, and academic writing skills in junior faculty members. From a broader perspective, strengthening doctoral training throughout the nation seems necessary, and in fact, Peking recently moved from the normal three-year PhD to a four-year period of study.

Our findings also indicate that women faculty members are likely to face additional challenges in their roles as professors, and faculty development programs should serve the needs of this population in particular. As many of the women academics with whom we spoke noted, they often assume one or two additional jobs beyond their faculty workload: their work in managing their household and sometimes their role as a tutor for their child.

A final issue relating to faculty empowerment concerns the degree to which Chinese universities are prepared for the forms of academic citizenship most typically coinciding with faculty life at elite research universities around the world. Professors at such universities are afforded the highest levels of professional autonomy, given the tendency for many of them to be leaders in their fields. They also are more likely to have a strong sense of connection and obligation to their disciplines, sometimes more than to their home institutions. Scholars such as Burton Clark have written about this type of academic citizenship in terms of cosmopolitans versus locals, drawing on the early work of Alvin Gould-ner.[6] The key point is that such forms of academic citizenship may exist in oppo-sition to an administratively dominated university, wherein faculty may lack the degree of professional autonomy associated with more cosmopolitan forms of academic citizenship. Given the status of the Chinese professoriate as a managed body, it is conceivable that administrative restrictions on faculty activity could place faculty at a disadvantage in certain disciplinary circles and research-related activities. We are not suggesting that China does not already have cosmopolitan professors but rather asking whether the system of higher education—and most notably those universities striving for world-class standing—are prepared for greater and greater percentages of their professoriate operating in such a manner.

Faculty Evaluation and Assessment

A consistent concern voiced by faculty was that too much emphasis was placed on quantitative measures of scholarly production as opposed to a more serious assessment of the actual quality of publications. Several professors pointed out that an emphasis on quantity discouraged serious, long-term empirical work. Others noted that the quantitative focus also tended to encourage faculty to write more essay-style publications, which arguably are easier to produce than empirically based pieces. Although faculty generally saw the number of publica-tions as increasing, several professors expressed grave concerns about publica-tion quality. Several faculty members argued that the tendency to emphasize numbers was in part tied to the strong role senior administrators played in evaluating faculty productivity, hypothesizing that senior administrators lack-ing the necessary expertise to judge the merit of a particular publication would evaluate publications by their quantity. Accordingly, faculty believed that quali-fied scholars in the field ought to be more involved in the process of assessing faculty productivity. Along these lines, some faculty suggested that too many journal articles with faculty listed as first authors are likely written by their graduate students and that too many papers are simply literature reviews of research in the West.

Relating to issues of faculty evaluation and assessment were concerns about faculty peer review processes. For example, faculty consistently discussed the need to strengthen peer review systems, especially with regard to three particular aspects of scholarly life: the faculty promotion process, publishing in journals, and competing for funding opportunities. The preceding paragraph highlighted the major concern about faculty promotion, that too much emphasis was placed on quantity over quality. A second concern, though, was raised with regard to publishing in journals, where some faculty believed the process was too tied to a particular individual's reputation or institutional status. Some faculty pointed out the challenges junior faculty face in publishing and noted that often they have to add a senior scholar as a co-author in order to publish a particular article. This issue will not be addressed simply by peer review but rather by *blind* peer review and a more merit-based system for evaluating scholarship. A similar concern was raised with regard to competition for grants, where it seems too much emphasis presently is placed on building personal relationships (*guanxi*) or the stature and title of the faculty member submitting a grant proposal. Many faculty expressed that the actual quality of the proposed research ought to be the key.

Another key concern relating to faculty evaluation and assessment, especially noted by many junior faculty, involved a critique of what was often described as a "quota system." This phrase referenced changes to the academic personnel system by which the government sets limits on the number of full and associate professor positions within particular universities. These changes were adopted at many top universities following the personnel reform at Peking University in the early 2000s. Because the government is involved in determining the number of positions universities will have on an annual basis, not every faculty member who qualifies for a promotion to associate or full professor will in fact be promoted. This creates intense competition, as even faculty in the same department may be competing against one another for a single position. Faculty deemed the general competition among faculty members detrimental to the overall goals of the university and in opposition to other important societal and institutional values, such as collectivism. The quota system, since the allocations are made at the university level, also contributes to intense deliberations and politicking among the various schools and departments that must compete against one another to acquire various slots.

Another issue arising in discussions of faculty evaluation and assessment concerned the growing emphasis on income generation, or what some might refer to as academic capitalism. Several faculty, especially those operating in the social sciences and humanities, openly questioned the strong shift toward the marketization of research, particularly expressing concerns about the growing pressure on faculty to generate revenue in the form of grants and to engage in entrepreneurial activity. There was a sense, especially at Tsinghua, that hierarchies were being created among faculty working in more applied science areas, especially engineering, versus those working in less applied areas. More than a few alluded to the idea that some Chinese universities were starting to exhibit forms of academic capitalism that are resulting in a more hierarchical faculty structure—complete with "haves" and "have nots." Some expressed a strong desire to reject this facet of leading Western research universities. Such a situation was seen as alienating and marginalizing for faculty working in the social sciences and humanities and even for some in less applied areas of the natural or hard sciences.

An issue that arose mostly in the context of more informal settings was plagiarism, although there was a wide range of opinion about the degree to which it occurs among the Chinese professoriate. We mention plagiarism here, though, because in part it may be tied to the extreme pressure some Chinese faculty members feel to publish, as a consequence of the quantitative focus of personnel reviews and of limited positions at the associate and full professor levels due to the above-noted quota system. Faculty also raised concerns about student plagiarism. Some faculty members specifically pointed to the practice of students "pulling" text from the Internet and then turning it in as their own work—both at the undergraduate and graduate level. Several suggested that some of their colleagues tend to "look the other way" rather than dealing with the hassle of confronting students.

Ethnic Affairs and Diversity

Another issue that was not mentioned outside of Minzu University concerns the role top universities ought to play in promoting social equality, most notably in terms of the nation's ethnic diversity. Although quite obviously these issues are vital to the mission and educational activities of Minzu, it was quite rare for them to come up in our discussions with faculty at the other three universities. In this regard, it appears as though ethnic diversity issues relative to higher education access and participation are mostly compartmentalized at the *minzu* college and university system. This seems problematic given the leading role universities such as Peking, Renmin, and Tsinghua could play in influencing increased participation and academic success of the nation's minority populations, including their representation and participation in academic life as faculty and staff. This is not to suggest that the three aforementioned universities do not admit or support ethnic minority students, as in fact they do. However, there is a lack of visibility at these three leading universities of the overall research and social agenda that ethnic minority affairs encompasses. For example, when a foreign scholar specializing in the study of ethnic minority issues in education was suggested as a possible faculty candidate for an opening at one of the universities (which was seeking a foreign scholar), it was suggested that the person's research was more suitable for working at Minzu University. Research and service to ethnic minorities and to addressing social equality relative to the nation's ethnic diversity needs to go beyond simply the work and concern of the *minzu* colleges and universities. We find it more than disappointing that the global ranking schemes that are so much a part of framing what constitutes a world-class university in China and elsewhere completely ignore social justice issues such as those related to addressing ethnic or racial inequality.

Questions of Colonialism

We conclude with what is perhaps the most paradoxical issue of those highlighted in this concluding chapter—the reality that as China seeks to build stronger research universities it finds itself adopting policies and practices common to Western universities. A key point here is that the essence of the modern university model that has caught the attention of China's leaders is in effect a Western invention. As Chinese universities strive for elite standing as top research universities they find themselves subscribing to and adopting a whole host of Western academic norms and values. Hence, the paradoxical challenge concerns how to follow a model based on Western norms and ideals and yet at the same time retain one's own cultural distinctiveness. Some well-known scholars have questioned the degree to which Chinese universities are being colonized by the West. This is most obvious in some examples brought to our attention by several professors at Renmin University, who openly wondered how some scholarly practices—such as expecting Chinese scholars to publish in English in international journals, in accord with growing international standards—actually benefit China. A specific case in point was mentioned with regard to scholars working to address China's rural development problems. As one scholar pondered, how do scholars working in such areas help to address the nation's needs by publishing articles in English for an international audience? A second scholar, from Minzu University, noted that English is the only common subject of the written admissions exams for graduate studies.

The key point here is that compliance with international scholarly norms may not at times be in the best interest of China. One might question whether this is in fact an example of colonialism, given that China's leaders are making choices to move more and more into international arenas, such as in terms of academic science. But the reality is that the arena of academic science is increasingly a global one, framed to a great extent by leading Western universities and scientists. Participation necessarily involves a certain degree of compliance on the part of Chinese universities. This surely is a challenge that will be continually confronted in the coming years if not decades.

The challenges delineated in this chapter point to a host of issues that the nation's leading universities are likely to face as they continue their quest for world-class standing. The issues and related changes that arise will likely reveal a unique version of the modern-day research university. If the nation's top universities are to succeed, it is quite likely that a hybrid form of the modern research university will emerge, although only time will tell the degree to which such institutions are able to maintain elements of China's distinctive society and culture.

Final Thoughts: China's Era of Global Ambition

In early 2013, *University World News* reported that the Chinese and Egyptian governments were collaborating to establish the Egyptian Chinese University in Cairo. The university represents a partnership between Liaoning University, a

Project 211 university in the northeast city of Shenyang, and Egypt's International Education Institution. As Wagdy Sawahel noted, "It will have four faculties —economy and international trade, physical therapy, pharmacy technology and medicine, and engineering and technology—and will be home to a Confucius Institute that will promote the Chinese language and culture" (Sawahel 2013). The article went on to point out that China also had established universities in Vientiane, Laos, and Florence, Italy, and that a two-year MBA program was offered through Myanmar's Chinese Chamber of Commerce. These types of global endeavors may be seen as signposts for the nation's growing ambitions in the higher education arena.

China's higher education ambition is also revealed through the expansion of its Confucius Institutes. In a December 2012 article published with *China Daily*, it was noted that China had established more than four hundred Confucius Institutes in 108 countries and regions and more than five hundred Confucius Classrooms, adding up to six hundred thousand registered students (Qu, Zhao, and Cheng 2012). The article also noted that seventy of the world's top two hundred universities had opened Confucius Institutes and that there were more than four hundred universities in more than seventy countries on the waiting list to add such institutes. Many commentators in the Western world have described the growth of Confucius Institutes as an expression of China's rising status in the world and its efforts to employ soft power to advance its own culture and political agenda. For example, Jeffrey Gil noted that China's Ministry of Education points to Chinese language instruction as a critical tool in advancing the nation's interests, extracting the following passage from the Ministry's website: "Teaching Chinese as a foreign language (TCFL) is an integral part of China's reform and opening up drive. To promote TCFL is of strategic significance to popularize the Chinese language and culture throughout the world, to enhance the friendship and mutual understanding as well as the economic and cultural cooperation and exchanges between China and other countries around the world, and to elevate China's influence in the international community" (Gil 2008).

The fact that China has become a key player in the deployment of soft power through education was also noted at a panel discussion at the March 2013 British Council "Going Global" conference, wherein one participant posited, "The purpose of China investing so much money is to improve the image of China, globally, to help people understand China. . . . So obviously China has been very serious about using higher education to cultivate soft power" (Sharma 2013). This should not be taken as a criticism of the Chinese government, as most powerful nations around the world employ forms of soft power in such a manner. Indeed, organizations and programs such as the United Kingdom's British Council and the U.S. Fulbright Program, the latter sponsored by the U.S. Department of

State's Bureau of Educational and Cultural Affairs, may be interpreted as serving similar kinds of soft-power objectives. China has joined the world powers in terms of its resources and desire to use such forms of influence—and primarily in conjunction with higher education endeavors.

The rising status and potential global contributions of China's higher education institutions, most notably its leading universities, is also evident by the 2013 creation of a global network of research universities that includes the Association of American Universities (AAU), the League of European Research Universities (LERU), the Australian Group of Eight (Go8), and the China 9 League of leading universities (Maslen 2013). The China group is comprised of Fudan, Harbin Institute of Technology, Nanjing, Peking, Shanghai Jiao Tong, Tsinghua, University of Science and Technology of China, Xi'an Jiao Tong, and Zhejiang. These are the original nine universities first included as part of Project 985 funding, and "collectively, the nine absorb about 10 percent of China's R&D expenditures and generate more than 20 percent of the nation's output of journal articles" (Maslen 2013). The broad plan of the global network is for these leading research-intensive universities "to join forces to tackle what the groups see as the challenges facing research institutions around the world" (Maslen 2013). Again, our point is that China's leading universities are once more included among the most elite in the world. This further supports our claim that university reform in China is in the midst of a new era—the global ambition period.

We started this book by highlighting the present-day achievements and challenges confronting China and the expectations government leaders have that their universities will help to advance the nation's primary interests. We wrote about China's growing economic clout, evidenced by it surpassing Japan as the world's second-largest economy. We noted the nation's technological advances, such as development of the Chinese supercomputer in Tianjin and the Jinping Underground Laboratory in Sichuan province. We also pointed out that militarily speaking China was looking to assert itself in new ways, as evidenced by its advances in intercontinental ballistic and submarine-launched missiles, which have extended its ability to deliver nuclear warheads. We also turned to problems the nation faces, including concerns related to widespread environmental degradation and ethnic differences resulting in regional tensions. In regard to all of these advances and problems, the nation's universities are increasingly implicated, especially its top universities, such as those included in Projects 211 and 985.

In closing, we turn to another aspect of China's progress: its increasing deployment of soft power to advance the nation's interests. Here, too, its leading universities, and the nation's higher education system in general, are implicated. Examples of the intersection of China's soft power strategies with higher education include the expansion of China's higher education system abroad and the MoE efforts in support of Confucius Institutes around the world. These are further examples of what we sought to highlight throughout this book—that Chinese higher education has reached a new era in the reform and development of its universities. It is an era characterized by the modern-day zeitgeist of the nation, captured by its growing ambition to assert itself on a global stage. The present era of global vision obviously extends beyond the realm of higher education, but we have tried to remain focused on what we know and study, university life. Through in-depth case studies of four of the nation's leading universities—Tsinghua, Peking, Renmin, and Minzu—we have tried to capture important cultural facets of this new age of optimism and achievement in the nation's higher education trajectory. It is indeed an age of unquenchable global ambition.

NOTES

Introduction · *The Chinese University and the Quest for World-Class Standing*

1. Although China's university reform movement reflects powerful global trends, as well as national objectives to expand research capacity and advance internationalization, we contend that changes at the nation's top universities may be best examined and understood by employing a more localized and particularized focus, in a manner consistent with the way Rhoads and Xuehong Liang (2006) studied the influence of globalization on one university in southern China. Our thinking also builds on the work of Allan Luke and Carmen Luke (2000), who argued that the challenge of understanding complex global processes is often best met through an intense examination of more localized contexts.

2. Our understanding and use of case study methodology is informed by Robert Yin (1989).

3. The sampling of key sites for this study was informed by David Arnold's (1970) notion of dimensional sampling, wherein key variables are identified upfront and then respective sampling decisions are made to intentionally minimize or maximize variation. We selected Minzu, Peking, Renmin, and Tsinghua because they are all included in Projects 211 and 985 and thus represent a narrowly defined group of the nation's top universities; this serves to limit variability based on institutional status. Second, we selected the four universities on the basis of their diverse origins and missions, thus enabling us to observe changes across important institutional differences (a strategy to maximize variability). The uniqueness of each of the universities is highlighted in the case study chapters. Finally, we controlled geographic variability by selecting institutions in the same locale—Beijing. This was in keeping with our view that geographic differences might overly complicate our analysis and detract from potential findings (a strategy intended to minimize variability).

4. Our theoretical orientation favors a methodological approach stressing particularizability over generalizability; hence, our methodological goal is to provide rich description in terms of background and data, thus enabling readers to make judgments about the usefulness and applicability of the particular cases we present. Such a perspective is consistent with arguments advanced by Clifford Geertz (1973, 1983), which advocate the importance of thick description while grounding interpretive work in more localized contexts. Thus, for us, the beauty and relevance of social science is its potential to make sense of complex social phenomenon through a rich understanding of the details of lived experience.

5. See Clark (1970, 1972, 1983, 1987a, 1987b) and Tierney (1988a, 1988b, 1993).

6. We draw a great deal from the work on organizational culture. For example, key orga-

nizational theorists such as Gareth Morgan (1986), William Ouchi (1982), and Linda Smircich (1983) advanced organizational culture as a theoretical lens in the early 1980s, but its roots in the study of higher education can be traced back to the early work of Charles Percy (C. P.) Snow (1959) and his classic *The Two Cultures and the Scientific Revolution*, wherein he delineated the essential differences among faculty working in the sciences and those working in the humanities. For Snow, the "hard" quality of science was reflected in the stability (hardness) of the general theories and facts brought to bear on scientific concerns, while the humanities were termed "soft" because theories and opinions were often challenged and overturned (they were on soft ground, so to speak). Anthony Biglan (1973a, 1973b) later built on Snow's original idea of the two cultures, adding additional layers of complexity to the framework by including pure versus applied and life versus nonlife systems, thus creating a multidimensional model for considering the nature of scholarly work. In subsequent years, scholars such as Burton Clark (1970, 1972) took up the idea of academic culture, suggesting that universities as unique organizations reveal observable patterns reflected in common norms, values, and beliefs. To understand the nature of university life necessitated coming to terms with the complexities and subtleties of academic culture. For Clark, as for Tony Becher (1987, 1989), this required a focus on professors, given their key role in shaping the norms, values, and attitudes of particular colleges and universities. Others have followed the path paved by Snow and Clark, including William Tierney (1988a, 1988b). For example, Tierney and Rhoads (1993) furthered this line of inquiry by examining faculty socialization as a cultural process. Of course, viewing faculty life as a cultural experience has led many scholars working in this area to adopt methodologies consistent with the interpretive tradition in social science, often conducting institutional case studies.

7. The data collection phase of our project covered roughly a three-year period, from 2009 through 2011, with development of the written case studies mostly occurring in the latter months of 2011 and throughout 2012.

8. Over 70 semistructured interviews were conducted, with most lasting about one hour. The vast majority of these interviews were digitally recorded and transcribed verbatim. These interviews were conducted in either Chinese or English, typically depending on the preference of the interview subjects.

9. Throughout this book, we use the term *professor* in a generic sense, akin to the terms *faculty member* or *faculty*. To refer to the faculty rank of professor, we use the term *full professor* or the Chinese equivalent *zheng jiaoshou*.

10. Our first three periods of higher education development and reform reflect to a great extent Hayhoe's (1996) work in this area, but our thinking is also informed by additional key works, including that of Yeh (2000). The fourth stage—the era of global ambition—reflects our own take on recent developments in higher education reform in China.

11. Although in this book we often discuss national initiatives to *build* world-class research universities, it is the position of the authors of this book that China in fact already has several world-class universities, including at least two of the universities highlighted in this project: Peking University and Tsinghua University. Furthermore, and depending on how one defines *world-class*, other universities, such as Renmin University, have common features typically associated with world-class universities, including internationally regarded professors, high levels of internationalization, and expansive research capacity. Thus, from our perspective, national initiatives such as Project 985 may be more accurately described as seeking to build or further develop world-class universities.

12. See D. Chen (2004), Cheng (1995, 1999), Hayhoe (1995), F. Huang (2003, 2005), Mok (2003), Pretorius and Xue (2003), and R. Yang (2004).

13. For an earlier discussion of ideas associated with elite, mass, and universal academic systems, see Trow (1973).

14. Student enrollment data in China tends to include two general types of students: (1) students enrolled in regular college and university programs, who predominantly attend full-time, and (2) adult learners enrolled in specialized training programs, who tend to be part-time. The latter might be compared with U.S. community college–based training or certificate programs.

15. See chart for "School enrollment, tertiary (%)" (for China) at http://data.worldbank .org/indicator/SE.TER.ENRR.

16. See Rhoads (2011) for a deeper discussion of this entrepreneurial trend in the U.S. research university.

17. The Chinese term *minzu* is often translated as *nationality* in English, but *ethnic group* or *national ethnic group* is probably a better translation in terms of actual meaning and usage. For example, the Chinese government recognizes 56 ethnic groups (*minzu*), including the Han majority, but sees the nation as having only one nationality—Chinese. We discuss these matters extensively in the chapter about Minzu University.

18. See Liu and Zhou 2007; Liu, Wang, and Cheng 2011.

19. Data reported in this section come from the website of the Chinese Ministry of Education unless otherwise noted; MoE data may be accessed at www.moe.edu.cn/publicfiles/ business/htmlfiles/moe/moe_2792/index.html.

Chapter 1 · Tsinghua University and the Spirit of Innovation and Entrepreneurialism

1. For a detailed discussion of the circumstances surrounding China's overpayment to the United States, see Hunt (1972).

2. See Hu 2011; Y. Huang 2000, 2006; Miao 2010; Su 2001.

3. Our discussion of Southwest United University is informed by Israel (1998).

4. The total international student enrollment reported here differs from that reported earlier simply because the figure here also includes nonformalized student enrollment.

Chapter 2 · Peking University and the Pursuit of Academic Excellence the "Beida Way"

1. Comments as part of the 1931 inaugural speech of Qinghua University President Mei Yiqi. http://blog.renren.com/share/2059708302/527234781.

2. Faculty comments adapted from meeting minutes of the PKU Guanghua Business School on January 9, 2008.

3. These points derive from a document titled, "The Strategic Plan for Shaping a World-Class University from 1999–2015," obtained from the PKU Office of Planning and Policy Research.

4. A multitude of publications by Ka Ho Mok (1997a, 1997b, 1997c, 1999, 2000, 2001, 2002) address the marketization and commercialization of Chinese higher education.

5. The use of "all-tenure" is meant to convey the reality that Chinese faculty typically have career-long employment at their respective university as long as they meet the most basic

expectations. This does not amount to tenure as defined by U.S. university norms, which is also tied to the ideal of academic freedom, but it does reflect a measure of career security.

6. Speech by Min Weifang in September 2010 delivered before the PKU Graduate School of Education faculty.

Chapter 3 · *Internationalization of Academic Life and the Changing Face of Renmin University*

1. Portions of the findings presented in this chapter derive from an earlier publication of the same study: Robert A. Rhoads and Juan Hu. 2012. "The Internationalization of Faculty Life in China." *Asia Pacific Journal of Education* 32 (3): 351–365.

2. We want to acknowledge Dr. Hu Juan, executive dean of the School of Education and director of Renmin University's Higher Education Studies Office, and her staff for their support throughout our field work. Without their assistance, our data collection at Renmin would not have been so successful.

3. President Ji retired in 2011 and was replaced by Professor Chen Yulu.

4. These figures were provided by the Renmin Higher Education Studies Office (HESO).

5. Data reported to us by the Renmin Higher Education Studies Office.

6. *Renmin University of China Fact Book 2010.*

7. Based on data from the Renmin Higher Education Studies Office.

8. Based on data from the Renmin Higher Education Studies Office.

Chapter 4 · *China's Ethnic Diversity and the Critical Role of Minzu University*

1. Our understanding of China's preferential policies for higher education is informed by a combination of personal experience and the research literature, including the work of Rebecca Clothey (2005) and Barry Sautman (1998, 1999). There are several facets to China's preferential policies. One facet involves adding points to the overall *gaokao* (the national college entrance exam) score, but this practice only applies to certain ethnic minorities and then only under very particular conditions (e.g., such as in areas where the schools or the economy are less developed); a variation of this involves waiving the requirement of a minimum *gaokao* score or lowering the required score for certain ethnic minorities at particular universities or academic programs. A second facet of the preferential policies allows some ethnic minority students to take the *gaokao* in their native language, but these students typically must subsequently enroll at a *minzu* college or university, where they receive a special classification as *min kao min* students. This option only applies to groups having their own written language, such as many Kazakhs, Kirghiz, Koreans, Tibetans, Mongols, and Uyghurs, and is an important practice given that some of China's minority groups do not speak Mandarin Chinese as their first or primary language. A third aspect of the preferential policies involves Chinese universities setting aside a number of spots or quotas for students from certain ethnic areas, a practice sometimes followed for students from Tibet or Xinjiang. A fourth involves financial support for some ethnic minority students in the form of reduced or free tuition or stipends from the government. A fifth facet centers on the *minzu* colleges and universities offering preferential admission for large numbers of ethnic minority students.

2. The work of Mary Helen Brown and Jill McMillan (1991) was particularly helpful in our framing of "narratives of change."

3. See, for example, Harrell 1995a, 2001; He 2008; Kaup 2002; Mackerras 2004; Oakes 2000; Shih 2002.

4. For a discussion of ethnic minority migration patterns in China see Iredale, Bilik, Su, Guo, and Hoy 2001.

5. The Bai are one of the fifty-five official ethnic minority groups officially recognized by the Chinese government. They predominantly live in the southwest region of China, with the majority located in Yunnan Province.

6. June 4 is the date typically seen as the dramatic culmination of the 1989 Tiananmen Square protests, which were mostly led by university students from the Haidian District in Beijing.

7. Here, the faculty member references both the State Ethnic Affairs Commission and the Ministry of Education as having some involvement in the faculty promotion process. As we noted earlier, the national-level *minzu* universities have complex governance arrangements in that both of these agencies have some jurisdiction over university operations. Hence, Minzu University in Beijing reports to both of these governmental agencies, depending on the particular issue and its related funding source.

Conclusion · Achievements and Challenges in the Quest to Build Leading Universities

1. See "University of California Partners with Fudan University to Establish Center on China," http://ucsdnews.ucsd.edu/pressreleases; "McGill to expand ties with China's top university," http://www.mcgill.ca/research/node/42517; "Carnegie Mellon Partners with Sun Yat-sen University to Develop Graduate Engineering Degree Programs," www.cit.cmu.edu/media/press/2012/11_12_sysu.html.

2. The Mandarin term for China is *Zhongguo*, which may be translated as *middle* or *central nation* or *land*.

3. Here we refer to massive open online courses, or MOOCs for short; the madness to which we refer pertains to one university after another signing on to the MOOC movement without anyone knowing for sure whether revenue will flow or not.

4. "Why VU China Research Centre?" www.feweb.vu.nl/nl/afdelingen-en-instituten/management-en-organisatie/vcrc/index.asp.

5. See Kerr (1963) and Hayhoe (1995).

6. Clark (1987a), among others, applied Gouldner's (1957, 1958) distinction between cosmopolitans and locals as types of organizational roles to an examination of academic life and citizenship.

Adams, Jonathan, David Pendlebury, and Bob Stembridge. 2013. *Building Bricks: Exploring the Global Research and Innovation Impact of Brazil, Russia, India, China and South Korea.* Research report. New York: Thomson Reuters.

Altbach, Philip G. 2001. "Why Higher Education Is Not a Global Commodity." *Chronicle of Higher Education, The Chronicle Review* (11 May). http://chronicle.com/weekly/V47/i35/35 bo2001.htm.

———. 2003. "Globalization and the University: Myths and Realities in an Unequal World." *Current Issues in Catholic Higher Education* 23: 5–25.

———. 2004. "Globalisation and the University: Myths and Realities in an Unequal World." *Tertiary Education Management* 10: 3–25.

———. 2009. "Peripheries and Centers: Research Universities in Developing Countries." *Asia Pacific Education Review* 10: 15–27.

Altbach, Philip G., and Gerard A. Postiglione. 2012. "Hong Kong's Academic Advantage." *International Higher Education* 66: 22–27.

Altbach, Philip G., and Jamil Salmi, eds. 2011. *The Road to Academic Excellence: The Making of World-Class Research Universities.* Washington, DC: International Bank for Reconstruction and Development / The World Bank.

Altbach, Philip G., and Ulrich Teichler. 2001. "Internationalization and Exchanges in a Globalized University." *Journal of Studies in International Education* 5: 5–25.

Andreas, Joel. 2009. *Rise of the Red Engineers: The Cultural Revolution and the Origins of China's New Class.* Stanford, CA: Stanford University Press, 2009.

Arnold, David O. 1970. "Dimensional Sampling: An Approach for Studying a Small Number of Cases." *American Sociologist* 5: 147–150.

Bagilhole, Barbara. 2002. "Challenging Equal Opportunities: Changing and Adapting Male Hegemony in the Academy." *British Journal of Sociology of Education* 23 (1): 19–33.

———. 2007. "Challenging Women in the Male Academy: Thinking about Draining the Swamp." In *Challenges and Negotiations for Women in Higher Education,* edited by Pamela Cotterill, Sue Jackson, and Gayle Letherby, 21–32. Dordrecht, Netherlands: Springer.

Barboza, David. 2010. "China Passes Japan as Second-Largest Economy." *New York Times* (15 August). www.nytimes.com/2010/08/16/business/global/16yuan.html.

Becher, Tony. 1987. "The Disciplinary Shaping of the Profession." In *The Academic Profession: National, Disciplinary, and Institutional Settings,* edited by Burton R. Clark (pp. 271–303). Berkeley, CA: University of California Press.

————. 1989. *Academic Tribes and Territories: Intellectual Enquiry and the Cultures of Disciplines*. Bristol, PA: Open University Press.

Biglan, Anthony. 1973a. "The Characteristics of Subject Matter in Different Academic Areas." *Journal of Applied Psychology* 57 (3): 195–203.

————. 1973b. "Relationships between Subject Matter Characteristics and the Structure and Output of University Departments." *Journal of Applied Psychology* 57 (3): 204–213.

Bloemraad, Irene. 2007. "Unity in Diversity? Bridging Models of Multiculturalism and Immigrant Integration." *Du Bois Review* 4 (2): 317–336.

Bradsher, Keith. 2012. "China Is Said to Be Bolstering Missile Capabilities." *New York Times* (24 August). www.nytimes.com/2012/08/25/world/asia.

Brandenburg, Uwe, and Jiani Zhu. 2007. "Higher Education in China in Light of Massification and Demographic Change." Research Report. Gustersloh, Germany: Centre for Higher Education Development.

Branigan, Tania. 2009. "China Locks Down Western Province after Ethnic Riots Kill 140 People." *Guardian* (6 July). www.guardian.co.uk/world/2009/jul/06.

————. 2010. "China's Tianhe-1A Takes Supercomputer Crown from US." *Guardian* (28 October). www.guardian.co.uk/technology/2010/oct/28.

————. 2011. "Chinese Students Screened for 'Radical Thoughts' and 'Independent Lifestyles.'" *Guardian* (28 March). www.guardian.co.uk/world/2011/ mar/28.

Bresnahan, Timothy, and Alfonso Gambardella, eds. 2004. *Building High-Tech Clusters: Silicon Valley and Beyond*. Cambridge, UK: Cambridge University Press.

Bristow, Michael. 2011. "Chinese Premier Calls for Political Reform." *BBC News* (14 March). www.bbc.co.uk/news/world-asia-pacific-12729687.

Brown, Mary Helen, and Jill J. McMillan. 1991. "Culture as Text: The Development of an Organizational Narrative." *Southern Communication Journal* 57 (1): 49–60.

Calderone, Shannon, and Robert A. Rhoads. 2005. "The Mythology of the 'Disappearing Nation-State': A Case Study of Competitive Advantage through State-University Collaboration." *Education and Society* 23 (1): 5–23.

"Campus Collaboration." 2013. *Economist* (5 January). www.economist.com.

Cao, Cong. 2013. "Culture Change Needed to Counter Brain Drain." *University World News* (20 July). www.universityworldnews.com/article.php?story=20130719150700309.

Chao, Loretta. 2011. "China Media Push into the Web." *Wall Street Journal* (8 March). www .evri.com/media/article.

Chen, David Y. 2004. "China's Mass Higher Education: Problems, Analysis, and Solutions." *Asia Pacific Education Review* 5 (1): 23–33.

Chen, Jia. 2011. "Students Go Overseas in Record Numbers." *China Daily-USA* (18 April). http://usa.chinadaily.com.cn/china.

Chen, Terence. 2011. "The Scourge of Plagiarism in China." *Asia Sentinel* (29 April). www.irrawaddy.org/article.

Chen, Xiangming. 2003. "The Academic Profession in China." In *The Decline of the Guru: The Academic Profession in Developing and Middle-Income Countries*, edited by Philip G. Altbach, 107–134. New York: Palgrave Macmillan.

Cheng, Kai Ming. 1986. "China's Recent Education Reform: The Beginning of an Overhaul." *Comparative Education* 22 (3): 255–269.

————. 1995. "Education—Decentralization and the Market." In *Social Change and Social*

Policy in Contemporary China, edited by Linda Wong and Stewart MacPherson, 70–87. Aldershot, England: Avebury.

———. 1999. "Education and Market: How Could It Be Different and What Is New?" *Current Issues in Comparative Education* 1 (2): 73–81. www.tc.columbia.edu/cice.

"China Lacks Global Top-Ranking Universities, Says Academic." 2010. *People's Daily Online* (16 April). http://english.people.com.cn/90000l/90782/90873/6953072.html.

"China's Amazing Half-Century: The 50 Places that Define Modern China." 1999. *TIME Asia* (27 September). www.cnn.com/ASIANOW/time/magazine/99/0927.

Chow, Tse-tsung (also Zhou Cezong). 1960. *The May Fourth Movement: Intellectual Revolution in Modern China*. Cambridge, MA: Harvard University Press.

Clark, Burton R. 1970. *The Distinctive College: Antioch, Reed and Swarthmore*. Chicago, IL: Aldine.

———. 1972. "The Organizational Saga in Higher Education." *Administrative Science Quarterly* 17: 178–184.

———. 1983. *The Higher Education System: Academic Organization in Cross-National Perspective*. Berkeley, CA: University of California Press.

———. 1987a. *The Academic Life: Small Worlds, Different Worlds*. Princeton, NJ: Carnegie Foundation for the Advancement of Teaching.

———, ed. 1987b. *The Academic Profession*. Berkeley, CA: University of California Press.

Clothey, Rebecca. 2005. "China's Policies for Minority Nationalities in Higher Education: Negotiating National Values and Ethnic Identities." *Comparative Education Review* 49 (3): 389–409.

Collins, Christopher S., and Robert A. Rhoads. 2010. "The World Bank, Support for Universities, and Asymmetrical Power Relations in International Development." *Higher Education* 59: 181–205.

"Confucius Makes a Comeback." 2007. *Economist* (17 May). www.economist.com/node/920 2957?story_id=9202957.

"Dangerous Shoals." 2013. *Economist* (19 January). www.economist.com/news/ leaders.

Dasgupta, Saibal. 2011. "China Student Poses Nude for Fees, Sparks Row." *Times of India* (18 January). http://findarticles.com/p/news-articles/times-of-india-the/mi_8012/is_20110118 /china-student-poses-nude-fees/ai_n56693090/

Denzin, Norman K. 1989. *The Research Act*, 3rd ed. New York: Prentice-Hall.

DesRoches, Catherine M., Darren E. Zinner, R. Rao Sowmya, Lisa I. Iezzoni, and Eric G. Campbell. 2010. "Activities, Productivity, and Compensation of Men and Women in the Life Sciences." *Academic Medicine* 85 (4): 631–639.

De Wit, Hans. 2011. "Misconceptions about Internationalisation." *University World News* 166 (10 April). www.universityworldnews.com/article.php?story=20110408181353543.

DiMaggio, Paul J., and Walter W. Powell. 1983. "The Iron Cage Revisited: Institutional Isomorphism and Collective Rationality in Organizational Fields." *American Sociological Review* 48 (2): 147–160.

Erlanger, Steven. 1998. "U.S. Reports China Has Agreed to Free Tiananmen Leader." *New York Times* (2 April). www.nytimes.com/1998/04/02/world.

Etzkowitz, Henry, and Andrew Webster. 1998. "Entrepreneurial Science: The Second Academic Revolution." In *Capitalizing Knowledge: New Interactions of Industry and Academia*, edited by Henry Etzkowitz, Andrew Webster, and Peter Healy, 21–46. Albany, NY: SUNY Press.

Fei, Xiaotong. 1980. "Ethnic Identification in China." *Social Sciences in China* 1: 94–107.

———. 1989. "Zhongguo Minzu de Duoyuan Yiti Geju" ("The Pattern of Unified Diversity among China's Nationalities"). *Beijing Daxue Xuebao (Journal of Beijing University)* 4: 1–19.

———. 1992. *From the Soil: The Foundations of Chinese Society* (a translation of Fei Xiaotong's *Xiangtu Zhongguo*). Berkeley, CA: University of California Press.

Friedman, Peter. 2010. "China's Plagiarism Problem." *Forbes.com* (26 May). www. forbes.com/2010/05/26/china-cheating-innovation-markets-economy-plagiarism.html.

Froumin, Isak. 2011. "Establishing a New Research University: The Higher School of Economics, the Russian Federation." In *The Road to Academic Excellence: The Making of World-Class Research Universities*, edited by Philip G. Altbach and Jamil Salmi, 293–319. Washington, DC: International Bank for Reconstruction and Development / The World Bank.

Gan, Yang, and Meng Li. 2004. *Zhongguo Daxue Gaige Zhidao (A Road to Chinese University Reform)*. Shanghai: Shanghai People's Publishing House.

Geertz, Clifford. 1973. *The Interpretation of Cultures.* New York: Basic Books.

———. 1983. *Local Knowledge: Further Essays in Interpretive Anthropology.* New York: Basic Books.

Gil, Jeffrey. 2008. "The Promotion of Chinese Language Learning and China's Soft Power." *Asian Social Science* 4 (10): 116–122.

Gladney, Dru C. 2004. "Ethnic Identity in China: The Rising Politics of Cultural Difference." In *Democratization and Identity: Regimes and Ethnicity in East and Southeast Asia*, edited by Susan J. Henders, 133–152. Lanham, MD: Lexington Books.

Gouldner, Alvin W. 1957. "Cosmopolitans and Locals: Toward an Analysis of Latent Social Roles." *Administrative Science Quarterly* 2 (3): 281–306.

———. 1958. "Cosmopolitans and Locals: Toward an Analysis of Latent Social Roles—II." *Administrative Science Quarterly* 2 (4): 444–481.

Gregory, Sheila T. 2006. "The Cultural Constructs of Race, Gender and Class: A Study of How Afro-Caribbean Women Academics Negotiate Their Careers." *International Journal of Qualitative Studies in Education* 19 (3): 347–366.

Hansen, Metta Halskov. 1999. *Lessons in Being Chinese: Minority Education and Ethnic Identity in Southwest China.* Seattle, WA: University of Washington Press.

Harrell, Stevan, ed. 1995a. *Cultural Encounters on China's Ethnic Frontier.* Seattle, WA: University of Washington Press.

———. 1995b. "Introduction: Civilizing Projects and Reactions to Them." In *Cultural Encounters on China's Ethnic Frontier*, edited by Stevan Harrell, 3–36. Seattle, WA: University of Washington Press.

———. 2001. *Ways of Being Ethnic in Southwest China.* Seattle, WA: University of Washington Press.

Harvey, David. 2003. *The New Imperialism.* Oxford: Oxford University Press.

Hayhoe, Ruth. 1989. *China's Universities and the Open Door.* Armonk, NY: M. E. Sharp.

———. 1995. "An Asian Multiversity? Comparative Reflections on the Transition to Mass Higher Education in East Asia." *Comparative Education Review* 39 (3): 299–321.

———. 1996. *China's Universities 1895–1995: A Century of Cultural Conflict.* New York: Garland.

———. 2005. "Peking University and the Spirit of Chinese Scholarship." *Comparative Education Review* 49 (4): 575–583.

Hayhoe, Ruth, Jun Li, Jing Lin, and Qiang Zha. 2011. *Portraits of 21st Century Chinese Universities: In the Move to Mass Higher Education.* Hong Kong: Comparative Education Research Center / Hong Kong University Press.

He, Yue. 2008. "Regionalism and Cross-Border Ethnicalism: On the Cross-Border Ethnicalism in the Border Region of Southwest China." *Journal of Yunnan Nationalities University: Social Sciences* 1: 11–16.

Hickman, Leo. 2011. "China's Coal Reserves 'Will Make It New Middle East', Says Energy Chief." *Guardian* (8 March). www.guardian.co.uk/environment/2011/mar/08/china-coal -new-middle-east.

Hilton, Isabel. 2011. "Under This Surreal 'Rule by Law', Ai Weiwei Is Guilty." *Guardian* (8 April), 36.

Hinton, William. 1972. *Hundred Day War: The Cultural Revolution at Tsinghua University.* New York: Monthly Review Press.

Hu, Xianzhang. 2011. *Shuimu Qinghua, Renwen Rixin (A Century at Tsinghua of Reviving Humanism).* Beijing: Tsinghua University Press.

"Hu Calls for Harmony amid Spread of Jasmine Revolution." 2011. *Want China Times* (20 February). www.wantchinatimes.com/news-subclass-cnt.aspx?id=20110220000018&cid=1101.

Huang, Futao. 2003. "Policy and Practice of the Internationalization of Higher Education in China." *Journal of Studies in International Education* 7 (3): 225–240.

———. 2005. "Qualitative Enhancement and Quantitative Growth: Changes and Trends of China's Higher Education." *Higher Education Policy* 18 (2): 117–130.

Huang, Yanfu. 2000. *Er San Shi Niandai de Qinghua Xiaoyuan Wenhua (Tsinghua Campus Culture in the 1920s and 1930s).* Guilin, Guangxi: Guangxi Normal University Press.

———. 2006. *Qinghua Chuantong Jingshen (Tsinghua Traditional Spirit).* Beijing: Tsinghua University Press.

Huang, Zhixun. 1986. "Xi Nan Lian Daxue yu Zhongguo de Ziran Kexuejia" ("South-West United University and China's Natural Scientists"). *Baike Zhishi (Encyclopedia of Knowledge)* 7: 7–9.

Hunt, Michael H. 1972. "The American Remission of the Boxer Indemnity: A Reappraisal." *Journal of Asian Studies* 31 (3): 539–559.

Hvistendahl, Mara. 2009. "China: Attract Talent First, and Outstanding Universities Will Follow." *Chronicle of Higher Education* (5 October). http://chronicle.com/article/China -Attract-Talent-First/48684.

Iredale, Robyn, Naran Bilik, Wang Su, Fei Guo, and Caroline Hoy. 2001. *Contemporary Minority Migration, Education and Ethnicity in China.* Glos, UK: Edward Elgar Publishing.

Ismail, Maimunah, and Roziah Mohd Rasdi. 2006. "High-Flying Women Academics: A Study at Selected Universities in Malaysia." *Asia Pacific Journal of Education* 26 (2): 155–171.

Israel, John. 1998. *Lianda: A Chinese University in War and Revolution.* Stanford, CA: Stanford University Press.

Jackson, Ben. 2010. "Chimneys of Hell." *Sun* (6 November). www.thesun.co.uk/sol/ home page/news/Green/3214555/Worlds-most-polluted-cities.html.

Jacques, Martin. 2009. *When China Rules the World: The End of the Western World and the Birth of a New Global Order.* New York: Penguin Books.

Jencks, Christopher, and David Riesman. 1969. *The Academic Revolution.* Garden City, NY: Doubleday.

Johnson, Ian, and Thom Shanker. 2012. "Beijing Mixes Messages over Anti-Japan Protests." *New York Times* (16 September). www.nytimes.com/2012/09/17/world/asia.

Jones, Jennifer M., and Frances H. Lovejoy. 1980. "Discrimination against Women Academics in Australian Universities." *Signs: Journal of Women in Culture and Society* 5 (3): 518–526.

Kaup, Katherine Palmer. 2002. "Regionalism versus Ethnicnationalism in the People's Republic of China." *China Quarterly* 172: 863–884.

Kerr, Clark. 1963. *The Uses of the University*. Cambridge, MA: Harvard University Press.

Kirk, Kate, and Charles Cotton. 2012. *The Cambridge Phenomenon: 50 Years of Innovation and Enterprise*. London: Third Millennium Information.

Knight, Jane. 2004. "Internationalization Remodeled: Definition, Approaches, and Rationale." *Journal of Studies in International Education* 8 (1): 5–31.

LaFraniere, Sharon. 2010. "Fighting Trend, China Is Luring Scientists Home." *New York Times* (6 January). www.nytimes.com/2010/01/07/world/asia.

Leibold, James. 2010. "The Beijing Olympics and China's Conflicted National Form." *China Journal* 63: 1–24.

Levin, John S. 1999. "Missions and Structures: Bringing Clarity to Perceptions about Globalization and Higher Education in Canada." *Higher Education* 37 (4): 377–399.

Li, Jiao. 2011. "World's Deepest Lab to Hunt Dark Matter." *IOP Asia-Pacific* (7 September). http://asia.iop.org/cws/article/news/47110.

Lin, Xiaoqinq Diana. 2005. *Peking University: Chinese Scholarship and Intellectuals, 1898–1937*. Albany, NY: SUNY Press.

Liu, Niancai, Qi Wang, and Ying Cheng, eds. 2011. *Paths to a World-Class University: Lessons from Practices and Experiences*. Rotterdam: Sense Publishers.

Liu, Niancai, and Ling Zhou. 2007. *Mianxiang Chuangxinxing Guojia de Yanjiuxing Daxue Jianshe Yanjiu (Building Research Universities for Achieving the Goal of an Innovative Country)*. Beijing: Renmin University Press.

Long, Xicheng. 2004. "Xu Zhihong: We Must Reform but Should Remain Steady as We Advance." *Chinese Education and Society* 37 (6): 48–54.

Luke, Allan, and Carmen Luke. 2000. "A Situated Perspective on Cultural Globalization." In *Globalization and Education: Critical Perspectives*, edited by Nicholas C. Burbules and Carlos Alberto Torres, 275–297. New York: Routledge.

Ma, Rong. 2004. "Guanyu Minzu Yanjiu de Ji ge Wenti" ("Some Issues about the Research of Nationality Groups"). *Beijing Daxue Xuebao (Beijing University Journal)* 4: 132–143.

———. 2007a. "Bilingual Education for China's Ethnic Minorities." *Chinese Education and Society* 40 (2): 9–25.

———. 2007b. "A New Perspective in Guiding Ethnic Relations in the Twenty-First Century: 'De-Politicization' of Ethnicity in China." *Asian Ethnicity* 8 (3): 199–217.

———. 2010. "The 'Politicization' and 'Culturization' of Ethnic Groups." *Chinese Sociology and Anthropology* 42 (4): 31–45.

Mackerras, Colin. 1994. *China's Minorities: Integration and Modernization in the Twentieth Century*. New York: Oxford University Press.

———. 2004. "Ethnicity in China: The Case of Xinjiang." *Harvard Asia Quarterly* 8 (1): 4–14.

Marginson, Simon. 1995. "Markets in Higher Education: Australia." In *Academic Work: The Changing Labour Process in Higher Education*, edited by John Smyth, 17–39. London: Open University Press, 1995.

———. 2006. "Dynamics of National and Global Competition in Higher Education." *Higher Education: The International Journal of Higher Education and Educational Planning* 52: 1–39.

———. 2010a. "The Rise of the Global University: 5 New Tensions." *The Chronicle of Higher Education* (30 May). http://chronicle.com.

———. 2010b. "World Potential." Keynote speech given at the Going Global Conference, March 25, London.

Marginson, Simon, and Mark Considine. 2000. *The Enterprise University: Power, Governance, and Reinvention in Australia*. Cambridge, UK: Cambridge University Press.

Marginson, Simon, and Marijk C. van der Wende. 2007. "To Rank or to Be Ranked: The Impact of Global Rankings in Higher Education." *Journal of Studies in International Education* 11 (3/4): 306–329.

Marshall, Jane. 2011. "Global: UNESCO Debates Uses and Misuses of Rankings." *University World News* (22 May). www.universityworldnews.com/article.php?story=20110521105752138.

Maslen, Geoff. 2013. "Research Universities to Establish Global Network." *University World News* (21 March). www.universityworldnews.com/article.

Meredith, Robyn. 2007. *The Elephant and the Dragon: The Rise of India and China and What It Means for All of Us*. New York: W.W. Norton.

McCurry, Justin, and Julia Kollewe. 2011. "China Overtakes Japan as World's Second-Largest Economy." *Guardian* (14 February). www.theguardian.com/business/2011/feb/14/china-second-largest-economy.

Miao, Li-xin. 2010. *Investigation of Xichun Park and Tsinghua Park (Xichun Yuan Qinghua Yuan Kao)*. Beijing: Tsinghua University Press.

Min, Weifang. 2004. "Chinese Higher Education: The Legacy of the Past and the Context of the Future." In *Asian Universities: Historical Perspectives and Contemporary Challenges*, edited by Phillip G. Altbach and Toru Umakoshi, 53–84. Baltimore, MD: Johns Hopkins University Press.

Mohrman, Kathryn. 2008. "The Emerging Global Model with Chinese Characteristics." *Higher Education Policy* 21: 29–48.

Mohrman, Kathryn, Yiqun Geng, and Yingjie Wang. 2011. "Faculty Life in China." In *The NEA 2011 Almanac of Higher Education*, edited by the National Education Association, 83–99. Washington, DC: National Education Association.

Mohrman, Kathryn, Wanhua Ma, and David Baker. 2008. "The Research University in Transition: The Emerging Global Model." *Higher Education Policy* 21: 5–27.

Mok, Ka Ho. 1997a. "Private Challenges to Public Dominance: The Resurgence of Private Education in the Pearl River Delta." *Comparative Education* 33 (1): 43–60.

———. 1997b. "Privatization or Marketization: Educational Development in Post-Mao China." *International Review of Education* 43 (5–6): 547–567.

———. 1997c. "Retreat of the State: Marketization of Education in the Pearl River Delta." *Comparative Education Review* 41 (3): 260–276.

———. 1999. "Education and the Market Place in Hong Kong and Mainland China." *Higher Education* 37 (2): 133–158.

———. 2000. "Marketizing Higher Education in Post-Mao China." *International Journal of Educational Development* 20 (2): 109–126.

———. 2001. "From State Control to Governance: Policy of Decentralization and Higher Education in Guangdong." *International Education Review* 47 (1): 123–149.

————. 2002. "Policy of Decentralization and Changing Governance of Higher Education in Post-Mao China." *Public Administration and Development* 22: 261–273.

————. 2003. "Globalisation and Higher Education Restructuring in Hong Kong, Taiwan, and Mainland China." *Higher Education Research & Development* 22 (2): 117–129.

————. 2005a. "Globalization and Educational Restructuring: University Merging and Changing Governance in China." *Higher Education* 50 (1): 57–88.

————. 2005b. "Riding over Socialism and Global Capitalism: Changing Education Governance and Social Policy Paradigms in Post-Mao China." *Comparative Education* 41 (2): 217–242.

————. 2007. "Questing for Internationalization of Universities in Asia: Critical Reflections." *Journal of International Studies in Education* 11 (3/4): 433–454.

Mok, Ka Ho, and Yat Wai Lo. 2007. "The Impacts of Neoliberalism on China's Higher Education." *Journal for Critical Education Policy Studies* 5 (1). www.jceps.com/index.php?p/ageID=article&articleID=93.

Moore, Gordan, and Kevin Davis. 2004. "Learning the Silicon Valley Way." In *Building High-Tech Clusters: Silicon Valley and Beyond*, edited by Timothy Bresnahan and Alfonso Gambardella, 7–39. Cambridge, UK: Cambridge University Press.

Morgan, Gareth. 1986. *Images of Organizations*. Beverly Hills, CA: Sage.

Normile, Dennis. 2001a. "Women Academics Propose Steps to Equity." *Science* 292 (5516): 416.

————. 2001b. "Women Faculty Battle Japan's Koza System." *Science* 291 (5505): 817–818.

————. 2009. "Chinese Scientists Hope to Make Deepest, Darkest Dreams Come True." *Science* 324 (5932): 1246–1247.

Nye, Joseph. 2011. "Viewpoint: China's Hubris Colours US Relations." *BBC News* (18 January). www.evri.com/media/article?title=Power+slide?&page=.

Oakes, Tim. 2000. "China's Provincial Identities: Reviving Regionalism and Reinventing 'Chineseness.'" *Journal of Asian Studies* 59 (3): 667–692.

Ouchi, William G. 1982. *Theory Z*. New York: Avon Books.

Ozkanli, Ozlem, and Kate White. 2008. "Leadership and Strategic Choices: Female Professors in Australia and Turkey." *Journal of Higher Education Policy and Management* 30 (1): 53–63.

Pan, Su-Yan. 2007. "Intertwining of Academia and Officialdom and University Autonomy: Experience from Tsinghua University in China." *Higher Education Policy* 20: 121–144.

Perlez, Jane. 2012a. "Close Army Ties of China's New Leader Could Test the U.S." *New York Times* (3 November). www.nytimes.com/2012/11/04/world/asia.

————. 2012b. "Dispute Flares over Energy in South China Sea." *New York Times* (4 December). www.nytimes.com/2012/12/05/world/asia.

Peters, Michael A., and Tina A. C. Besley. 2006. *Building Knowledge Cultures: Education and Development in the Age of Knowledge Capitalism*. London: Rowman & Littlefield.

Postiglione, Gerard. 2009. "The Education of Ethnic Minority Groups in China." In *The Routledge International Companion to Multicultural Education*, edited by James Banks, 501–511. New York: Routledge.

Pretorius, S. G., and Yang Qing Xue. 2003. "The Transition from Elite to Mass Higher Education: A Chinese Perspective." *Prospects* XXXIII (1): 89–101.

Probert, Belinda. 2005. "'I Just Couldn't Fit In': Gender and Unequal Outcomes in Academic Careers." *Gender, Work and Organisation* 12 (1): 50–72.

Qiu, Jane. 2009. "China Targets Top Talent from Overseas." *Nature* 457: 522.

Qu, Yingpu, Huanxin Zhao, and Yingqi Cheng. 2012. "Confucius Institutes Go beyond Borders." *China Daily* (2 December). www.chinadaily.com.

Rampell, Catherine. 2012. "Putting China's Economic Power in Perspective." *New York Times* (15 June). http://economix.blogs.nytimes.com/2012/06/15.

Rhee, Byung Shik. 2011. "A World-Class Research University on the Periphery: The Pohang University of Science and Technology, the Republic of Korea." In *The Road to Academic Excellence: The Making of World-Class Research Universities*, edited by Philip G. Altbach and Jamil Salmi, 101–128. Washington, DC: International Bank for Reconstruction and Development/The World Bank.

Rhoads, Robert A. 2011. "The U.S. Research University as a Global Model: Some Fundamental Problems to Consider." *InterActions* 7 (2): art. 4. http:// escholarship.org/uc/item/8b91s24r.

Rhoads, Robert A., and Juan Hu. 2012. "The Internationalization of Faculty Life in China." *Asia Pacific Journal of Education* 32 (3): 351–365.

Rhoads, Robert A., and Xuehong Liang. 2006. "Global Influences and Local Responses at Guangdong University of Foreign Studies." *World Studies in Education* 7 (2): 23–53.

Rhoads, Robert A., and Amy Liu. 2009. "Globalization, Social Movements, and the American University: Implications for Research and Practice." *Higher Education: Handbook of Theory and Practice* XXIV: 277–320.

Rhoads, Robert A., and Katalin Szelényi. 2009. "Globally Engaged Universities: The Changing Context of Academic Citizenship." *Education and Society* 27 (2): 5–26.

———. 2011. *Global Citizenship and the University: Advancing Social Life and Relations in an Interdependent World*. Stanford, CA: Stanford University Press.

Rhoads, Robert A., and Carlos Alberto Torres, eds. 2006. *The University, State, and Market: The Political Economy of Globalization in the Americas*. Stanford, CA: Stanford University Press.

Rizvi, Faval. 2006. "The Ideology of Privatization in Higher Education: A Global Perspective." In *Privatization and Public Universities*, edited by Douglas M. Priest and Edward P. St. John, 65–85. Bloomington: Indiana University Press.

Ross, Heidi A. 1993. *China Learns English: Language Teaching and Social Change in the People's Republic of China*. New Haven, CT: Yale University Press.

Rupesinghe, Kumar, Peter King, and Olga Vorkunova, eds. 1992. *Ethnicity and Conflict in a Post-Communist World: The Soviet Union, Eastern Europe, and China*. New York: St. Martin's Press.

Said, Edward W. 1993. *Culture and Imperialism*. New York: Vintage Books.

Salmi, Jamil. 2009. *The Challenge of Establishing World-Class Universities*. New York: International Bank for Reconstruction and Development/The World Bank.

Santos, Boaventura de Sousa. 2006. "The University in the 21st Century: Toward a Democratic and Emancipatory University Reform." In *The University, State, and Market: The Political Economy of Globalization in the Americas*, edited by Robert A. Rhoads and Carlos Alberto Torres, 60–100. Stanford, CA: Stanford University Press.

Sautman, Barry. 1998. "Affirmative Action, Ethnic Minorities and China's Universities." *Pacific Rim Law and Policy Journal* 7 (1): 77–116.

———. 1999. "Expanding Access to Higher Education for China's National Minorities: Policies of Preferential Admission." In *China's National Minority Education: Culture, Schooling, and Development*, edited by Gerard A. Postiglione, 173–210. New York: Falmer.

Sawahel, Wagdy. 2013. "Presidential Decree Creates First Chinese University." *University World News* (5 March). www.universityworldnews.com.

Saxenian, AnnaLee. 1996. *Regional Advantage: Culture and Competition in Silicon Valley and Route 128*. Cambridge, MA: Harvard University Press.

Scrutton, Alistair, and Chris Buckley. 2011. "Emerging Powers Join in Opposition over Libya Air Strikes." *Reuters* (22 March). www.evri.com/media/article.

Shanker, Thom, and Ian Johnson. 2012. "U.S. Accord with Japan over Missile Defense Draws Criticism in China." *New York Times* (17 September). www.nytimes.com/ 2012/09/18/world/asia.

Sharma, Yojana. 2011. "CHINA: Premiere in Surprise Visit to UK Branch Campus." *University World News* (24 April). www.universityworldnews.com/article.php?story=2011042120 3104837.

———. 2013. "Higher Education as Soft Power in the Age of Autonomy." *University World News* (8 March). www.universityworldnews.com.

Shi, Yigong, and Yi Rao. 2010. "China's Research Culture." *Science* 329(5996): 1128.

Shih, Chih-yu. 2002. *Negotiating Ethnicity in China: Citizenship as a Response to the State*. London: Routledge.

Shirk, Susan L. 1982. *Competitive Comrades: Career Incentives and Student Strategies in China*. Berkeley, CA: University of California Press.

Skachkova, Penka. 2007. "Academic Careers of Immigrant Women Professors in the U.S." *Higher Education* 53 (6): 697–738.

Slaughter, Sheila, and Larry L. Leslie. 1997. *Academic Capitalism: Politics, Policies, and the Entrepreneurial University*. Baltimore, MD: Johns Hopkins University Press.

Slaughter, Sheila, and Gary Rhoades. 2004. *Academic Capitalism and the New Economy: Markets, State and Higher Education*. Baltimore, MD: Johns Hopkins University Press.

Smircich, Linda. 1983. "Studying Organizations as Cultures." In *Beyond Method*, edited by Gareth Morgan, 160–172. Beverly Hills, CA: Sage.

Smith, David. 2007. *The Dragon and the Elephant: China, India and the New World Order*. London: Profile Books.

Snow, C. P. 1959. *The Two Cultures and the Scientific Revolution*. Cambridge, UK: Cambridge University Press.

Su, Yunfeng. 2001. *From Tsinghua School to Tsinghua University*. Shenghuo, Dushu: Xinzhi Joint Publishing Company.

Tang, Jiannan. 1996. "Jinhou Shiwu Nian Woguo Minzu Xueyuan de Fazhan Mubiao he Zhanlue" ("The Goals and Strategies for the Development of Minzu Colleges and Universities in the Next Fifteen Years"). *Minzu Luntan* (*Minzu Forum*) 2: 42–49.

Tempest, Rone. 1998. "Beijing University at 100 Years: A Symbol of China's Ferment." *Los Angeles Times* (3 May). http://articles.latimes.com/print/1998.

Thomas, William I., and Dorothy Swaine Thomas. 1928. *The Child in America: Behavior Problems and Programs*. New York: Knopf.

"Three Outspoken Academics." 2011. *Global Times* (30 March). http://en.huanqiu.com/spe cial/2011-03/639456.html.

Tierney, William G. 1988a. "Organizational Culture in Higher Education." *Journal of Higher Education* 59 (1): 2–21.

———. 1988b. *The Web of Leadership*. Greenwich, CT: Praeger.

————. 1993. *Building Communities of Difference: Higher Education in the Twenty-First Century*. Westport, CT: Bergin & Garvey.

Tierney, William G., and Robert A. Rhoads. 1993. *Enhancing Promotion, Tenure and Beyond: Faculty Socialization as a Cultural Process*. ASHE-ERIC Higher Education Reports, #6. Washington, DC: The George Washington University.

Trow, Martin. 1973. *Problems in the Transition from Elite to Mass Higher Education*. Berkeley, CA: Carnegie Commission on Higher Education.

————. 2006. "Reflections on the Transition from Elite to Mass to Universal Access: Forms and Phases of Higher Education in Modern Societies since WWII." In *International Handbook of Higher Education: Global Themes and Contemporary Challenges*), edited by James J. F. Forest and Philip G. Altbach, 243–280. Dordrecht, the Netherlands: Springer.

"Tsinghua Joins American Universities on US Patent Success List." 2011. *Asian Scientist* (20 September). www.asianscientist.com/biotech-pharma/tsinghua-joins-american-universities-patent-success-list.

Vaira, Massimiliano. 2004. "Globalization and Higher Education Organizational Change." *Higher Education* 48: 483–510.

Vance, Ashlee. 2010. "China Wrests Supercomputer Title from U.S." *New York Times* (28 October). www.nytimes.com/2010/10/28/technology/28compute.html?_r=2&scp =1&sq=Tianhe-1&st=cse.

Vidal, John, and David Adams. 2007. "China Passes US as World's Biggest CO2 Emitter." *Guardian* (20 June). www.guardian.co.uk/business/2007/jun/20/china.carbonemissions.

Wang, Guoming, and Liu Jianfeng. 2002. "Beida Qinghua Shei Geng Qiang? Liang Suo Dingjian Xuefu de Shiji Duihua (Xia Pian)" ("Which Is Stronger, Beida or Qinghua? A Century Dialogue of Two Top Universities"). *Zhongguo Jingji Shibao* (*Chinese Economic Times*) (9 May).

Wang, Qing Hui, Qi Wang, and Nian Cai Liu. 2011. "Building World-Class Universities in China: Shanghai Jiao Tong University." In *The Road to Academic Excellence: The Making of World-Class Research Universities*, edited by Philip G. Altbach and Jamil Salmi, 33–62. Washington, DC: International Bank for Reconstruction and Development / The World Bank.

Weston, Timothy B. 2004. *The Power of Position: Beijing University, Intellectuals, and Chinese Political Culture, 1898–1929*. Berkeley, CA: University of California Press.

Wildavsky, Ben. 2010. *The Great Brain Race: How Global Universities Are Reshaping the World*. Princeton, NJ: Princeton University Press.

Wong, Edward. 2010. "China Increases Security in Tibet to Prevent Protests." *New York Times* (11 March). www.nytimes.com/2010/03/12/world/asia/12tibet.html.

————. 2013. "China Lets Media Report on Air Pollution Crisis." *New York Times* (14 January). www.nytimes.com/2013/01/15.

Xiao, Chaoran. 1998. *Weiwei Shangyang Baisui Xingchen: Mingren yu Beida* (*Great Ancient Institutions and Centenarian Stars: Great Figures and Beida*). Beijing: Peking University Press.

"Xu Zhihong: Nine Years as President of Peking University." 2010. *CPC Encyclopedia* (17 November): 1–2. http://cpcchina.chinadaily.com.cn/people/2010-11/17.

Yang, Dongping. 2004. "*Daxue Gaige Lixiang yu Xianshi Zhijian*" ("University Reform: Between Idealism and Reality"). *Xinjing Bao* (*New Beijing News*) (31 March). http://edu.sina.com.cn/l/2004-03-31/63721.html.

Yang, Rui. 2000. "Tensions between the Global and the Local: A Comparative Illustration of the Reorganisation of China's Higher Education in the 1950s and 1990s. *Higher Education* 39: 319–337.

———. 2002. *Third Delight: Internationalisation of Higher Education in China.* New York: Routledge.

———. 2004. "Toward Massification: Higher Education Development in the People's Republic of China since 1949." *Higher Education: Handbook of Theory and Research* XIX: 311–374.

Yeh, Wen-Hsin. 2000. *The Alienated Academy: Culture and Politics in Republican China, 1919–1937.* Cambridge, MA: Harvard University Asia Center.

Yeung, Linda. 2011. "CHINA: Ex-Premier Criticises Higher Education Reform." *University World News* (1 May). www.universityworldnews.com/article.php?story=20110429170813 946.

Yi, Lin. 2008. *Cultural Exclusion in China: State Education, Social Mobility and Cultural Difference.* Oxford: Routledge.

Yin, Robert K. 1989. *Case Study Research: Design and Methods,* rev. ed. Newbury Park, CA: Sage.

Ying, Xie. 2010. "Chinese Businessman Draws Fire for Yale Donation." *Global Times* (12 January).

Young, Jeffrey R. 2010. "Chinese Research Park Incubates Hope for Scholarly Spinoffs." *Chronicle of Higher Education* (14 September). http://chronicle.com/article/Chinese-Research-Park/124420.

Zhang, Donghui. 2012. "*Tongshi* Education Reform in a Chinese University: Knowledge, Values, and Organizational Changes." *Comparative Education Review* 56 (3): 394–420.

Zhang, Weiying. 2004. *Daxue de Luoji (The Logic of the University).* Beijing: Peking University Press.

Zhao, Zhenzhou, and Gerard A. Postiglione. 2010. "Representations of Ethnic Minorities in China's University Media." *Discourse: Studies in the Cultural Politics of Education* 31 (4): 1–18.

Zhou, Faqin. 1990. *"Xi Nan Lian Da De Li Shi Gong Xian"* ("The Historic Contribution of South-West United University"). *Kexue yu Yanjiu (Science and Research)* 8 (2): 97–102.

Zhou, Ji. 2004. "The Full Implementation of the 2003–2007 Action Plan for Invigorating Education." Minister of Education speech, March 24. www.china.org.cn/e-news/news040324.htm.

Zhu, Yuchao, and Dongyan Blachford. 2006. "China's Fate as a Multinational State." *Journal of Contemporary China* 15: 329–348.

Zhu, Zhiyong. 2010. "Higher Education Access and Equality among Ethnic Minorities in China." *Chinese Education and Society* 43 (1): 12–23.

Zitan, Gao. 2011. "Official Corruption and Debauchery in China Exposed by Lawyer." *Epoch Times* (17 February). www.theepochtimes.com/n2/china/official-corruption-and-debauchery-in-china-exposed-by-lawyer-51445.html.

ROBERT A. RHOADS is Professor of Higher Education and Organizational Change in the Graduate School of Education and Information Studies (GSEIS) at the University of California, Los Angeles (UCLA). He also holds the title of University Chair Professor at Renmin University of China. His work focuses on the impact of globalization on universities in the United States and China, multiculturalism and university life, and ethnographic/qualitative methods in the social sciences. Professor Rhoads also examines the intersection of social movements and the university with a particular concern for the ways in which universities contribute to advancing democracy and open societies. His most recent books include *Qualitative Research Methods in Ethnic Education: Theory, Strategy, and Exemplars* (in Chinese) with Su De and Ulla Ambrosius Madsen (2013); *Global Citizenship and the University: Advancing Social Life and Relations in an Interdependent World*, co-authored with Katalin Szelényi (2011); and *The University, State, and Market: The Political Economy of Globalization in the Americas*, edited with Carlos Alberto Torres (2006). The latter two books were published with Stanford University Press, with the former being awarded as Publication of the Year by both the American Educational Research Association (AERA) Postsecondary Education Division and the Association for the Study of Higher Education (ASHE) Council for International Higher Education (CIHE).

XIAOYANG WANG is Associate Professor of Higher Education and Director of the Higher Education Institute at Tsinghua University. His research focuses on higher education and institutional culture, comparative higher education with a particular interest in the United States and Chinese higher education systems, and international education. His most recent scholarly works include the following papers: "University Culture Change and Creative Talents Cultivation," a paper presented at Sichuan University-Arizona State University Joint Research Conference in Chengdu; "Chinese Talents Programs, Progress, and Problems," presented at the Annual Conference of the Canadian Society for the Study of Higher Education; and "Present American Education Reform: Issues and Trends," published in the journal *Education Research* (in Chinese).

XIAOGUANG SHI is Professor of Higher Education and Director of the Center for International Higher Education Research in the Graduate School of Education at Peking University. His academic interests include international and comparative higher education policy and higher education theory. He is a member of the Chinese Higher Education Society, the Chinese Comparative Education Society, and the Comparative International Education Society (CIES). Professor Shi has authored or edited numerous publications (mostly in Chinese), including *Studies of Makiguti Tunezaburo's Educational Thought* (2012); *Higher Education in the Globalist Knowledge Economy* (2012); *American Higher Education Thought* (2001); and *The Idea of Western Higher Education: A Historical Perspective* (2002).

YONGCAI CHANG is Professor of Comparative Education and Cultural Anthropology and Psychology in the School of Education at Minzu University of China. His academic interests focus on intercultural learning, indigenous education and community development, comparative higher education, and educational anthropology. Professor Chang has been a visiting professor in Canada, where he studied at Queen's University and at the Ontario Institute for the Studies of Education (OISE) of the University of Toronto (2006–2007). He has published in prestigious international journals such as *Comparative Education Review*. His recent books include *Cultural Diversity and Acculturation of Ethnic Minority Students in China* (2007); *Sociocultural Change and Educational Innovation in China's Rural Ethnic Minority Areas* (2008); and *The Pedagogy of Today's Ethnic Minority Students in Universities and Colleges for Ethnic Groups: Issues and Innovation* (2010).

204, 59, 68, 82, 89, 92–94, 123, 130–131, 134,